Beginning Scribus

Robert White

Apress®

Beginning Scribus

ISBN-13 (pbk): 978-1-4842-0723-9

ISBN-13 (electronic): 978-1-4842-0722-2

Managing Director: Welmoed Spahr
Lead Editor: Ben Renow-Clarke
Technical Reviewer: Garry Patchett
Editorial Board: Steve Anglin, Louise Corrigan, Jim DeWolf, Jonathan Gennick, Robert Hutchinson, Michelle Lowman, James Markham, Susan McDermott, Matthew Moodie, Jeffrey Pepper, Douglas Pundick, Ben Renow-Clarke, Gwenan Spearing
Coordinating Editor: Melissa Maldonado
Copy Editor: Mary Behr
Compositor: SPi Global
Indexer: SPi Global
Artist: SPi Global

Distributed to the book trade worldwide by Springer Science+Business Media New York, 233 Spring Street, 6th Floor, New York, NY 10013. Phone 1-800-SPRINGER, fax (201) 348-4505, e-mail orders-ny@springer-sbm.com, or visit www.springer.com. Apress Media, LLC is a California LLC and the sole member (owner) is Springer Science + Business Media Finance Inc. (SSBM Finance Inc). SSBM Finance Inc is a Delaware corporation.

For information on translations, please e-mail rights@apress.com, or visit www.apress.com.

Apress and friends of ED books may be purchased in bulk for academic, corporate, or promotional use. eBook versions and licenses are also available for most titles. For more information, reference our Special Bulk Sales–eBook Licensing web page at www.apress.com/bulk-sales.

Any source code or other supplementary material referenced by the author in this text is available to readers at www.apress.com. For detailed information about how to locate your book's source code, go to www.apress.com/source-code/.

To my parents, Peter and Pauline.

Contents at a Glance

Contents

About the Author

Robert White is a freelance writer who uses Scribus to edit a local magazine. He spent much of his life working in the library, museum and archive sector, and has worked for such diverse companies as The British Library, The National Archives, and G.E.C. A former spreadsheet developer, he spent a year at Oxford and has a degree in History.

About two years ago, after using QuarkXPress 5 for several years, he was offered the chance to edit a local magazine that operated on a modest budget. Frustrated by the cost involved in using the world's industry-leading application for page layout and publication design, he converted to Scribus, the free and open source alternative, and has never looked back. He also used it to produce a brochure for the heritage sector.

In his spare time, Robert is a keen rambler, and an avid supporter of Watford Football club.

About the Technical Reviewer

Garry Patchett has worked in IT and engineering for more than 20 years designing products, creating software, and administering and documenting systems. With a Master's Degree in Project Management, he is a dedicated "systems nerd" whose interests vary from the technological to the philosophical. Garry is currently working freelance and is involved in various open source projects.

Acknowledgments

First of all, I feel that I ought to thank Mick Dobson of the Watford Enterprise Agency in Hertfordshire, England. It was Mick's idea to market the idea I had for this book in the first place. WENTA is an impressive organization, and at the time that we were thinking about the book, I had been attending one of Mick's thought-provoking seminars on pay-per-click advertising in North Watford. When I eventually followed up on his idea, Mick was there to offer plenty of advice and encouragement.

The result is this book. However, although it bears my name, the book's contents are the result of a three-way collaboration between myself, Apress Editor Ben Renow-Clarke, and Technical Reviewer Garry Patchett.

Ben was keen to publish a more project-oriented work, one that contained plenty of exercises for the reader, and he provided enough positive feedback for me to think that my idea for the book might have some potential. So together we spent the next few months reappraising the original proposal and fleshingout the table of contents.

Of equal importance is the contribution made by our Technical Reviewer, Garry Patchett. Garry is a gifted graphic designer and technical communicator with very exacting standards. I like to pride myself on being well-read, but Garry has an astounding insight into the inner workings of Scribus, and I learned a lot from his feedback. While it was not always possible to act on all of Garry's suggestions for improvements to this book, the result, I feel, has been a more tightly-focused book and a more definitive account of the way in which Scribus really works. And his technical review saved me many weeks of arduous proofreading.

Finally, I would like to thank the coordinating editors and copy editors at Apress in New York-Melissa Maldonado, Christine Ricketts, Mark Powers, James Markham, and Mary Behr-who maintained patience, politeness, and goodhumor even when things got a bit frantic.

Introduction

This book was originally intended as an aide memoire for use in the compilation and publication of a parish magazine. Gradually, though, it evolved from a basic list of DOs and DON'Ts into a more project-oriented piece that shows you how Scribus actually works.

This book is the end result. It offers a way into the world of professional desktop publishing for those who cannot afford the more celebrated commercial alternatives. It teaches you what you need to know in order to produce professional-looking printed documents and stunning, interactive digital magazines. It also provides a useful companion to Akkana Peck's book Beginning Gimp.

It is aimed specifically at the desktop publishing newbie, those who want to learn more about open source desktop publishing, and those who cannot afford the prices of the top-ranking, commercial applications.

But it should also prove a valuable resource for impoverished higher education studentswho cannot afford the student rates for the commercial software being offered for graphic design courses. It will enable them to produce visually appealing, professional-looking documents for their coursework, even if they do not have the money to use Adobe Creative Suite or QuarkXPress.

Above all, we hope that this book will provide you with hours of fun. Think of the fun you will have turning your word-processed greyscale newsletters into graphics-rich and intensely colorful e-magazines, complete with gradient-filled backgrounds and full-page bleeds for your color photos.

Structure of the Book

Chapter 1 assumes that you have no knowledge of Scribus or desktop publishing. It takes you through the process of downloading and installing Scribus for the first time.

Chapter 2 introduces you to the Scribus interface.

Chapter 3 looks at the way text is managed and manipulated in Scribus. It also introduces you to some of the typographical effects available in Scribus.

Chapter 4 introduces you to the various image formats that are available in desktop publishing, and shows youhow to manage yourimages, how to modify lines and shapes, and how to create a Bezier curve.

Chapter 5 delves into the wonderful world of color models and color space. It looks at the differing methods by which Scribus manages color, both in its image input files and in its PDF output files.

Chapter 6 examines the diagnostic checks that are built into Scribus, and shows you how to export your documents for printing.

Chapter 7 introduces you to the image-processing editor known as GIMP. It shows how GIMP can be used to augment the creative work that is done in Scribus. It demonstrates how to crop an image, how to apply image effects, and how to add alpha channels so that you can remove an object from its background.

Chapter 8 shows you how Scribus can help cut down on repetitive tasks by using styles, templates, and master pages. You are also shown how to go about designing a threefold brochure.

In Chapter 9, you get to design four pages of a magazine. You are shown how to layout a front page, how to design a masthead/imprint, and how to design an advert.

Finally, in Chapter 10, you get to try your hand at a bit of scripting and are shown how to create interactive PDFs.

Exercises

In order to complete the exercise in the book, you will need to have access to some digital photographs. If you want to use the photographs featured in the book, they are available for download from the Apress website at `www.apress.com`.

■ ■ ■

CHAPTER 1

Scribus Basics

Most word processing systems are, by their very nature, limited in what they will allow you to do in terms of document layout. They are mainly concerned with creating textual content, and with copying and editing texts. However, they are not the most appropriate tools for preparing a publication for professional printing, as there is no real design element.

Desktop publishing applications, on the other hand, allow the user to complement the text by introducing images and graphic design elements as part of a more flexible page layout system. The emphasis, therefore, shifts from the processing of text to the design of page layouts; layouts, moreover, that enable the reader to absorb the content as quickly and efficiently as possible.

Up until now, the professional desktop publishing market has been dominated by commercial applications. Happily, for those of us who cannot afford these applications, there is now an alternative. It is called Scribus.

This chapter will cover the following:

- How to download and install Scribus

- How to get around in the graphical user interface of Scribus

- How to open your first document

- How to use the frames that will hold your content

- How to view and navigate your documents

Welcome to Scribus!

Scribus is an award-winning, cross-platform program for creating professional page layouts and designs. At the heart of Scribus is the page. You build a publication in Scribus by setting up its framework: its page size, page orientation, and margins. Then you "paste-up" the individual pages by adding text frames and graphical elements. Scribus is remarkably flexible from a design perspective. It provides a variety of fonts, colors, visual effects, and object positions. Using the Properties Palette, the user can manipulate pages and text frames, image frames, lines, text paths, and tables with a level of precision and flexibility that would normally be the preserve of other, more expensive desktop solutions. Repetitive tasks can be automated using templates, styles, master pages, and Python scripts.

Scribus offers precision control over the final arrangement of the document. The page design that results can be exported as a Postscript file or an Adobe PDF file. Scribus is a great tool for creating Adobe PDF documents with advanced features such as interactive forms and buttons. It can also handle beveling, gradient filling, and text path setting.

But Scribus need not be used in isolation, for Scribus can be used in conjunction with other open source programs such as OpenOffice, Gimp, and Inkscape. OpenOffice can be used to format your Word documents and import paragraph styles into Scribus; Gimp provides a cheap way of editing photographic images, screen shots, and transparencies; and Inkscape can be used to produce vector drawings, which is useful if you need a logo.

Scribus is free to download. It is distributed under the GNU General Public License and may be obtained freely to use, distribute, copy, and modify using the program's source code. The original programming code that was used to create the program has been made available for users to improve, develop, and distribute.

Download and Installation

Before you install Scribus, you will need to decide whether to download and install a piece of software called Ghostscript.

Ghostscript

Ghostscript is an open source tool that is used for rendering Postscript and PDF files. Many software applications use it as a background library, but Scribus uses it to import PDF files as image files, and to import and export Postscript files.

It is not strictly necessary to install Ghostscript in order to use Scribus; there is nothing to "run" once it is installed, and it does not have a desktop icon. But it is essential if you intend to import EPS or PDF files into Scribus, or if you intend to export your documents as Postscript files.

If you decide to install Scribus without installing Ghostscript first, you will receive a warning telling you that Ghostscript is missing and that it ought to be installed.

You can download the version of Ghostscript that is right for your operating system by visiting the official Ghostscript website at `www.ghostscript.com` and following these steps:

- Select the Download page.

- Select the latest GPL release version of the Postscript and PDF renderer.

- Select the correct version of Ghostscript for your operating system.
  You can choose from:

    - Windows 32-bit

    - Windows 64-bit

    - Linux 32-bit

    - Linux 64-bit

Windows users should save the download as an `.exe` file on their desktop, and then double-click the .exe file to install. The program works in the background, so no shortcut icon will appear on the desktop or in the Start menu.

Scribus 1.4.5

At the time of writing, the stable version of Scribus is 1.4.5, which is available for Windows XP, Windows Vista, Windows 7, Windows 8, and Mac OSX. So download and install Scribus 1.4.5. The minimum disk space required is 65MB and the minimum level of memory necessary to run Scribus is 512MB. The official document site is `www.scribus.net`. The Scribus download page also contains Scribus download links for Gentoo, Ubuntu, Red Hat, Solaris, OpenSuse, FreeBSD, OpenBSD, and NewBSD.

The files for the Scribus downloads are often served from a web-based code repository called SourceForge, so do not be alarmed if the download link takes your web browser to the SourceForge download page. It's perfectly safe.

Go to the Download page and select the current stable version of Scribus for your operating system.

How to Install Scribus on Windows

As mentioned, before you install Scribus, you will probably want to download and install a Windows version of Ghostscript, which you can download from www.ghostscript.com.

Having installed Ghostscript, go to the Scribus website, follow the link for the stable Windows version of Scribus, download the .exe file for Scribus 1.4.5 and save it to your desktop. Double-click the executable file to commence the installation, and select the Program Files folder as your default program destination.

Scribus sometimes takes a while to install. This is due to the checks that it makes in order to establish which fonts are installed on your computer.

How to Install Scribus on a Mac

As mentioned, before you install Scribus, you need to think about whether you should install Ghostscript. If you decide that you do want to install it, the easiest way is to install the Mac version from the Ghostscript download page (www.ghostscript.com/download).

Locate the latest version of Ghostscript for the Mac, and click it. This will begin the download of the Ghostscript Package Installer. Once you have downloaded the PKG file, go to your Downloads folder, locate the PKG file, double-click the icon, and follow the on-screen instructions, accepting the default settings you are offered if you are unclear about the choices.

Once the installation process has finished, Ghostscript should be running in the background, and you can turn your attention to the installation of Scribus.

Assuming that your Mac is running Mac OSX 10.5 or later, the easiest way to install Scribus is to download the Scribus Package Installer. Go to www.scribus.net and download the package to your Downloads folder. When the download is complete, double-click the Scribus PKG file to install it.

When the installation process has finished, open your Applications folder and look for the Scribus icon. Double-click the icon to start Scribus.

How to Install Scribus on Linux Distros

Most of the mainstream Linux distros include Ghostscript in their software repositories. Ubuntu 14.04 includes a version of Ghostscript in the Ubuntu Software Centre, and once you install it, it will keep itself updated. If not, go to www.ghostscript.com and select the download page for the Postscript and PDF interpreter and renderer. Then select either a 32-bit or a 64-bit download for Linux. When the download opens in your browser, click to save the download or to open it with the Archive Manager. At the time of writing, you should be able to find a stable version of Scribus (1.4.5) in the Ubuntu Software Centre.

You can also install an unstable SVN version of Scribus 1.5.0 by using the Terminal. If you want to try this version, bring up the Terminal, and enter the following command:

```
Sudo apt-get update
```

Then press Enter and add:

```
Sudo apt-get install scribus-trunk
```

Press Enter again. This will bring up your launcher.

Scribus Documentation

The Scribus installation will include some documentation, but the Scribus community also provides three other sources of help. Further documentation can be found on the Scribus Wiki at `wiki.scribus.net` and at the home of the Scribus Documentation project (`Documentation.scribus.net`).

The Scribus Wiki represents the official documentation site for Scribus. It was created in order to give users a place to put HOW TOs, tips, and ideas on using and enhancing Scribus. It contains information taken from Scribus Help and from the Scribus Official Manual. As of December 2010, the Scribus Wiki has also hosted the "official" documents provided by the Scribus team (contributors include Gregory Pittman and Christophe Schaffer).

Finally, there is the Scribus User mailing List which you can join at `http://lists.scribus.net/mailman/listinfo/scribus.` The mailing list is useful for obtaining quick responses to questions that have not been addressed in the FAQ, and cannot be found in the archives. Prominent members of the Scribus Development Team, such as Craig Bradney, Christophe Schaffer, and Gregory Pittman, are said to be active on the list.

Organizing Your Workflow

In Scribus, you lay out your page contents by inserting image and text frames onto the page, and then placing image files and text files inside those frames. Having said that, Scribus is unlikely to be the only piece of software that you will want to use when creating a document.

Different documents have different layout requirements and require different working methods. In desktop publishing, it is important to keep the content-producing processes (such as word processing, image editing, proofreading, and layout) separate from each other. So we recommend using a plain text editor to compose your text, an image editor (such as GIMP) to edit your photos, and a vector graphics editor (such as Inkscape) to create your logos. You will also need a PDF viewer to view the finished product; Scribus is tested against Adobe Acrobat, and Adobe Acrobat Reader is the recommended PDF reader of the Scribus Development Team.

■ **Note** It is possible to use Microsoft Word to create your documents; it is, after all, said to be the world's most pervasive word processing program. However, at the time of writing, Scribus does not have an import filter for Microsoft Word. You can import text from Word files into your text frames, but you will lose all of the formatting when you do so. If you want to retain your formatting, you are better off opening your Word documents in OpenOffice Writer, and then saving them as ODT files. Scribus cannot handle the character formatting in ODT files (and it handles bold and italics formatting differently from Word), but it can at least import paragraph formatting at a basic level, which is all that many of us require.

Scribus will be the system you use to mix all these elements together in your final layout. So use other programs to create your content, and use Scribus for the final layout of your content. This process of separation between content and layout is known as a *publishing workflow*. A properly organized workflow will help make the editorial process a lot easier.

Use a Separate Folder and Subdirectories for Your Content

As a central part of your workflow organization, you would be well advised to create a separate folder for each of your publishing projects (and some people prefer to store all of their images in a separate folder). You can then keep your text files, image files, and other sources of content in separate subdirectories within that folder. Scribus can handle a project that uses a diverse placement of resources, but having all your resources in one location makes it less likely that things will get moved or that images will go missing.

Scribus Files

When you have finished laying out your content, and you come to name your file, Scribus will save your document in its native Scribus Layout format, which has the `.sla` extension.

Having finished laying out your content, go to the Preview Mode by clicking the eye icon at the bottom right of the Scribus main window, and use a tool known as the Preflight Verifier in order to check for errors. The Preflight Verifier is a quality control tool that is used to flag errors before the document is exported as a PDF file. It runs a series of tests on your Scribus document, and issues a warning about any potential errors that it finds. The Preflight Verifier is an important tool within Scribus, and we will be showing you how to use it in a later chapter. Once you've fixed the errors (or chosen to ignore them), you can export the finished layout to PDF or Postscript.

Before You Open Scribus

Before you open Scribus, it is good to have a rough idea of the sort of document you wish to create. You need to get some idea of the requirements of your layout before you can start work. For instance, do you want to create a single page document, a double-sided document, or a folded brochure, and in what page size and orientation? You need to consider these options *now* because you will be prompted to make a selection when you open Scribus.

Opening Scribus: The New Document Window

When you open Scribus, the first window that you will encounter is the New Document window, as shown in Figure 1-1. This window opens by default when you open Scribus.

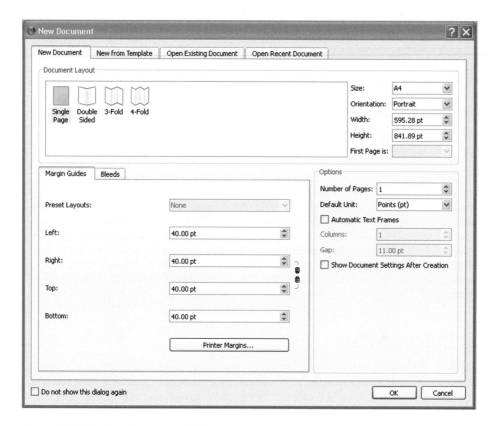

Figure 1-1. *The New Document window*

This window presents the user with the various options and presets that are needed for the creation of a document, but before you select them, you will need to decide which size and type of page layout you require.

You will notice that there are four tabs that run horizontally along the top of the window: New Document, New from Template, Open Recent Document, and Open Existing Document.

The New Document window also enables the user to select a document layout, a default unit of measurement, the number of pages you wish to add, and the size, width, height, and orientation of those pages. Clicking OK to the selected settings will take you into the main Scribus window.

Document Layout

The top left hand corner of the window provides options for document layout. You can choose from Single Page, Double Sided, 3-Fold, and 4-Fold layouts.

The Single Page option will create pages in a single column, with one page following another. This format is ideal for creating certificates, letters, CVs, and business cards (and some digital printers prefer to use single-page layouts when printing double-sided magazines).

The double-sided option will produce two pages that sit side-by-side with a fold in the middle; this format is ideal for printing codex-type publications such as books, newspapers, and magazines.

The 3-fold and 4-fold options are used to design brochures (though some users prefer to start with a single-page layout in landscape format, which they then divide into three or four sections using grids and guides).

Page Size

To the right of the Document Layout section is a section containing page size options, which is used for selecting the size, orientation, and width of the intended document. In the Size drop-down list, you can select from a range of paper sizes, and if the option you want is unavailable, Scribus gives you the option of creating your own custom page size by choosing from the width and length measurements available in the spin boxes. Once you enter your own size measurements, the Size option will set itself to "custom."

Orientation

There are two choices available for page orientation: portrait and landscape. Portrait is the standard orientation for most letters, books, and posters, and landscape is the orientation used in the production of maps, pictures, and some brochures.

Default Units

On the right hand side of the New Document window, the Options section lets you select the number of pages that you require in your document and the default unit of measurement in which you will be working.

The default units of measurement that are selected in Scribus are points. Points are a throwback to the days of hot metal printing, but with the arrival of desktop publishing, the point became standardized as 1/72 of an inch. Today, points represent an international standard for typographical and printing measurements. However, some users might prefer to use millimeters.

Margin Guides

This section allows you to set the Left, Right, Top, and Bottom alignments for your margins. Margins represent the space between the edge of your paper and the printable area. They are necessary in order to provide a space for the printer to grip the paper when the document is being printed. If you wish, you can alter these settings at a later date.

Automatic Text Frames

In the Options section of the New Document window, there is a checkbox for creating automatic text frames. This feature enables the user to insert the necessary number of pages and text frames when importing large amounts of text into Scribus. The Automatic Text Frames dialog also enables the user to set the number of text columns and the size of the gap between the columns.

Opening Recent Documents

If a document has been opened recently, you will find an entry for it in the Open Recent Documents tab (you will also find it if you follow the File ➤ Open Recent menu.

Creating Documents from Templates

The second tab in the New Document window is for creating a document that is New from Template. This tab can also be accessed by using the File ➤ New from Template menu.

If you decide to open a new document that is based on a template, the choices regarding the page size and layout will have already been made for you. These documents already have some graphical, textual, and stylistic content added. In fact, Scribus contains its own collection of built-in templates, though it is relatively easy to create your own (as you will see later).

The left side of the template dialog lists the available template categories. The middle column displays the thumbnails of templates belonging to particular categories (such as a brochure, two newsletters, and a presentation) as shown in Figure 1-2. The right-hand column lists details of the currently selected template.

To open a template, either double-click the thumbnail image, or select a template and click OK. It is also possible to save a document as a template by using the File ➤ Save as template menu option.

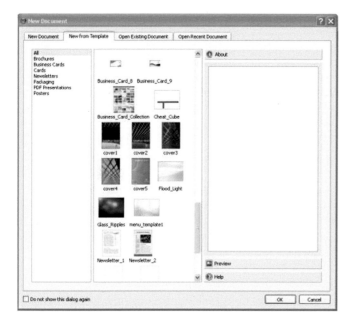

Figure 1-2. *A selection of templates comes built in to Scribus*

The Main Scribus Windows

The Scribus workspace consists of the main Scribus window, which contains a title bar, menu bar, toolbar, document window, and scratch space, as displayed in Figure 1-3.

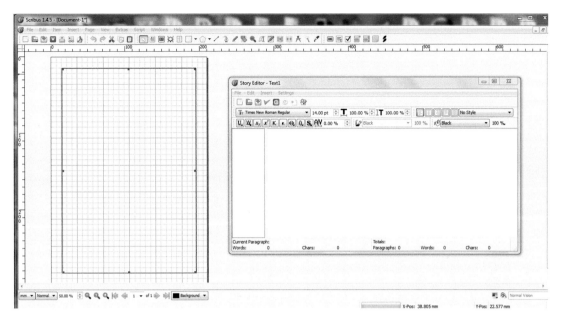

Figure 1-3. *The main Scribus window*

The Scribus main window (displayed in Figure 1-3) has a toolbar running along the top, but this can be customized to suit the way that you work. There are four vertical, dotted lines spaced out along the toolbar.

If you select one of these lines with your mouse, you will be able to detach a section of tools from the toolbar and move them to any spot you like on your workspace.

At the bottom of the main window are controls for selecting the default unit of measurement, as well as the image preview quality and current zoom level. The area to the lower left of the page also contains three other zoom controls and four arrows to aid in page navigation.

To the right are controls that enable and disable color management, controls that enable and disable the Preview mode, and controls that alter the visual appearance of the display.

There are two other panels that I will be introducing you to a little later. The first is the Story Editor, which is the Scribus text editor. It is a tool that you will use a lot when inserting text into your documents. It has a menu bar, a row of icons, and a row of text and font controls that enable you to select the font family, font size, style, and text alignment of their choice. The Story editor enables you to insert and edit the text in your text frames.

The second panel that you will be learning more about later is the Properties Palette, which is a floating panel that lets you control the properties of the objects on your page. Both of these panels are illustrated in Figure 1-4.

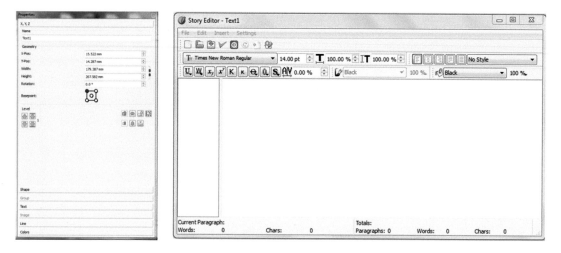

Figure 1-4. *The Properties Palette and Story Editor*

You can interact with Scribus in one of five ways, via the Menu bar, the Toolbar, the Properties Palette, the Context menu, or your keyboard shortcuts.

The Context Menu

The Context menu, which can be produced by right-clicking an image or text frame, provides a range of context-sensitive operations that are relevant to the selected object type.

An Introductory Tour of the Scribus Workspace

Open Scribus now and look at the New Documents window, like the one shown in Figure 1-5.

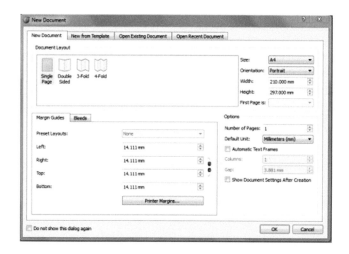

Figure 1-5. *The New Document window*

Without examine it in detail, note that it is set to create a document with a single page of A4 size by default. Click the OK button at the bottom and let it open the first page of your document, as shown in Figure 1-6.

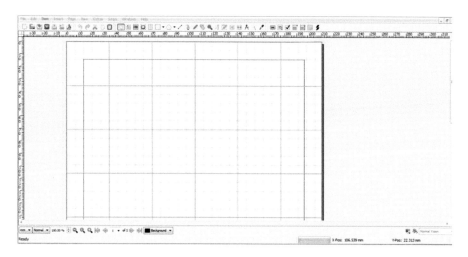

Figure 1-6. *Creating a New Document*

If the page is too big, you can zoom down until the entire page can be viewed in the window by using the zoom controls.

Using your mouse, click the Insert Text Frame icon.

Your cursor will turn into a crosshair cursor with a text box at the side. Using the cursor, draw a rectangle on the page. The exact shape does not matter, but the page and text frame should look similar to the ones in Figure 1-7.

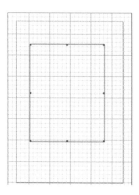

Figure 1-7. *A Scribus page with a text frame inserted on the page*

Now, with the text frame still selected, go to the Edit menu, and select Edit ➤ Text. This will produce the Story Editor displayed in Figure 1-8.

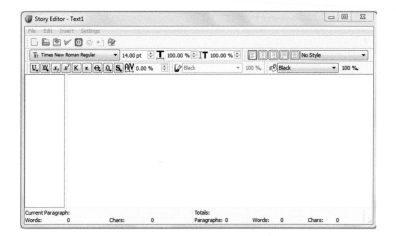

Figure 1-8. *The Story Editor and the Properties Palette*

Now close the Story Editor by clicking the white diagonal cross in the top right of the toolbar. ⬚

With the text frame still highlighted, go to the Windows menu, and select Properties. This will produce the Properties Palette shown in Figure 1-8. Close the Properties Palette by clicking the diagonal cross in the top right corner. Close Scribus by clicking the red cross in the top right corner of the main Scribus window.

Congratulations! You've now completed your first exploration of Scribus.

Setting Your Preferences and Document Settings

At this point, I recommend that you master the use of your Preferences and Document Setup windows; they are closely related, and they play an important part in achieving a successful workflow. Mastering them at this stage will save you a lot of editing time later on.

Both of these windows allow you to change your default settings in Scribus. However, the Preferences window represents the application-wide settings that allow you to change the default settings of any future documents that you create in Scribus, whereas any changes you make in the Document Settings window will only affect the document that is currently being edited.

Please note, however, that any changes you make in Preferences will not take effect until you create a new document. Some changes, such as those for spelling and short words, are made instantly. Other changes, such as those for font family and size, will only take effect when you create a new document.

The Preferences and Document Setup menus can both be accessed via the File menu.

The Document Setup Window

The Document Setup window, shown in Figure 1-9, lets you change the properties of the document you are currently working on. You can open the Document Setup window by selecting Document Setup from the File menu. Amongst other things, it enables you to change the document's layout, page size, and fonts.

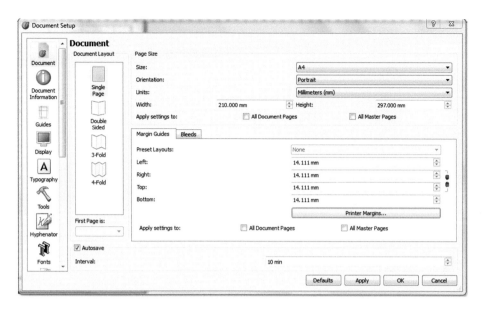

Figure 1-9. *The Document Setup window*

The options found in the Document Setup window are similar (but not the same) as the ones found in the Preferences window. The main difference is that the setup options refer to the active document, whereas the Preferences can be set for all future documents.

Preferences

The Preferences Window is displayed in Figure 1-10.

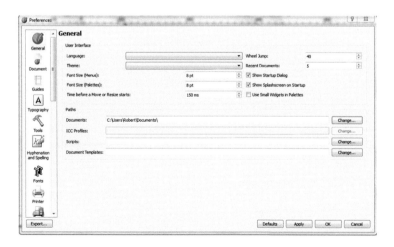

Figure 1-10. *The Preferences window*

The Preferences menu that runs along the left side contains a set of tabs that allow you to make permanent changes to the categories shown in Figure 1-11.

Figure 1-11. *The Preferences menu*

Preferences: The General Tab

In the User Interface section of the General tab, there are settings available for the GUI (graphical user interface), Language, Themes, and Font Size, and a setting allowing you to alter the number of documents available to view in the Recent Documents tab (see Figure 1-12).

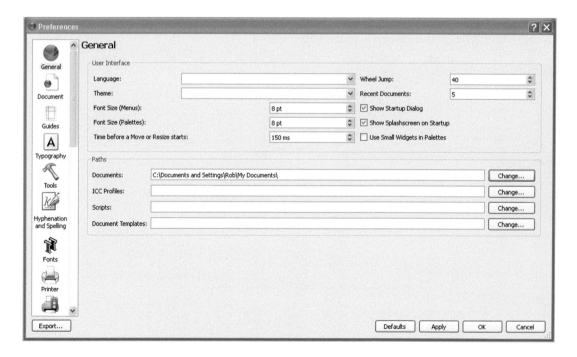

Figure 1-12. *The General tab in the Preferences window*

The Language setting refers to the languages available in Scribus menus and dialogs. The choices range from Afrikaans to Welsh and include UK English.

The Theme setting refers to the appearance of Scribus on your operating system. There are different themes available for Windows, such as Windows XP, Motif, Plastique, and Cleanlooks.

The Wheel Jump setting refers to the number of lines that Scribus will scroll through for each move of the mouse wheel.

The Recent Documents setting allows you to adjust the number of recently edited documents available in the File menu.

Finally, the Paths setting enables you to set the default paths for documents, templates, OCC profiles, and scripts. (This setting is not available in Document Setup.)

Setting Your Preferences

Before you start working in Scribus, there are three Preference settings that are useful to know about: The Documents tab, the Tools tab, and the Fonts tab.

In the Documents tab, the Units setting allows you to choose your default setting from a selection of units of measurement such as points, millimeters, inches, picas, centimeters, and cicero. Should you wish to create some custom page sizes, Scribus allows you to select the width and height of the page.

The Tools Tab (as shown in Figure 1-13) lets you select the type, size, and color of font to be used when you open a new text frame.

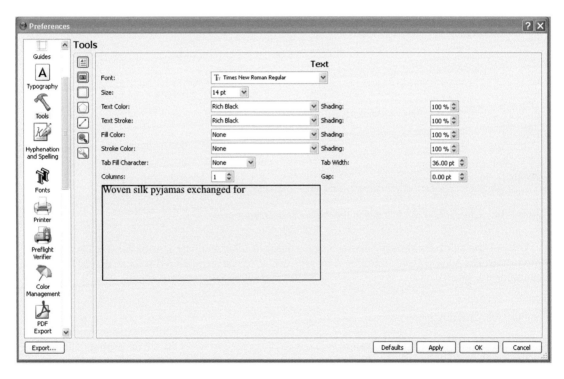

Figure 1-13. *The Tools tab in the Preferences dialog*

Finally, there is the Fonts tab. This tab provides a list of the fonts that are available to Scribus. It allows you to de-select those fonts that you do not intend to use, and (more importantly) it allows you to automate your font substitutions so that you can nominate other fonts in place of those that are not installed on your computer.

It also enables you to set the path to your font files. If you have fonts hidden away in a directory other than you standard fonts folder, you can use "additional paths" to enable Scribus to locate these fonts.

Adjusting the Scratch Space

It is possible to use Preferences to adjust the scratch space in your Scribus workspace. You can adjust the scratch space between the borders of the page and the canvas by setting the Minimum Scratch Space in the Preferences ➤ Display tab (as shown in Figure 1-14).

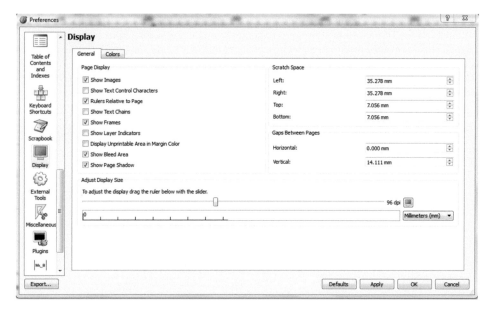

Figure 1-14. *Setting the Scratch Space in the Preferences/Display tab*

You can also adjust the distance between single pages in a document by altering the Gap Between the Pages setting. The Adjust Display Size area allows the user to adjust the Scribus display so that 100% zoom is the same size as printed.

Keyboard Shortcuts

To find a list of your keyboard shortcuts, got to File ➤ Preferences and select the tab for Keyboard Shortcuts. This tab gives you the ability to set a shortcut for anything in the program, as shown in Figure 1-15.

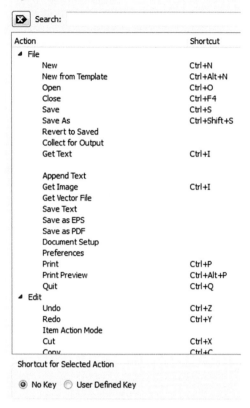

Keyboard Shortcuts

Action	Shortcut
▲ File	
New	Ctrl+N
New from Template	Ctrl+Alt+N
Open	Ctrl+O
Close	Ctrl+F4
Save	Ctrl+S
Save As	Ctrl+Shift+S
Revert to Saved	
Collect for Output	
Get Text	Ctrl+I
Append Text	
Get Image	Ctrl+I
Get Vector File	
Save Text	
Save as EPS	
Save as PDF	
Document Setup	
Preferences	
Print	Ctrl+P
Print Preview	Ctrl+Alt+P
Quit	Ctrl+Q
▲ Edit	
Undo	Ctrl+Z
Redo	Ctrl+Y
Item Action Mode	
Cut	Ctrl+X
Copy	Ctrl+C

Shortcut for Selected Action

◉ No Key ◯ User Defined Key

Figure 1-15. *The listing for Keyboard Shortcuts in Preferences*

The activities that are listed on the left side coincide with actions that can be found in the Scribus menu. So look for an action that you use all the time and make a note of the shortcut.

Creating Your Document

Clicking OK to the settings in the New Document window will result in the creation of your first document, as displayed in Figure 1-16.

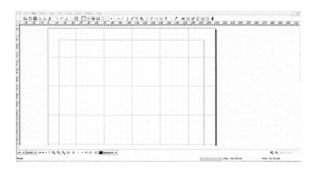

Figure 1-16. *Your first document*

If you have created a document that uses a double-sided format, you will be given the option of deciding whether the first page is a right-hand page or a left-hand page. It is set to the right by default, and you should leave it as it is when creating a document in traditional book (or codex) format.

Laying Out Your Document

A good desktop publishing workflow requires the designer to import text and objects from different sources. Once this has been done, the designer can then proceed to the layout process, laying objects out onto the page in such a way that they communicate information clearly and simply, and in a way that is pleasing to the eye.

Often the best form of layout is that which adapts itself to the content, so it is a good idea to assemble your text and your graphics on the page first, and then decide how they should be arranged so as to aid assimilation. In Scribus, you place your text and images on the page using objects called frames.

Introduction to Frames

In most desktop publishing systems, the text and pictures are held in place by a frame. This frame is like an invisible bounding box that is used to house an object on the page. Frames in Scribus can (in theory) be made to any size or shape. They help the user to position their text and their images very precisely on different parts of the page.

You can move your frames across the page with your mouse, and you can lock their contents in position by right-clicking them and selecting Lock Frame from the Context menu. You can also make the boundary of your frames visible by using the Line tab of the Properties Palette.

EXERCISE

Begin by opening Scribus, then select an A4-sized page for your document and click OK. This will take you to your Scribus workspace, which consists of a white page and a grey background known as the scratch space.

The easiest way to insert a Text frame is to select the Insert Text

Frame icon on the toolbar.

Begin by clicking the Text Frame icon, and then draw a rectangular shape on the page. At the border of the text frame, click one of the control handles that appears along the border, and drag it out to your desired size and shape, as shown in Figure 1-17.

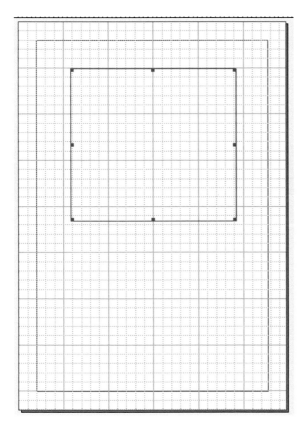

Figure 1-17. *Inserting a text frame. Note that I have also made the grid visible here*

How to Insert Sample Text

From the context menu, select Insert Sample Text. You will then be presented with a list of languages from which you can choose your sample text.

Select the Latin text referred to as Standard Lorem Ipsum. Lorem Ipsum is the original Latin version of the sample text. The text (which is taken from a passage by the Roman philosopher Cicero) was often used as sample text in typeface catalogues, and was later adopted by Aldus PageMaker.

You can also double-click the text frame to select it, or you can right-click the frame and select Get Text to insert text from an external file. The Latin Text will appear in the frame, as shown in Figure 1-18.

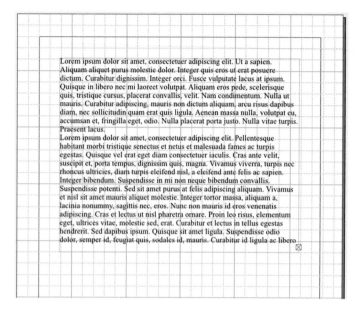

Figure 1-18. *Text frame displaying Standard Lorem Ipsum*

When you have finished, right-click the text frame again, and select the Edit Text option from the context menu. This will take you into the Story Editor, where you can edit your text, as shown in Figure 1-19.

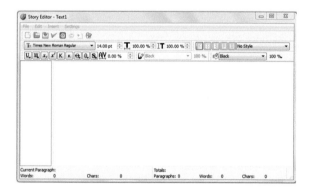

Figure 1-19. *The Story Editor*

To exit the Story editor, simply click the red and white cross in the top right-hand corner of the Editor, or select Exit from the File menu.

Working with Image Frames

Now click the Image Frame icon on the toolbar and draw a rectangular shape in the space below the text frame. Then right-click the image frame, and, using the context menu, select Get Image. You can now select an image from one of your graphics files. For my first image frame, I chose to insert a copy of the Scribus logo (see Figure 1-20).

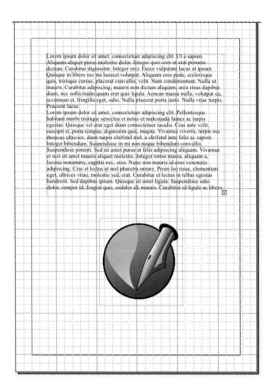

Figure 1-20. *The Sample text and the Scribus logo occupy separate frames*

You can find a non-copyright version of this logo at `commons.wikimedia.org/wiki/File:scribus-logo.svg`. You can, if you wish, use the Shape tab in the Properties Palette to refine the size of your image frame. Later on, you will see how to get your text frames to flow around an image.

Creating Inline Characters

In Scribus, it is also possible to input images into your text frames by pasting the image into the frame. These are known as inline characters.

Saving a Document

When you have finished importing your text and rearranging your images, you can save your document in the Scribus native format as an `.sla` file.

The `.sla` format will save the textual content of your file, but not the images. The file also contains other things, such as color definitions, patterns, etc. Instead of actually saving the image, Scribus saves the links to the images, and the links themselves refer to the original location from where the image was selected. It is for this reason that we recommend that you save all your document images in the same folder. If the `.sla` file is moved or renamed, the links will need to be recreated.

The various **Save** options (Save, Save As, Save As Template and Collect for Output) can be found under the File menu. You can save a document by selecting the Save icon on the toolbar, or by choosing File ➤ Save from the menu. This will save all unsaved changes since the document was last saved.

Alternatively, if the document has yet to be named and saved, selecting the Save action will bring up the Save As dialog (as shown in Figure 1-21) and you will be required to choose a file name and select a directory in which to save the document.

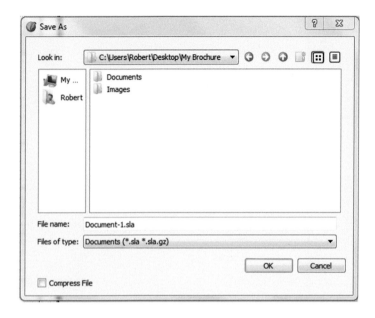

Figure 1-21. *The Save As dialog box*

Collect for Output

The Collect for Output function enables you to gather all the elements of your document together in one folder. Selecting the Collect for Output action creates a folder with all your document files inside, ready for export. This folder and its files can then enable you to recompile your original document on another computer.

The Autosave function saves your document automatically at a given interval. The interval can be set in the File Preferences window (File ➤ Preferences ➤ Document).

Viewing Your Documents

The View Menu contains several options that enable the user to change the display of pages or documents on the computer screen, and it also contains the following set of zoom levels:

- Fit to Height
- Fit to Width
- 50%
- 75%
- 100%
- 200%
- 400%

How to Zoom In on Your Documents

When working on a document, it is important that you get an overview of your work. You may feel the need to establish a set of zoom levels with which you feel comfortable working, so that you can perform different tasks. For my own screen size, I use a zoom level of 50% for opening documents and navigating between them, but I increase the zoom level to 100% if I need to move objects around on the page, or snap them to grid. I increase the zoom level to at least 200% for more detailed work involving the alignment of objects on the page. But each user, each monitor, and each Scribus installation will be different, and you need to find a set of zoom levels with which you feel comfortable.

For Windows users, a quick way of zooming in and out while working is to press Ctrl and Shift and the + key to zoom in, and Ctrl and Shift and the - key to zoom out. I prefer to use the spin box's zoom-increment settings at the bottom of the page, but I sometimes use the magnifier buttons as well.

The Spin Box

You can enter your required zoom level using the spin box. `pt ∨ Normal ∨ 50.00 % ⇕`

The Zoom Tool

Alternatively, you can zoom in on your documents using the zoom tool, which is located on the toolbar.

If you click the arrow repeatedly, the page will grow progressively larger. Then, when you have found the size you want, simply de-activate the zoom tool icon (i.e. click it again).

The View/Fit to Height Menu

Selecting the View ➤ Fit to Height menu (Ctrl + 0 in Windows) will adjust the page you are working on so that it fits the height of your screen.

The View Menu

Selecting Show Frames from the View menu will switch off the thin black lines that delineate a frame outline. This will enable you to get a better idea of what the finished page will look like. However, you can get a much better idea of what the finished product will look like by using the Preview mode. You can enable the Preview mode from the View menu, or you can click the eye icon on the lower right side of the screen.

The drop-down list for the Preview mode includes Normal Vision, which is designed to show how colors will look to someone who has normal vision. The other options show how the colors will look to someone who has a problem with their vision.

The Menu ➤ Show Grid setting provides a set of grid lines that will help you position objects on the page.

Another useful positional aid is the Show Guides setting, which displays any guides that have been created in order to assist the user to place objects on the page.

It is possible to switch between documents using the Windows menu. The Windows menu enables you to tile (Windows ➤ Tile) or cascade (Windows ➤ Cascade) their document windows, and you will find all your open documents listed at the end of the menu. The Windows menu also provides access to other useful dialogs such as the Layers dialog, the Scrapbook, the Properties Palette, and the Preflight Verifier.

Preferences

You can adjust the space between the borders of the page and the canvas by setting the Minimum Scratch Space in the Preferences/Display tab (see Figure 1-22). You can also adjust the distance between single pages in a document, by altering the Gap Between Pages setting.

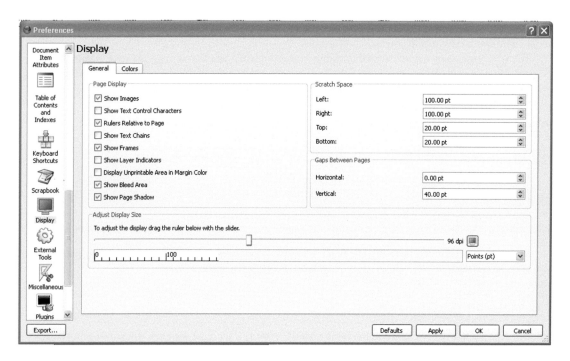

Figure 1-22. *Setting the Scratch Space in the Preferences/Display tab*

Navigating Your Documents

The following sections explain how to navigate your documents.

The Page List

The easiest way to navigate your documents is to use the page list, which is located on the status bar, as shown in Figure 1-23. You can jump between pages by clicking the arrow next to the drop-down list at the bottom of the screen. 1 ▼ of 1

Figure 1-23. *The Page List in the Navigation Bar*

Page Arrows

You can also move between pages by clicking the arrows at the bottom of the screen (status bar).

Document Outline

You can also choose a page by selecting the Windows ➤ Outline dialog (see Figure 1-24).

Figure 1-24. *The Outline dialog box*

Switching Between Documents

If you are working on more than one document in Scribus and you need to switch between documents, select the document you wish to move to by choosing the document name that you will find displayed at the bottom of the Windows menu.

Adding and Deleting Pages

To insert a page in your document, you can use the Page ➤ Insert menu (see Figure 1-25).

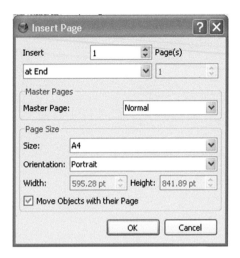

Figure 1-25. *The Page ➤ Insert Page dialog*

Scribus offers you the option of choosing how many pages to insert and where to insert them within the document. Scribus also offers you the ability to move and copy pages. Using the Page ➤ Copy option is a valuable way of editing your pages. It is also a good habit to get into.

The process of copying a page for editing purposes ensures that, should an edit go wrong, you still have the original page to fall back on.

EXERCISE

Go to the Page ➤ Insert menu.

Enter 2 pages.

Choose your insertion point. You can choose to insert your pages at the end, before a page number, or after a page number.

So choose to insert the new pages "After page: 1." Then click OK. You should now have two new empty pages following page 1.

Deleting Pages

You can also delete pages by using the Page menu. Simply go to the page you wish to delete, ensuring that it is selected, and then follow the Page ➤ Delete menu. The relevant page, and all its contents, will then be deleted. To delete several pages at once, use the Page ➤ Delete menu, and then enter the range of the pages that you wish to delete.

Arranging Pages

If you wish to rearrange the sequence of pages in your document, you can do so by using the Arrange Pages window (Windows ➤ Arrange Pages). Once you are in the Arrange Pages window, select the page that you wish to move with your mouse, drag it to its desired location, and then release it.

The Arrange Pages window (displayed in Figure 1-26) is a tool that lets you alter the running sequence of your pages so that they end up looking exactly the way that you want them.

Figure 1-26. *The Arrange Pages window*

To move the pages manually, go to the Arrange Pages window. The pages in your document are listed in the lower section of the window entitled Document Pages. With your mouse, highlight the page number that you wish to move and (while keeping the left mouse button depressed) move the page to its new position above or below the other pages.

The top of the Arrange Pages window displays a list of the available master pages (a master page is like a transparent underlay template on which you can place uneditable objects like page numbers, and headers and footers. These objects will then appear on every page to which the master page is applied. You will be looking at master pages later in the book). The area below the available master pages displays the pages in your document in a numbered sequence.

At the bottom of the Arrange Pages window, the Document Layout section displays the document format that was chosen when the document was first created.

You can use this section to change the document layout and first page layout. Simply click the arrow on the right and you will be given a choice of single page, double sided, 3-fold, or 4-fold.

Navigating with Bookmarks

Scribus can also aid the navigation within a document through the creation of bookmarks. To create a bookmark in Scribus, select a text frame that contains some text, and bring up the Context menu with a right click of the mouse. Then select PDF Options ➤ Is PDF Bookmark. The text frame will now be bookmarked.

If you open the bookmarks dialog (Windows ➤ Bookmarks) you should see your bookmark. Clicking a bookmark will take you back to the original text frame. Bookmarks can also be exported when a PDF is created so that the reader of the PDF can navigate between items.

Rules and Guides

The main Scribus window has a rule running along the top of the page, and there is another one running down the left side. You can toggle them on and off by going to the View menu and checking or unchecking the entry for Rules. You can use these rules to create guides.

Guides are horizontal and vertical lines that can be dragged onto the page in order to help you position objects on the page with a high level of precision, but which are not seen after the document is exported to PDF. The use of guides can help you increase your sense of visual space, and thus achieve more of a balance when it comes to positioning objects on the page.

You can place a guide line on the page by using the rules introduced earlier. Using the mouse, simply drag the rule onto the page, as shown in Figure 1-27.

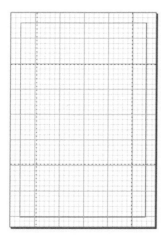

Figure 1-27. *Showing four rules after they have been dragged onto the page to form guides*

You can create the guides that you need by right-clicking the page, and selecting Manage Guides from the Context menu. This brings up the Guide Manager, as shown in Figure 1-28. You can start making guides by clicking ADD beneath the horizontal or vertical guide areas.

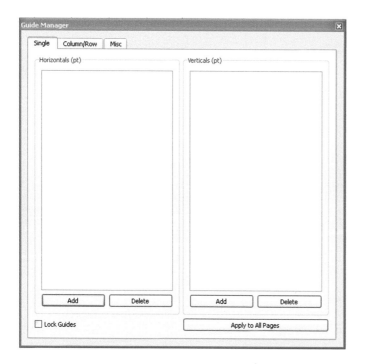

Figure 1-28. *The Guide Manager*

Once you are satisfied, you can check the box to lock the guides and a button that can apply them to all pages of your document, should you so wish.

You can snap an object to a guide by selecting Page ➤ Snap to Guides. To snap an object to a guide, select Page ➤ Snap to Guides.

Locking Your Guides

If you feel the need to lock your guides so that they cannot be moved, open the Guide Manager (Page ➤ Manage Guides) and check the Lock Guides box.

EXERCISE: CREATING A THREE-FOLD PANEL

Since you will be creating a three-fold brochure later on in the book, let's look at how to create three-fold panels from scratch using margins and guides.

Open Scribus, and in the New Document window, set the margins to 10mm. You can also select the Page Style, which will be Landscape. Set your default unit to millimeters and your four margin guides to 10mm. Then click OK.

Now, zoom out of the document so that you have a whole screen view (View ➤ Fit to height), and insert a second page (Page ➤ Insert).

Now you want to insert some guides so that your A4 page is divided equally into three panels. Open the Manage Guides window (Page ➤ Manage Guides), as shown in Figure 1-29.

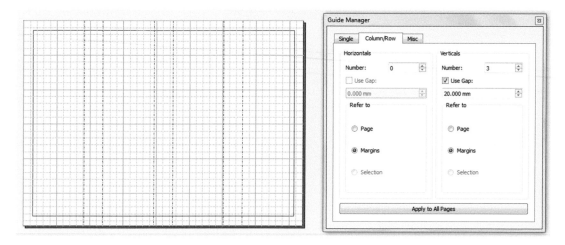

Figure 1-29. *The Guide Manager and three equal panels*

As you will need to include the margins when dividing up the page, select the Column/Row tab and then check the box "Refer to: Margins." You will need to insert three vertical columns and then establish a 20mm space for the gap between them for the panels.

To see how the changes will look, click the Apply to All Pages button at the bottom of the Guide Manager, and then click OK.

Once you are satisfied with the positioning of your guides, you can, if you wish, lock them to protect them from being accidentally moved on the page. To lock your guides, check the Lock Guides box, as shown in Figure 1-30.

Figure 1-30. *The Lock Guides box*

If you wish to snap some frames to your guides, select Snap to Guides from the Page menu. You can then insert some text frames in your three panels. Click the text frame icon and draw your first text frame so that it covers a panel up to the margin guides. You should find that the text box now "snaps" into place quite easily when you come to position it.

Working with Grids

Scribus also has a system of grids that you can use to aid your page layouts. The grids act like a sheet of graph paper, enabling you to align, distribute, and balance out the objects on your page. If your grid is not visible on the page, you can make it so by selecting View ➤ Show Grid. You can snap frames onto the grid system by selecting Page ➤ Snap to Grid.

Introducing Layers

Each document that you create will have at least one layer associated with it, but you can add and delete as many layers as you like. You can use layers to do the following:

- Aid the layout process (although you won't be able to align and distribute objects on different layers)

- Add guides, which can then be hidden during the printing process

- Adjust the transparency of a layer so that it appears partially visible over whatever is behind it.

- Overlap your graphics

- Separate objects that you wish to appear in the final print from those you wish to keep hidden

- Facilitate the editing of certain objects without affecting the others

Adding and Deleting a Layer

To add another layer, follow the Windows ➤ Layers menu. This will bring up the Layers dialog box shown in Figure 1-31.

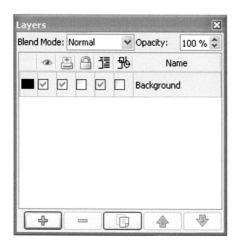

Figure 1-31. *The Layers window*

Click the + sign at the bottom to add a layer, and click the - sign alongside it to delete a layer. Click the Up or Down buttons to move between layers. Each layer can be locked or hidden. Using the Layers window, it is possible to redistribute the layers in the stack so that the objects on them appear above or below other objects.

Summary

Scribus is an impressive desktop publishing program, but it can sometimes appear a little confusing for the new user. In this chapter, I highlighted some of the things that the new user needs to bear in mind when loading Scribus for the first time.

You briefly looked at the system of frames that Scribus uses for its layouts, and you learned the importance of separating the process of content creation from that of page layout when creating a new document.

You were introduced to the New Document Dialog, to the Scribus templates, and to the use of Sample Text (which you can use as a filler), and you learned the importance of checking your default Preference settings when working with fonts and units of measurement. Finally, you learned how to navigate your documents.

In the next chapter, you will get more acquainted with the Scribus workspace and you'll learn about the Properties Palette, which lies at the heart of Scribus.

CHAPTER 2

■ ■ ■

Getting to Know the Workspace

In this chapter you will do the following:

- Familiarize yourself with Scribus

- Learn about your tools

- Customize the toolbar

- Learn to use the Story Editor

- Find your way around the Properties Palette

In the previous chapter, you learned about the New Document window, started a new document, and explored frames and preferences.

However, in order to use Scribus productively, it is important to familiarize yourself with the entire Scribus workspace. Chapter 2 is designed to get you acquainted with the toolbar and the menu bar, and to introduce you to the Story Editor, with which you will edit your texts in Scribus.

You will also be introduced to the Properties Palette, which lies at the heart of Scribus; this is where most of your detailed formatting and layout work will be done.

The Scribus Workspace

The first time you open Scribus, it will probably appear somewhat overwhelming. However, there is no need for panic; the Scribus interface has been designed so as to free the workspace of clutter.

Furthermore, Scribus gets easier to use the more you use it. Once you've used it a couple of times, you will start to adopt your own way of working, and you will create your own preferences, styles, and shortcuts.

Chapter 2 has been written with this process of familiarization in mind. Use it to familiarize yourself with the Scribus interface and the Properties Palette, and then proceed to customize Scribus so that it works for you just the way you want it.

The Scribus workspace, as it appears in Windows (and in Figure 2-1), is made up of the following five elements:

- **The Title Bar**, which is the topmost element of the application and bears the name of the active document

- **The Menu Bar**

- **The Toolbar**

- **The Canvas** (including the scratch space), which is the grey area surrounding the page that you can use as a test and storage area while you are experimenting with your text and image frames

- **The Status Bar**

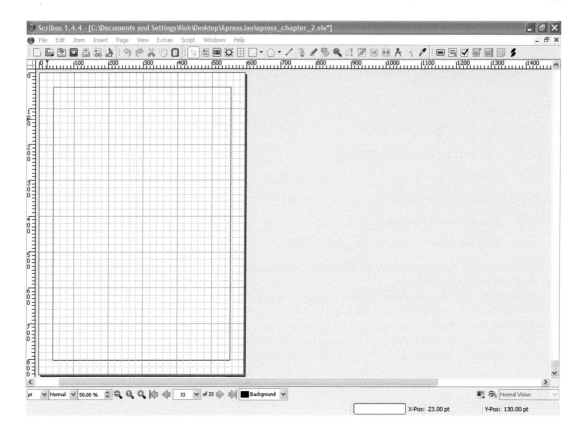

Figure 2-1. *The Scribus Workspace*

However, the Scribus workspace also utilizes a range of dialog boxes that can be opened and stored on the canvas. The most important of them all is the Properties Palette.

The Menu Bar

The menu bar, which is usually laid out across the top of the Scribus application window, contains eight menus: File, Edit, Item, Insert, Page, View, Extras, Script, Windows, and Help (see Figure 2-2). Each menu leads to a drop-down submenu containing a list of commands and associated shortcuts.

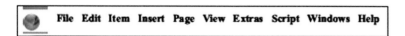

Figure 2-2. *The Menu Bar*

To display a menu, click the menu title, hold down the mouse button, and slide down the list of submenu commands. Inactive menu commands will have grayed-out letters.

If you wish to create a new document, select the New command in the File submenu (File ➤ New). This will bring up a dialog box in which you can set the size and orientation of your document. If you need to change how your documents (and their associated tools) are displayed, use the View menu.

The File menu (shown in Figure 2-3) contains a set of commands for opening, closing, saving, and printing files.

- **File ➤ Open** enables you to browse your Documents folder and locate your files using a variety of document formats as filters.

  With Scribus you can edit more than one document at a time. Moreover, if you have sufficient memory on your computer, it is possible to have two instances of Scribus running at the same time.

- **File ➤ Save** saves the document in the native .sla file format.

- **File ➤ Import** can be used to import text, image, or vector files.

- **File ➤ Export** saves the document as an EPS, PDF, Image, or SVG file.

- **File ➤ Print** brings up the Printer setup dialog box to help you print the document.

- **File ➤ Close** closes the document.

- **File ➤ Quit** closes Scribus.

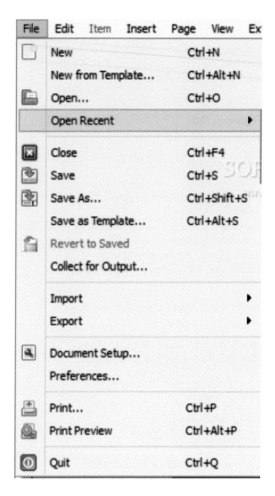

Figure 2-3. *The File Menu*

The File Menu: Preferences

Preferences are accessed from the File menu (although they are available through the Scribus menu in Mac OSX). The Preferences menu contains a set of tabs that allow you to make permanent changes to the following categories:

- General
- Document
- Typography
- Tools
- Hyphenator

- Fonts
- PreFlight Verifier
- Color Management
- PDF Export
- Document Item Attributes
- Table of Contents and Indexes
- Keyboard Shortcuts
- Display
- Miscellaneous
- Plugins
- Short Words
- Scripter

Preferences: The General Tab

In the Interface section of the General tab, there are settings available for the language, themes, and font size, and a setting allowing you to alter the number of documents available to view in the Recent Documents tab.

It is advisable to acquaint yourself with the Tools tab of the Preferences panel. The Tools tab lets you select the type, size, and color of the font to be used when you open a new text frame. If you overlook this tab and accept the default settings, you might find that an unwanted font, such as 12 point Arial Regular, appears every time you open a new text frame. Let's take a closer look at the Tools tab.

The Language setting refers to the languages available in Scribus menus and dialogs. The choice range from Afrikaans to Welsh and includes UK English.

The Theme setting refers to the appearance of Scribus on your O.S. There are different themes available for Windows, such as Windows XP, Motif, Plastique, and Cleanlooks.

There are two settings to enable you to alter the font sizes for the Interface menus and palettes.

The Wheel Jump setting refers to the number of pixels Scribus will scroll for each move of the mouse wheel.

The Recent Documents setting allows you to adjust the number of recently edited documents available in the File menu.

Finally, the Paths setting enables you to set the default paths for documents, templates, ICC profiles, and scripts. (An ICC profile is a set of international standards for the representation of color.)

The Document Tab

The Document tab (Figure 2-4) enables you to make changes to the default settings for document layers, page size, and margin guides.

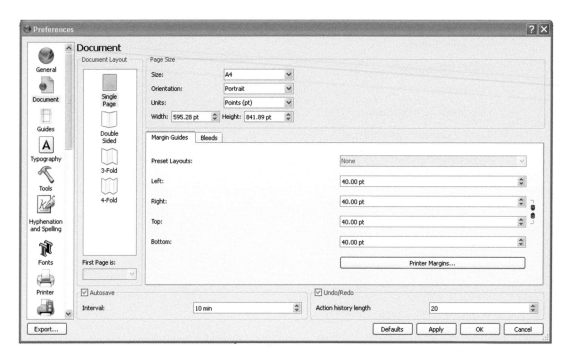

Figure 2-4. *The Document tab in Preferences*

On the left side, the Document Layout section lets you choose from single page, double-sided, 3-fold, and 4-fold layouts. It also lets you choose a left or right page as your first page.

The Page Size section allows you to choose from the following list of standard formats and custom sizes: A1 to A9, legal, letter, quarto, royal, and custom.

Under the Page Size section, you can also choose whether to have the portrait or landscape orientation as a default setting.

The Units setting allows you to choose your default setting from such typographical units of measure as points, picas, and ciceros as well as millimeters, inches, and centimeters. For custom page sizes, you can select the width and height of the page.

The default selections you can make for your margin guides vary according to your choice of document layout.

If you have opted for a single-page layout, you can adjust your margin guides for inside, outside, top, and bottom settings, but there are no preset layouts available; preset layouts only make sense for multipage documents.

Multipage Layouts

Preset layouts are, however, available if you select a double-sided, 3-fold, or 4-fold layout. You can choose from preset layouts such as Gutenberg, Magazine, Fibonacci, Golden Mean, and Nine Parts.

If printer drivers are installed, the Printer Margins button lets you choose between the printers available, and gets the margin values for the printers themselves (see Figure 2-4).

Bleeds

If you intend to print an image or background color right to the edge of a page, you will need to extend it over the edge of the current document, and to an area that will eventually be cut off. This area is called the **bleed**.

You can set your bleed when you set up the document for the first time, as shown in Figure 2-5. It will usually need a bleed area of between 3 and 5mm, but this depends on the printing process. I recommend checking the printer manual or asking the print shop where it will be printed. To show bleed guidelines, Select View ➤ Show Bleed.

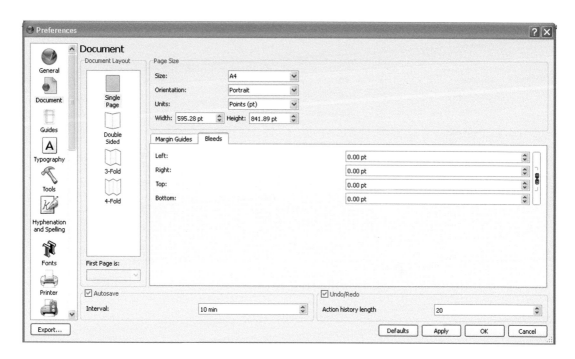

Figure 2-5. *The Bleeds panel in the Document window*

The Fonts Tab

The Fonts tab (shown in Figure 2-6) provides a list of the fonts that are available in Scribus. The tab tells Scribus which fonts should be available to you and, more significantly, it allows you to automate your font substitutions, enabling you to nominate serif and non-serif fonts in place of those that are unavailable on your computer.

It also enables you to set the path to your font files. If you have fonts stored in a directory other than your standard Fonts folder, you can use the Additional Paths option to enable Scribus to locate these fonts.

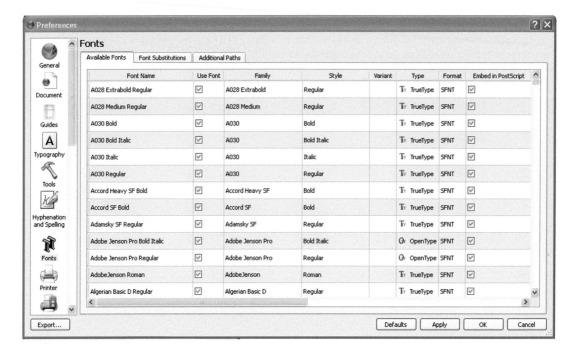

Figure 2-6. *The Fonts Tab in the Preferences Window*

The Guides Tab

The Guides tab (Figure 2-7) lets you choose whether you want to have guides and margins displayed, and whether they should be displayed in the foreground or the background.

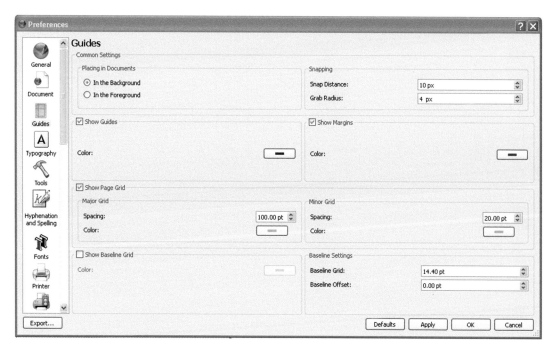

Figure 2-7. *The Guides Tab in the Preferences Window*

The Guides tab provides an option for displaying page grids (both major and minor) by default, as well as the distance between the baseline grids, which can be used to align text to the baseline. The baseline is the line on which each character, glyph, or line of text is based. Sometimes it is necessary to align text to a baseline in order to ensure that two columns of text are level with each other.

You can also set the snap distance (the distance within which an object will snap to your guides, which is useful when snapping objects to a grid) and something called a grab radius.

Grab Radius

The grab radius is the radius of the area where Scribus will allow you to grab an object's handles (see Figure 2-7). This setting determines the size of the area in which you can select those handles.

The Typography Tab

The Typography tab provides the ability to adjust the default settings for subscript, superscript, underline, strike-through, small capitals, and automatic line spacing.

The Tools Tab

The Tools tab (Figure 2-8) lets you select the type, size, and color of font to be used when you create a new text frame. It is important to be able to familiarize yourself with these settings. Simply ignoring them will result in a default setting, such as 12 point Arial Regular, appearing each time you start a new text frame.

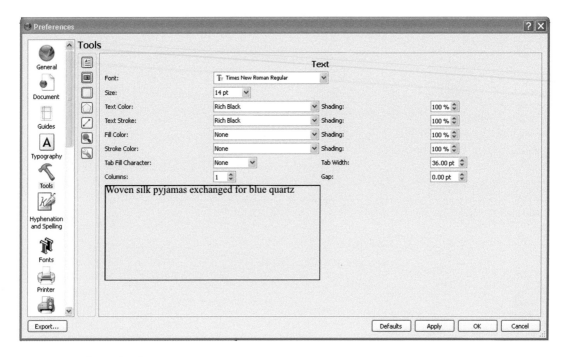

Figure 2-8. *The Tools tab*

The Hyphenation and Spelling Tab

This tab is useful if you want to use hyphenation automatically during typing, because hyphenation is not activated by default. It also lets you select the length of the smallest word to be hyphenated. The hyphenator hyphenates the text in your text frames, but you need to configure the tab carefully in order to be able to use it. For the current document you are working on, this can be done via Document Setup ➤ Hyphenation, or you can use File ➤ Preferences ➤ Hyphenation for all new documents.

The Preflight Verifier Tab

The Preflight Verifier runs automatically when you export your file in the Acrobat PDF format. It enables you to check your documents automatically for certain types of errors before they are exported as PDF files. The Preflight Verifier tab contains the default settings for the items that are checked.

The PDF Export Tab

When you follow the menu to save your file in PDF format (File ➤ Export ➤ Save as PDF), you will be given a lot of options. The PDF Export tab gives you the ability to select your default settings for PDF Export. It includes the settings for crop marks, printer marks, bleed settings, and registration marks.

It provides you with similar options to the ones that appear in the PDF Export dialog. You can compress text and vector graphics; set PDF output for color printing, greyscale, or the Web; and set the maximum image resolution.

Keyboard Shortcuts Tab

The Keyboard Shortcuts tab (shown in Figure 2-9) gives you the opportunity to add to and edit the default keyboard shortcuts in Scribus. For each shortcut, the tab lists a corresponding action. It also enables you to export their shortcuts as an XML file, so that you can copy them to another machine.

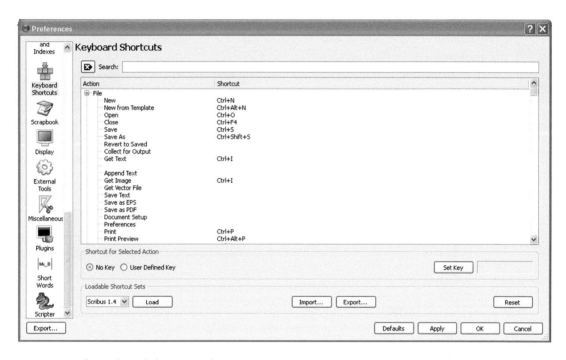

Figure 2-9. *The Keyboard Shortcuts Tab*

The Display Tab

The Display panel enables you to adjust your default page display and scratch space options. You can also use it to adjust the screen display size and the gaps between pages.

The Color tab of the Display panel enables you to customize the colors used to represent screen features such as pages, borders, and frames. This tab has a Pages section that lets you play with the fill color of the document background as it appears on your display. This document background fill color is not printed, but it can be used to check the result when printing onto colored paper.

Plugins

The Plugins panel (shown in Figure 2-10) contains a Plugin column that allows you to load and deselect the plugins that came with your Scribus installation, plugins such as Scripter, Barcode Generator, and Calendar.

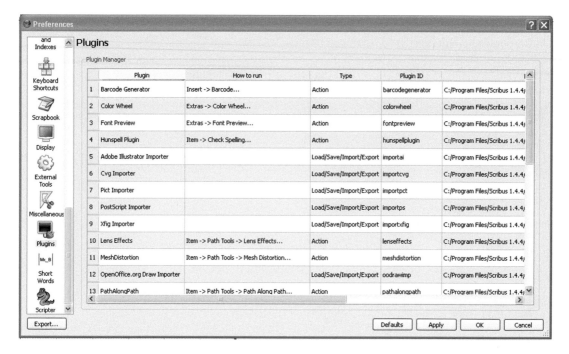

Figure 2-10. *The Plugins Panel*

The Scripter plugin is a Scribus scripting engine. It is intended for use with the Python programming language as a way of carrying out a series of operations within Scribus.

The Barcode Generator is a plugin that creates and inserts barcodes in your documents.

The Calendar wizard creates fairly professional-looking calendar layouts.

The Scrapbook

The Scrapbook is a way of storing your graphics, page objects, and page layouts in case you need to use them again. To save an object in your Scrapbook, right-click it and select Send to Scrapbook. You will be prompted to choose a name for your object. To open the Scrapbook, go the Windows menu and choose Scrapbook.

The Edit Menu

The Edit menu (Figure 2-11) is where you can undo recent actions in Scribus. You can cut, copy, and paste frames, and edit texts and images. You can also edit patterns and colors, and add JavaScript code.

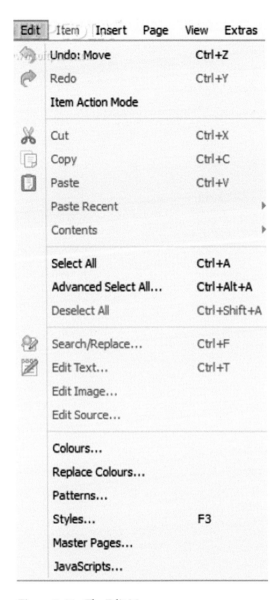

Figure 2-11. *The Edit Menu*

- **Edit ➤ Undo** undoes the last action and takes you back to the previous step.

- **Edit ➤ Redo** undoes the previous undo command.

- **Edit ➤ Cut** removes an object from the current document, and places it on the clipboard.

- **Edit ➤ Copy** copies an object in the open document to your clipboard.

- **Edit ➤ Paste** pastes the previously cut or copied element from the clipboard into the document.

- **Edit ➤ Select All** selects every object on the active layer on the active page.

- **Edit ➤ Advanced Select All** enables you to make a qualified selection of the objects you want to select.

- **Edit ➤ Colors** is where you make new colors for your color palette.

- **Edit ➤ Master Pages** is where you can change your Master Pages.

- **Edit ➤ Styles** is where you open the Style Manager. Styles help give a consistent look to your documents.

The Page Menu

The Page menu (Figure 2-12) is used for arranging pages in a document.

Figure 2-12. *The Page Menu*

- **Page ➤ Insert** inserts a new page.

- **Page ➤ Apply Master Page** enables you to specify which page is based on which master page.

- **Page ➤ Manage Guides** enables you to apply guidelines to your pages.

- **Page ➤ Snap to Grid** enables the automatic "snapping" of objects in relation to margins and guidelines.

- **Page ➤ Snap to Guides** enables you to force the objects on the page to snap to their guides.

The Insert Menu

Use the Insert menu to insert everything from a render frame or freehand line to a barcode or a sample text. Choosing to insert sample text will insert a sample (or placeholder) text inside the active text frame.

You can use the Insert menu to insert text frames or image frames into the active document; the menu provides shortcuts to enable you to do this. However, it is usually easier to select the appropriate tool in the toolbar.

The Item Menu

The Item menu contains options that enable you to manipulate the size and shape of an image frame, alter the level of a frame, or group and ungroup a set of frames.

- **Item ➤ Group** allows you to modify several items in the same way at the same time.

- **Item ➤ Ungroup** disperses the group. When you ungroup an object its constituent parts can be selected individually again.

- **Item ➤ Level** moves an object up or down in relation to other objects on the page using levels. A level is a stacking order control for objects that are on the same layer. Depending on what level an object is at, you can move it up or down in the stacking order.

- **Item ➤ Send to Layer** moves an object from one layer to another.

- **Item ➤ Adjust frame to Image** changes the size of an image frame so as to fit the size of the image.

- **Item ➤ Adjust Image to Frame** changes the size of an image so as to fit the size of an image frame.

- **Item ➤ Update Image** updates an image in Scribus immediately after it has been edited in an image editing program.

- **Item ➤ Link Text Frames** links two text frames together so that any overflowing text will flow from one text frame into the other.

- **Item ➤ Send to Scrapbook** sends a copy of the active item to the Scrapbook.

- **Item ➤ Duplicate** creates a copy of your selected object.

- **Item ➤ Multiple Duplicates** can make one or more copies of your selected objects.

- **Item ➤ Transform** modifies an object through scaling, rotation, skewing, or translation.

The View Menu

The View menu enables you to display your visual aids (such as grids or guides) and to alter how the document is shown on the screen. You can use it to try out different zoom levels, and to look at text under different magnifications.

The Extras Menu

Use the Extras menu to manage images, hyphenate text, generate a table of contents, preview your fonts, and use the color wheel.

You can manage images in the Extras menu by using the Manage Images dialog box. This displays a list of all the images imported into the document, together with graphics data about each image, and a path to the stored location of the image.

The Toolbar

Below the main menu bar is the Scribus toolbar. When Scribus is first installed, the toolbar is inserted across the top of the screen, but this arrangement can be changed at any time to suit your individual way of working.

Scribus has many floating panels, of which the toolbar is a good example. The idea is that you pull out just the panels that you need while you continue working on the layout. In the Windows versions of Scribus, the toolbar is divided into four groups of tools by faint dotted lines:

File Commands   Edit Commands   Tools   PDF Features

It is possible to move these groups of tools over onto another area of the canvas or against the left, right, and bottom edge of the Scribus window.

To relocate a group of tools, simply place the mouse over the faint dotted line and drag the tool group over to another place on the canvas.

If you move a group over to the left or right margins of the canvas, the items will group themselves in a vertical bar. Figure 2-13 explains the icons.

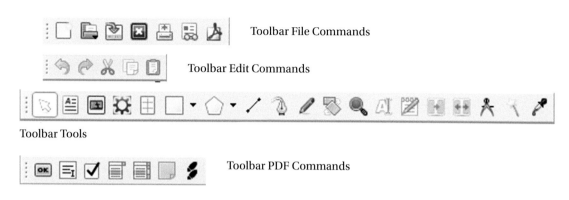

Toolbar File Commands

Toolbar Edit Commands

Toolbar Tools

Toolbar PDF Commands

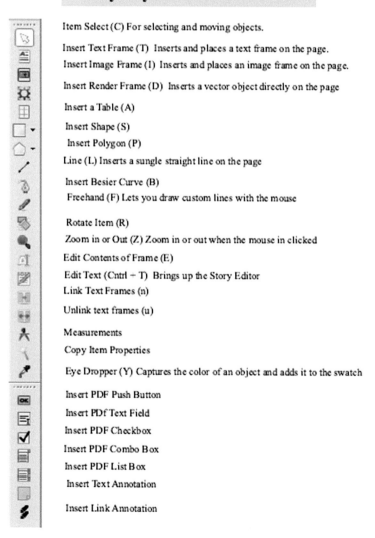

Key to your Toolbar Icons

Item Select (C) For selecting and moving objects.

Insert Text Frame (T) Inserts and places a text frame on the page.

Insert Image Frame (I) Inserts and places an image frame on the page.

Insert Render Frame (D) Inserts a vector object directly on the page

Insert a Table (A)

Insert Shape (S)

Insert Polygon (P)

Line (L) Inserts a sungle straight line on the page

Insert Besier Curve (B)

Freehand (F) Lets you draw custom lines with the mouse

Rotate Item (R)

Zoom in or Out (Z) Zoom in or out when the mouse in clicked

Edit Contents of Frame (E)

Edit Text (Cntrl – T) Brings up the Story Editor

Link Text Frames (n)

Unlink text frames (u)

Measurements

Copy Item Properties

Eye Dropper (Y) Captures the color of an object and adds it to the swatch

Insert PDF Push Button

Insert PDf Text Field

Insert PDF Checkbox

Insert PDF Combo Box

Insert PDF List Box

Insert Text Annotation

Insert Link Annotation

Figure 2-13. *Toolbar Icons Guide*

The Eye Dropper

The eye dropper is a really useful tool that lets you sample colors from an image, document, or photo, and then add them to your color palette.

This is very useful if, say, you want to match the background of a text or image frame with the exact color used in an accompanying photograph (see Figures 2-14, 2-15, and 2-16).

Figure 2-14. *The eye dropper can be used to capture colors like the blue in the Scribus logo*

3 May. Bistritz.--Left Munich at 8:35
P.M., on 1st May, arriving at Vienna early
next morning; should have arrived at 6:46,
but train was an hour late. Buda-Pesth
seems a wonderful place, from the
glimpse which I got of it from the train
and the little I could walk through the
streets. I feared to go very far from the
station, as we had arrived late and would
start as near the correct time as possible.
I did not sleep well, though my bed was
comfortable enough, for I had all sorts of
queer dreams. There was a dog howling
all night under my window, which may
have had something to do with it; or it
may have been the paprika, for I had to

Figure 2-15. *The background of the text frame now has the imported blue*

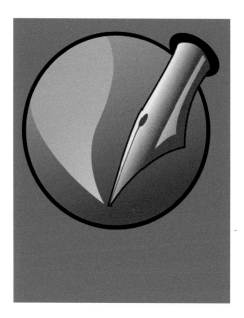

Figure 2-16. *The background of this image also now has the imported shade of blue*

The Eye Dropper dialog box requires you to supply your own name for the color, but after you have done that, it will be available to use in Scribus. Note that the Mac OS X version of Scribus has a bug with the eye dropper tool at the time of writing, which hopefully will have been fixed by the time you read this.

The Canvas

A really useful part of the Scribus environment is the canvas, which consists of the document page and the surrounding grey area, known as the "scratch space." Using the mouse, it is possible to drag text frames and graphics files onto the scratch space, which can act as a testbed for all your different page layouts. You can also use it as a way of storing items for later use.

The Select Item Tool

The Select Item tool is probably the single most important tool in Scribus. It is automatically selected after using another tool (unless Sticky Tools has been selected in the Insert menu).

Tooltips

As a beginner, you will almost certainly want to enable Tooltips. Tooltips appear whenever you hover your mouse over the icons and buttons in Scribus. They provide an easy and effective way of enabling new users to familiarize themselves with the Scribus workspace, so it is important to check that they are enabled.

To further encourage your familiarization with the Scribus workspace, make sure that the Tooltips are selected. To enable Tooltips, go to the Tooltips submenu under the Help menu, and ensure that the entry for Tooltips is marked with a tick.

The Status Bar

The status bar displays, from left to right, a points control, a layer selector, and a zoom selector (see Figure 2-17). It also displays the coordinates of your current mouse position, enabling you to read the location of your mouse and select the unit of measurement you will be working in, and it has several zoom levels to let you work up close to an object on the page. It also contains a button for activating color management and another for activating the Preview Mode. The status bar also enables you to read the location of your mouse and select the unit of measurement you will be working in.

Figure 2-17. *The Status Bar*

The Story Editor

Once you have inserted a text box, you will want to edit and format the text. This is when you use the Story Editor (Figure 2-18).

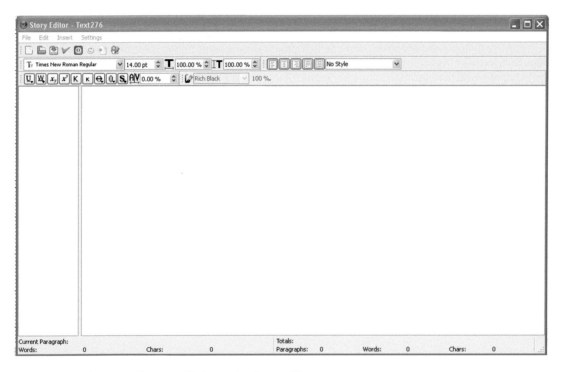

Figure 2-18. *The Story Editor is really just a simple text editor*

To open the Story Editor, simply right-click the text frame, and select Edit Text from the Context menu. The Story Editor is a simple text editing window with some formatting features added to it. It's not the right place for detailed formatting work (for that you need the Properties Palette) but it is where most users begin the process of text editing, and it is where most of your initial layout work will be done.

This is where you begin your initial edit of the text, selecting your desired type, size, and color of font, and applying superscript, shadowed text, and paragraph styles. Most of these tools are self-explanatory. The Underline tool underlines texts and spaces, whereas the Underline Words Only option leaves the spaces blank. The Shadow tool produces a duplicate behind the selected letter in order to create the effect of a shadow. The Kerning tool enables you to adjust the distance between letters. This is also where you format your left, right, or center-justified text.

The Story Editor provides a convenient way of editing text, but it is also rather basic, and you only get a real-time view of your edits when you click the Update Text Frame button on the Story Editor's toolbar.

When modifying your existing text, if you want to see the resulting text as it appears in the text frame, you need to click the Update button on the toolbar. If you make a mistake, you need to select the File ➤ Exit Without Updating Text Frame, which is the fifth button from the left. You can also update the text frame and exit the Story Editor by clicking the Update Text Frame and Exit button. There are also buttons for selecting the font family and a spin box for the font sizes.

The Justification and Style buttons (Figure 2-19) are located on the right side of the toolbar. There are buttons for left justification, center justification, right justification, full justification, and enforced full justification (where even short words are fully justified).

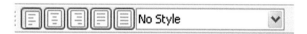

Figure 2-19. *The Justification and Style tools in the Story Editor*

If you use only a full justification for a block of text, you may find that the words in the final lines will look over-stretched. However, this can be remedied by using hyphenation properly with the current justification setting.

Closing

When you have finished formatting and editing your text and you've got it looking just how you want it, click the Update Text Frame and Exit button on the Story Editor toolbar. This will close the Story Editor and update the active frame.

The Properties Palette

So, you've added a frame, inserted some text, and formatted it using the Story Editor. If you want to do some more detailed work, you will need to customize your document's properties by opening the Properties Palette, as shown in Figure 2-20 (Windows ➤ Properties, or right-click the text frame and select Properties).

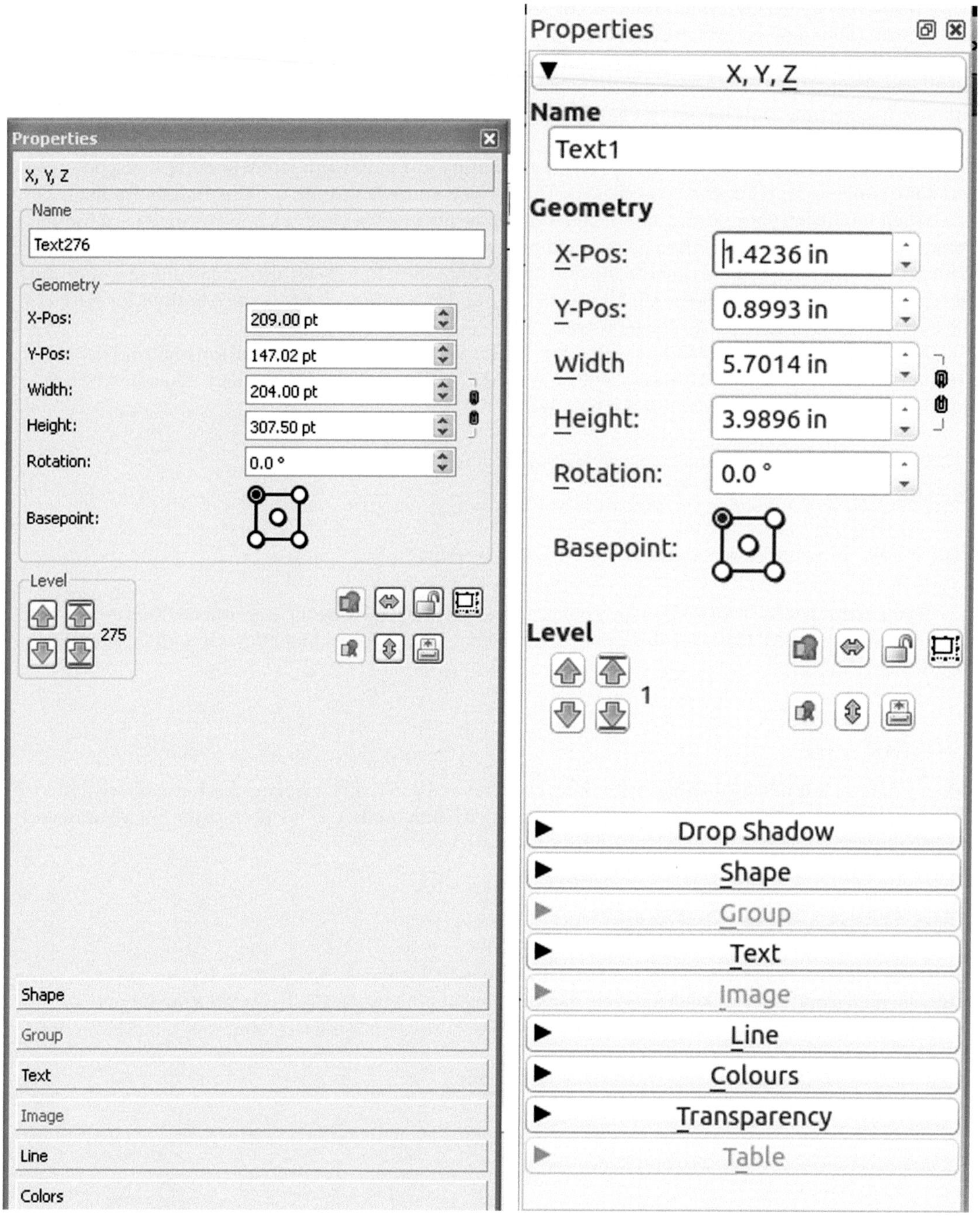

Figure 2-20. *The Properties Palette (the stable Windows 1.4.5 version on the left, the unstable Linux 1.5.0 version on the right)*

The Properties Palette could be said to be the control center of the Scribus page layout system. This is where you control, refine, and embellish the look of your text and image frames, with dazzling background color gradients and rotating images. It is where most of the really impressive functions reside, and it provides quick access to a wide range of properties so that you can customize the objects in an open document without the need to go through your menus.

It is advisable to practice using the Properties Palette; learn to use it well and you can turn a run-of-the-mill word-processed document into an elegant and feature-rich one.

The palette contains seven tabs, or panes, which can be expanded and reshaped as the palette is moved around the screen. In the current Windows version, these seven tabs are given over to XYZ positioning, line, color, text, shape, image, and group.

- **XYZ** enables you to locate and rotate your objects with detailed precision.

- **Shape** allows you to edit the borders of a frame shape and change how text flows around an object.

- **Text** enables you to change the settings for the font, text color, line-spacing, styles, and number of columns.

- **Image** lets you edit the position and scaling of your images.

- **Lines** lets you modify the type, width, and base point of lines, Bezier curves, freehand lines, and frame borders.

- **Color** lets you change the fill or stroke color of a frame or shape.

- **Group** allows you to modify grouped objects at the same time.

The XYZ Tab

The XYZ tab (Figure 2-21) provides a set of tools that lets you manipulate the width, height, and rotation of your frames on the page with a high degree of precision. You can rotate an item on the page by entering a range of plus or minus values in the rotation box.

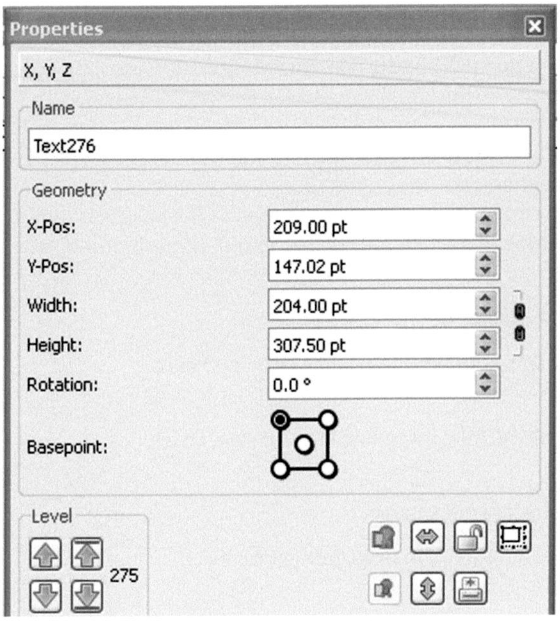

Figure 2-21. *The XYZ Tab of the Properties Palette*

Grouping Frames

The Groups tab gives you control over a group of objects. If you need to preserve the arrangement of frames on the paper, you can group them. You can do this by holding down the Shift key, selecting all the frames you want in your group, and then selecting Item ➤ Group (or Control+G). To ungroup them, simply select them all again and select Item ➤ Ungroup.

Properties: The Shape Tab

The Shape tab (shown in Figure 2-22) lets you manipulate shapes and edit the shape of your frames.

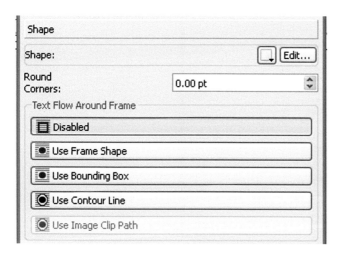

Figure 2-22. *The Shape Tab*

Text Flow Around Frame

Towards the bottom of the Shape tab is an area for controlling the flow of text around a frame. This is where you get to format your text so that it flows around an image. To do this, ensure that the image frame is positioned over the text frame. If it falls behind the image, right-click it and select Level ➤ Raise to Top from the context menu in order to restore it. You can flow text around an image in a precise way by manipulating the contour line, or you can use the bounding box of the image. Both the contour line and the bounding box are created when you create an image frame, and, initially, they occupy the same size and position. The bounding box is the rectangular shape that defines the boundary of a shape or image.

The contour line can be defined in editing mode by checking the Edit Contour Line box. It lets you add nodes and control points outside the bounding box. Selecting the Contour Line control will affect the flow of text around the selected image.

Properties: The Line Tab

The Line tab (Figure 2-23) enables you to select and format various types of lines. It also lets you add stroke colors to your frame borders.

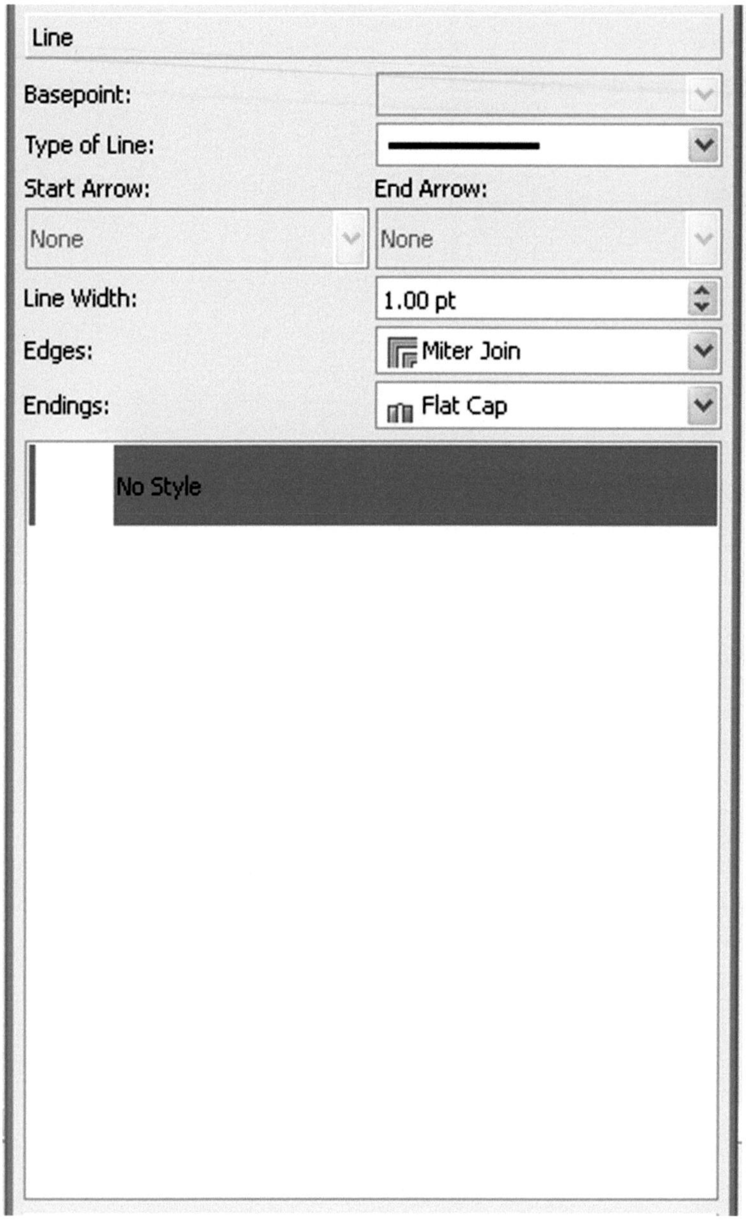

Figure 2-23. *The Line Tab*

Properties: The Colors Tab

You can use the Colors tab (Figure 2-24) to apply colors, shades, and patterns to your image and text frames. These colors can include the custom colors you have collected using the eye dropper tool on the toolbar, or colors you have created manually using other tools.

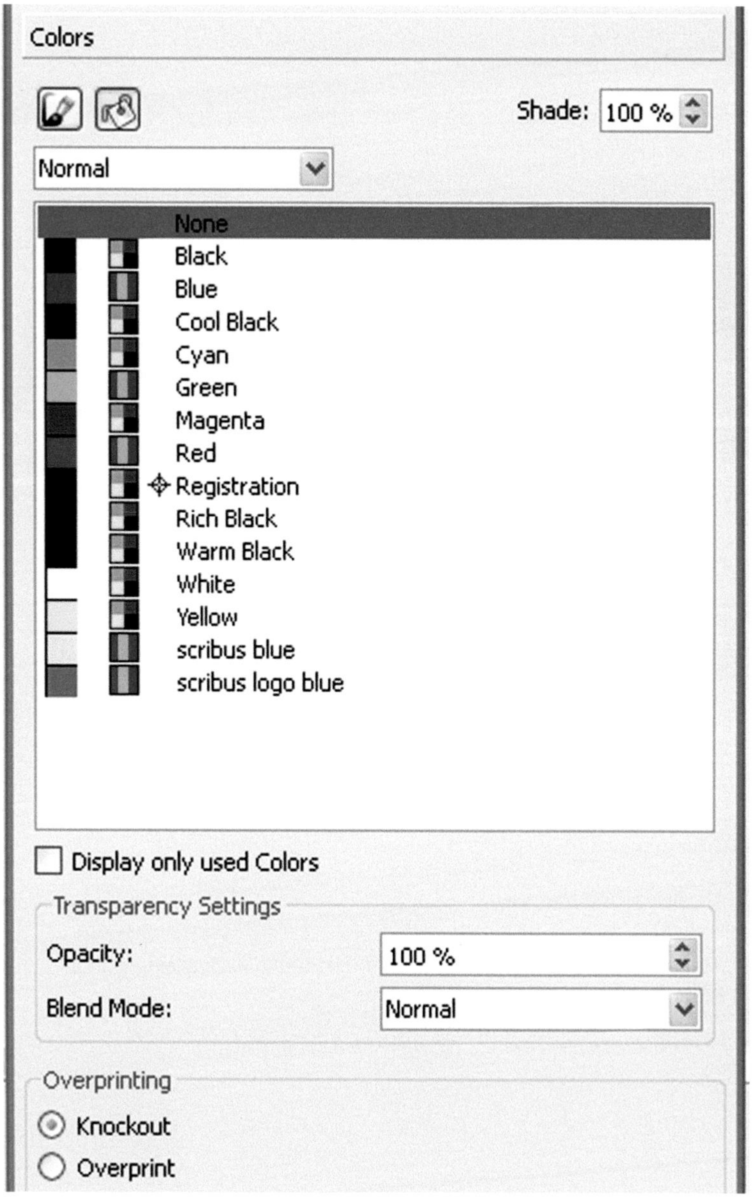

Figure 2-24. *The Colors Tab*

It will also let you create fill colors using gradients of two or more colors, a very impressive technique and one that is used in many glossy magazines. Let's give it a try.

EXERCISE

When you get time, try using the Gradient tool on the Colors tab of the Properties Palette (see Figure 2-25).

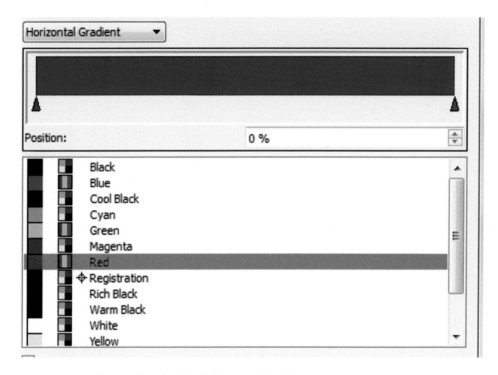

Figure 2-25. *Selecting the colors for the horizontal gradient*

You can try it out on a shape or a text box with a colored background. A text frame background with a plain color fill will have a default Normal setting in the Fill Type.

But when you click the arrow by the button marked Normal, you will see a list of fill types.

Horizontal Gradient

Vertical Gradient

Diagonal Gradient

Cross Gradient

Radial Gradient

Free Gradient

Go to the Colors tab of the Properties Palette, and select the drop-down list for the fill type that is set to Normal. You will be given a choice of Normal, Horizontal Gradient, Vertical Gradient, Cross-Diagonal gradient, Radial Gradient, Free Linear Gradient, and Free Radial Gradient.

Select the Horizontal Gradient setting. The Gradient Selector fill display will appear, as shown in Figure 2-26. It will have two triangular stops on the left and right side, which are set to the color black. The red triangle indicates the currently selected color stop.

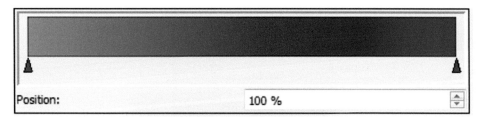

Figure 2-26. *The gradient is set and the colors have been imported into the text frame*

Select the first triangular color stop on the left and choose a color from the color swatch. Then select the color stop on the right and select another color. When you have done that, you should notice that your frame or shape now contains a horizontal gradient that runs from one color into the other, as in Figure 2-26.

If you want to add a third color, click the gradient fill selector somewhere in the middle of the display and a third triangular stop will appear. Select a third color, and you will now have three colors in your gradient. Note that you can slide your color stops left and right along the gradient selector in order to alter the mix of colors.

Properties: The Image Tab

The Image tab (see Figure 2-27) enables you to control the size and scale of your images. You can use it to play around with the scaling of your images. There is a checkbox that enables you to scale the image to frame size, and another for keeping the image scaling proportional.

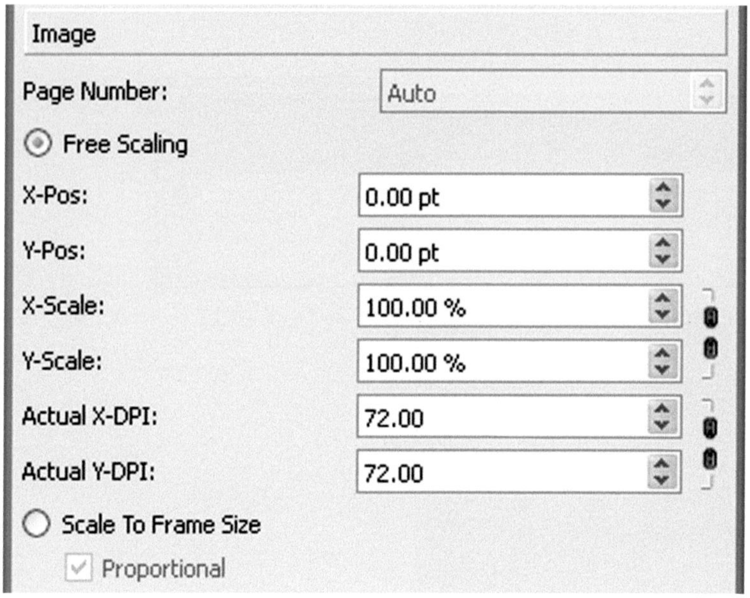

Figure 2-27. *The Image Tab*

If you select Free Scaling, you activate the scaling tools. Some of these tools can help you to offset your images to the left or the right, or up or down within the frame. Others enable you to rescale the image within the frame. You will be looking more closely at image effects in a later chapter.

THE IMAGE TAB

Insert another blank page in Scribus and then click the Insert Image Frame icon on the toolbar and draw an image frame onto the page (see Figure 2-28).

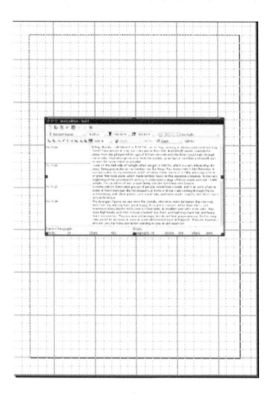

Figure 2-28. *Inserting an image onto the page*

Right-click the image frame and select Get Image from the context menu. Find a suitable image on your computer. (It does not matter too much what the image looks like at this stage; I have chosen a screen capture of the Story Editor from Scribus 1.5 svn for Linux.) Right-click the image and select Scale to Frame Size.

Now, with the image frame highlighted, right-click the frame and select Properties from the context menu. The Properties Palette will open, as displayed in Figure 2-29.

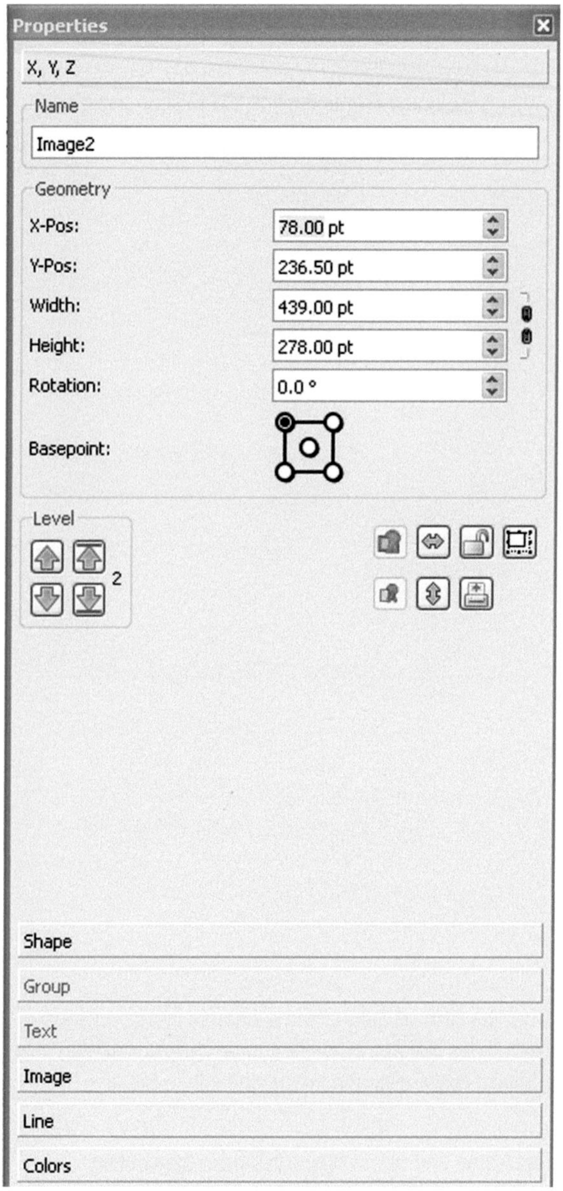

Figure 2-29. *The Properties Palette*

Select the tab marked Image, as shown in Figure 2-30.

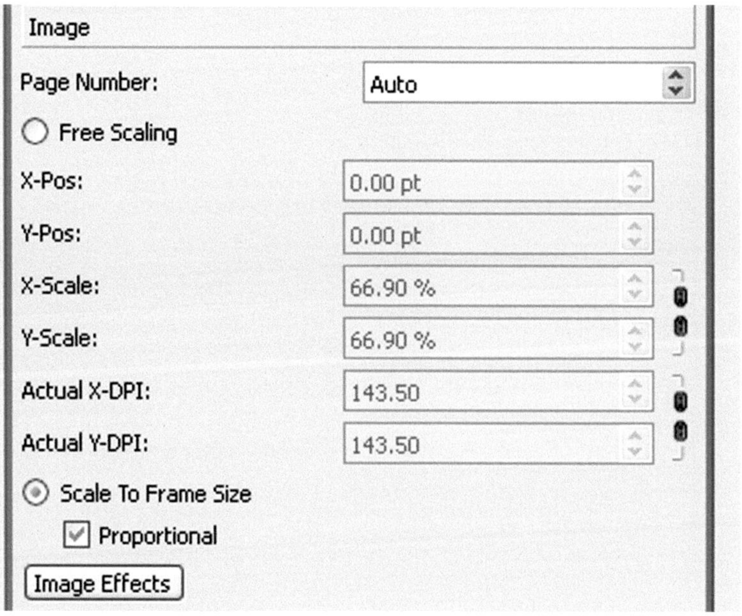

Figure 2-30. *The Image Tab*

Note that the Properties Palette has two fields entitled Scale to Frame Size and Proportional. If the Proportional field were left unchecked, the image would be stretched to fit the frame, and would, as a result, become quite distorted. When it is checked, the image is sized in proportion according to its frame size. Or you can select Free Scaling, which will enable you to crop the edges, reposition the image, or change the scaling.

The Image tab has a column of image manipulation tools. X-Pos and Y-Pos refer to the relative positions of the upper left corner of the image and the upper left corner of the frame. If you increase the X-Pos tool to 10 points, the image will move across to the right side of the frame. If you increase the Y-Pos by 10 points, the image will move down within the frame.

The X-Scale, Y-Scale, X-DPI, and Y-DPI fields are linked by default. X-Scale and Y-Scale refer to the magnification of the image compared to the actual DPI. Try increasing the X-Scale and you will notice that the image is rescaled and appears to stretch horizontally, as in Figure 2-31.

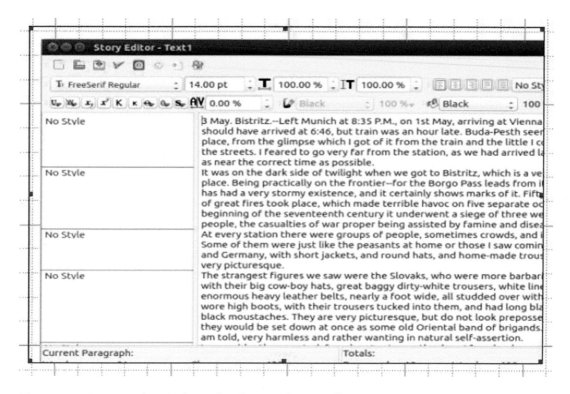

Figure 2-31. *Increasing the X-Scale stretches the image horizontally*

Try increasing the Y-Scale field. You will notice that the image is rescaled and appears to stretch vertically, as in Figure 2-32.

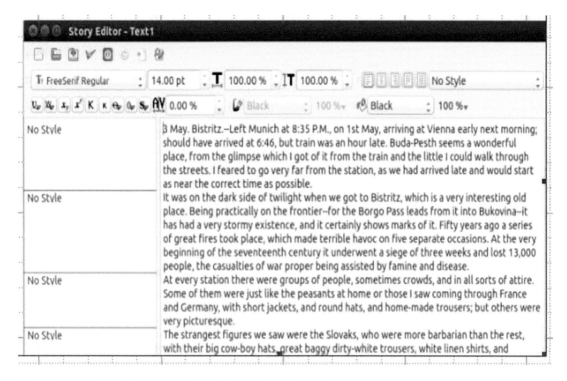

Figure 2-32. *Increasing the Y-Scale rescales the image vertically*

The Actual X- and Y-DPI fields are related to magnification. The measurement of 143-50 DPI refers to the final resolution to be exported to PDF. Now try increasing the Actual X-DPI field, as in Figure 2-33.

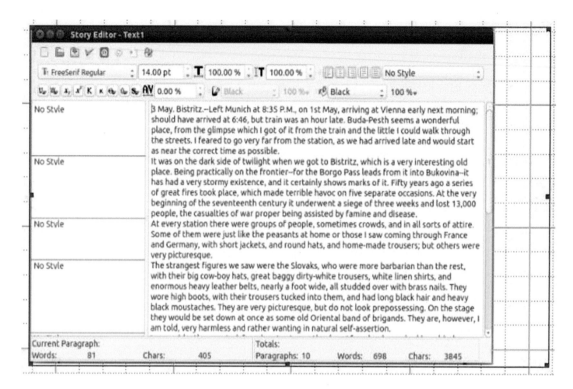

Figure 2-33. *Increasing the Actual X-DPI field rescales the image so that it looks squeezed*

Increasing the Actual X-DPI field rescales the image in such a way that it squeezes to the left within the frame, as in Figure 2-34.

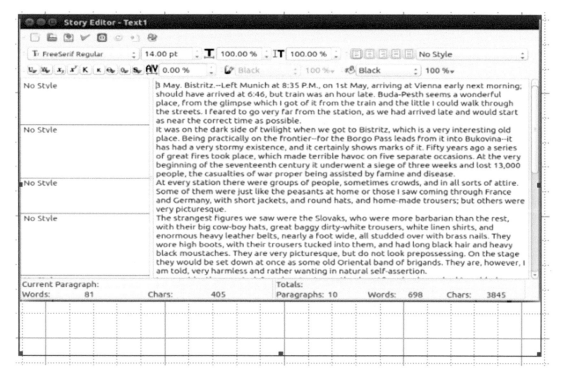

Figure 2-34. *Increasing the Actual X-DPI squeezes the image upwards*

Properties: The Text Tab

At the top of the Text tab (Figure 2-35) is a drop-down menu for selecting the required font family, and below that is another one for selecting font style, such as bold or italic. Below these are two columns of spin boxes that handle font size, linespacing, and the alignment of text on the baseline grid.

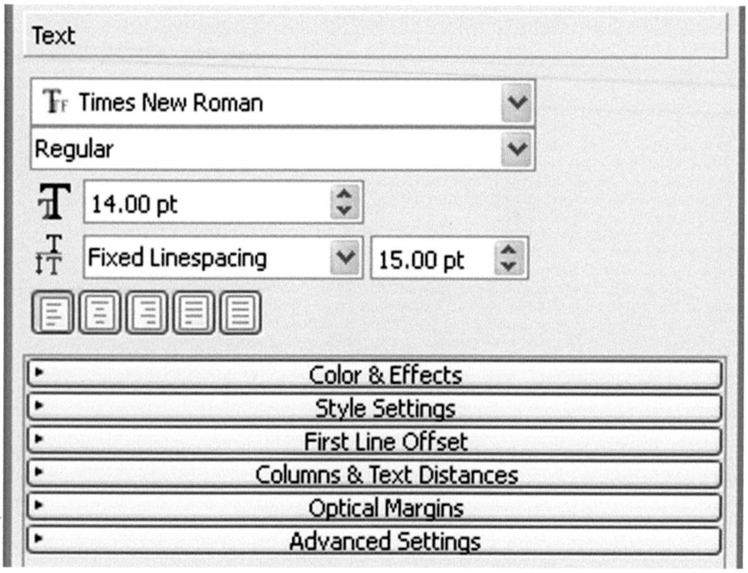

Figure 2-35. *The Text Tab*

Linespacing was once known as leading because typesetters in the days of hand typesetting used thin strips of lead to space their lines of text. The Linespacing spinbox offers a choice of fixed linespacing, automatic linespacing, or aligning to the baseline grid.

The baseline grid is a document-wide set of horizontal lines that are used, if baseline grid spacing is selected, as a way of aligning text to the same line.

There are also boxes for scaling, stretching, and shrinking the width of the font characters, and for scaling the height of the font.

At the bottom of the Text tab are a series of expanders. The first ones are the Color & Effects buttons, which provide the same tools as found on the Story Editor, enabling you to select the fill color of your text.

The Advanced Settings expander contains the manual tracking control, which alters the letter spacing that is applied within words. Kerning adjusts the space between individual letters.

There are also two drop-down menus for controlling the Font Stroke Color and Font Fill Color if the text has been given an outline.

There are also buttons for underlining text, or converting it to subscript, superscript, and shadowed text. Note that you can select fonts and font styles individually in the Text tab of the Properties Palette, but if you want to do this in the Story Editor, you need to select bold or italic variants as a separate font in the font selector.

Column and Text Distances

The button marked Column & Text Distances (Figure 2-36) enables you to set the number of text columns in your text frame as well as the width of the gap that will separate them (see Figure 2-37).

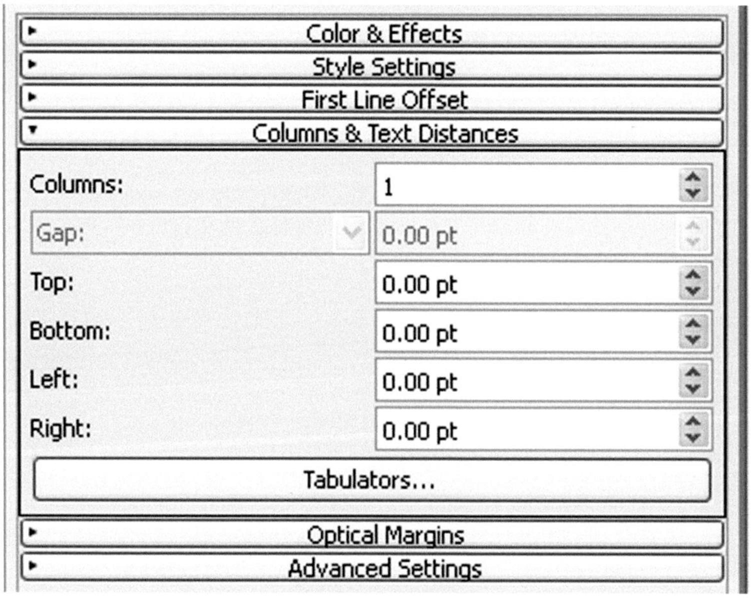

▸	Color & Effects	
▸	Style Settings	
▸	First Line Offset	
▾	Columns & Text Distances	

Columns:	1	▲▼
Gap: ⌄	0.00 pt	▲▼
Top:	0.00 pt	▲▼
Bottom:	0.00 pt	▲▼
Left:	0.00 pt	▲▼
Right:	0.00 pt	▲▼
Tabulators...		

▸	Optical Margins	
▸	Advanced Settings	

Figure 2-36. *The Columns and Distances Button*

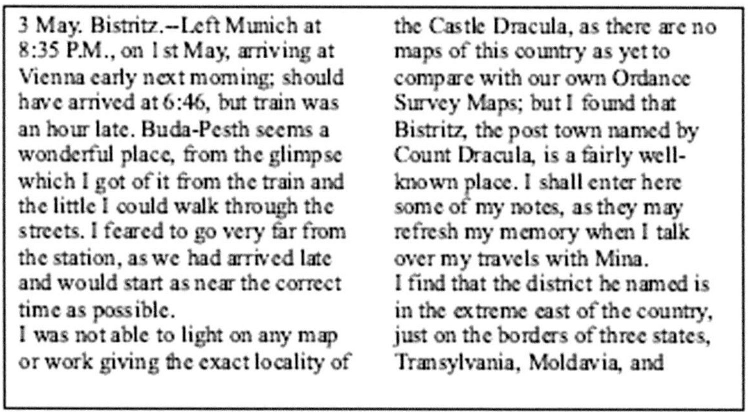

3 May. Bistritz.–Left Munich at 8:35 P.M., on 1st May, arriving at Vienna early next morning; should have arrived at 6:46, but train was an hour late. Buda-Pesth seems a wonderful place, from the glimpse which I got of it from the train and the little I could walk through the streets. I feared to go very far from the station, as we had arrived late and would start as near the correct time as possible.
I was not able to light on any map or work giving the exact locality of the Castle Dracula, as there are no maps of this country as yet to compare with our own Ordance Survey Maps; but I found that Bistritz, the post town named by Count Dracula, is a fairly well-known place. I shall enter here some of my notes, as they may refresh my memory when I talk over my travels with Mina.
I find that the district he named is in the extreme east of the country, just on the borders of three states, Transylvania, Moldavia, and

Figure 2-37. *A two-column layout in a text frame*

THE PROPERTIES PALETTE AND STORY EDITOR

Insert a new page in Scribus, click the Insert Text Frame icon on the toolbar, and draw out a new text frame onto the page.

Then right-click the frame and select Sample Text from the context menu. When prompted, select the version of Sample Text in the English language, and fill the frame with sample text, as in Figure 2-38.

Figure 2-38. *A text frame filled with sample text*

The text that appears will be in the default font setting, which in my case is Times New Roman, Regular, 14 points.

Now, right-click the text frame and select Properties. This will open the Properties Palette. Select the Text tab, as shown in Figure 2-39.

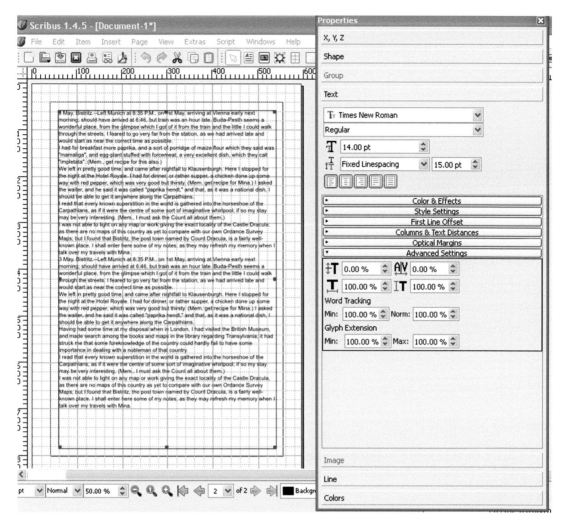

Figure 2-39. *The Text tab of the Properties Palette*

The text should appear as the default font, which (in my case) is 14 points Times New Roman Regular. You will notice two font fields, one for the font type, and one for the font style.

In the Font size field of the Properties Palette, select 12 points Arial and select Regular in the Font Style field. You should notice that the text frame updates automatically, as shown in Figure 2-40.

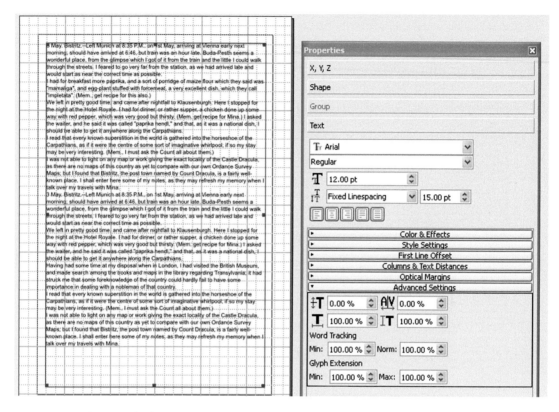

Figure 2-40. *The Text tab after a new font, font style, and font size have been selected*

Go back to the text frame, right-click it, and select Edit Text from the context menu. This will open the Story Editor, as shown in Figure 2-41.

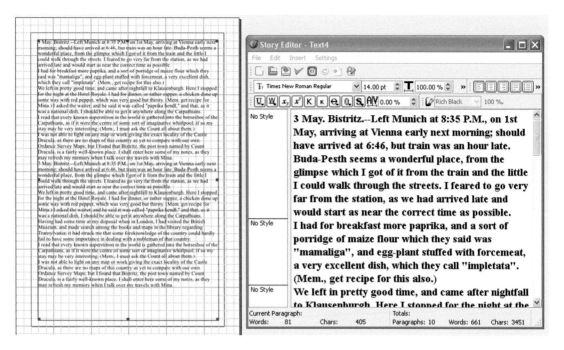

Figure 2-41. *The Story Editor*

As you can see, the text is now in Arial Regular 12 points. To change the text, you need to select it all first using the Font field in the toolbar. Notice, however, that the Story Editor has the same field for the font types and the font styles. Select Times New Roman Regular from the Font field, and select 14 points from the Font Size selector.

This time, nothing happens. If you want to update the text frame, you need to click the Update button, or the Update and Exit icon.

Click the Update and Exit icon.

Your text frame should now be set back in Times New Roman Regular, size 14.

So, to sum up, you can set the font size and style separately in the Properties Palette, but the Story Editor is better for highlighting and editing parts of the text separately. It also offers easy access to features such as underline, superscript, and subscript.

Right-click the text frame, and select Properties again. Select Blue in the Text Color field of the Color & Effects expander. The color of the text changes instantly to blue, as you can see in Figure 2-42.

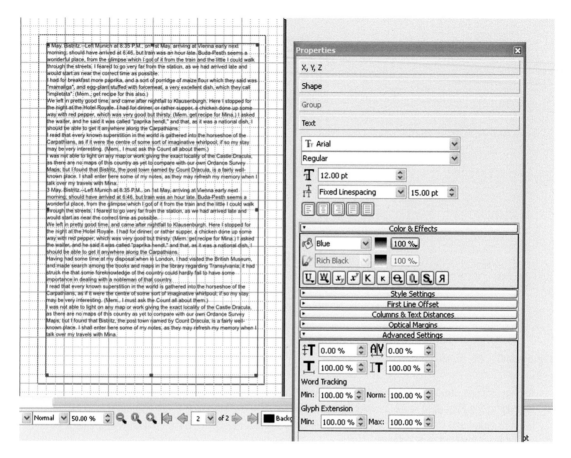

Figure 2-42. *Selecting Blue in the Color & Effects expander*

The Help Menu and Help Browser

The Help Menu and Help Browser are both useful if you need guidance on some aspect of the Scribus workspace (see Figure 2-43).

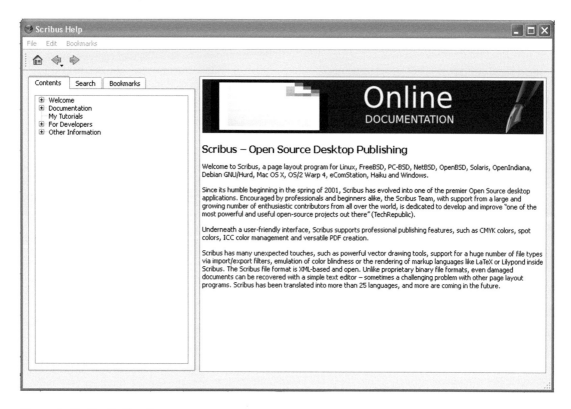

Figure 2-43. *The Scribus Browser*

The Help Menu contains the checkbox for Tooltips, as well as the Scribus Online Documentation, an Online Tutorial, and a built-in and searchable Scribus Manual. Note that the Scribus Manual is not available on all operating systems.

The Help Browser is useful for reading Help Files. It consists of three tabs: one that enables you to browse through the documentation, one from which you can perform a text search of the documentation, and one for bookmarks.

Grids and Guides

A key ingredient for good document design is the accurate placement of content on the page. Content should be positioned on the page in such a way that it enhances the look of the document, and makes the information it contains easy to assimilate. Grids and guides provide a handy way of achieving the accurate placement of content.

Grids

Grids provide a way of aligning your frames accurately on the page. You can also organize them so that your objects "snap" to them in an organized and linear manner. Each grid contains its own major and minor grids, which are based on default settings, but these can easily be changed to suit your needs.

To display a grid, choose View ➤ Show Grid. Your document will look like it has been overlaid with a sheet of graph paper.

Baseline Grid

The baseline grid displays a baseline on which the text in the text frame sits, and this tool enables you to raise or lower the type relative to the baseline. Should you wish to make adjustments to the height of your font characters from the baseline, you can do this via the Document Setup or Preferences.

Guides

Guides are horizontal or vertical lines that can help you with the alignment of your content, but which are not displayed when that content is exported as a PDF file. They are particularly useful if you need to position two or more frames along the same line.

The easiest way to create your guides is to click on the ruler running along the bottom of the toolbar, and drag it onto your page. (In order to do this, you need to ensure that guides are selected in the View menu).

If you wish to insert a vertical guideline, click and drag a line from the left-hand ruler onto the page. If you want to snap an object to a guideline, you first need to display the guide. Then select Snap to Guides from the page menu.

Managing Guides

If you wish to change the document settings for your guides (such as those for the snap distance or grab radius), you can change them for the current document using Document Setup (File ➤ Document Setup), and you can change them for all future documents by selecting File ➤ Preferences. But the actual management of guides is done by using Guide Manager in the Page ➤ Manage Guides menu. In the Guide Manager, your guides can be added, edited, and deleted.

Scrapbook

The Scrapbook has been designed as a place to store the objects that you use repeatedly within a document (see Figure 2-44). Using the Scrapbook avoids the hassle of having to import frequently-used objects from other Scribus documents, which can be time-consuming. You can view the Scrapbook dialog by using Windows ➤ Scrapbook.

Figure 2-44. *The Scrapbook Panel*

In the Scrapbook panel (Figure 2-30) there are five buttons, from which you can do the following:

- Create a new Scrapbook page

- Load an existing Scrapbook

- Save to a selected Scrapbook

- Import a Scrapbook from an older version of Scribus

- Close a selected Scrapbook

Summary

In order to develop effective layout skills, it is important to become familiar with the Scribus workspace. In this chapter, you toured that workspace. You looked at the commands available on the menu bar and the tools that are available in the toolbar, and you learned how to set your default preferences so that Scribus works just the way you want it to.

You saw how it is possible to refine and customize your document properties by making use of the Properties Palette, and you learned how to add sample colors to your color swatch, and how to use color gradients in your backgrounds.

In the next chapter, you will start working with text frames. You will learn how to rotate your text frames, and how to produce drop and raised capitals that highlight your text.

CHAPTER 3

◼◼◼

Text Frames and Font Management

In this chapter, you shall do the following:

- Explore text frame options

- Import and edit text

- Learn to manipulate the text

- Select and apply fonts

- Align text frames

- Control text placement with tabs and indents

- Create and edit drop caps

In Chapter 1, you learned how to start a new document. In Chapter 2, you had a good look around the Scribus interface. In this chapter, you will be taking a look at the text frame. You will look at how it can be used to handle text, and you will learn how to manipulate the visual aspects of its content.

When it comes to text creation and page layout, there is a balance to be struck between achieving the aesthetic preferences that you are striving for and producing a clear layout of your text. The way you handle your text will help to define the basic look of your documents, so I will promote a more thoughtful attitude towards the formatting of text, paying particular attention to the problems of text overflow and copyfitting.

You will also be looking at the variety, compatibility, and management of fonts within Scribus. I will also show you how to create impressive typographical effects such as drop caps and placing text on a curved path.

Using Frames

Scribus is a frame-based page layout system. It uses frames both to position the text and to position most of its graphical objects (in fact, all of them, except vector images). These frames can be inserted into the page by clicking the Image Frame and Text Frame icons on the Toolbar.

The frames can then be resized by clicking and dragging them using the small red squares around the frame, as shown in Figure 3-1.

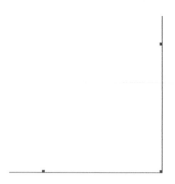

Figure 3-1. *Frame resizing*

The use of grids and guides can assist in this placement process, and can help you to structure the document. (You can also resize a frame by using the width and height spinboxes in the XYZ tab of the Properties Palette.)

It is possible to insert frames automatically when you create a new document. You can do this by selecting the checkbox for Automatic Frame Creation in the New Document window, as shown in Figure 3-2.

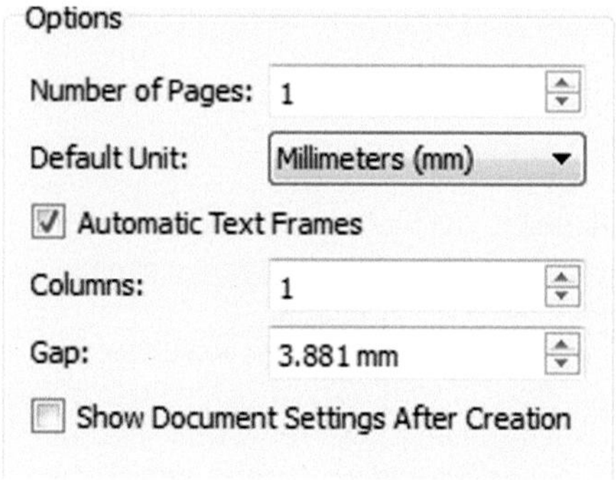

Figure 3-2. *Automatic Frame Creation*

When you do this, Scribus lets you specify the position of the margins, and the number of pages and columns that you require in your frames, as well as the size of the gap between them.

The text frames that result will occupy and link to each new page that you create using these presets. In Scribus, text frames are, by default, rectangular in shape.

Right-clicking inside a text frame brings up the context menu:

- Info
- Undo
- Get Text
- Append Text
- Edit Text
- Sample Text
- Attributes

- PDF Options
- Is Locked
- Size is Locked
- Send to Scrapbook
- Send to layer
- Level
- Convert to
- Cut
- Copy
- Delete
- Contents
- Properties

The context menu for a text frame provides you with the option of creating and editing the text in the Story Editor, or loading it from a text file.

The Append Text option enables you to add more text to the text that already exists in the text frame, while Sample Text gives you the option of filling your text frame with placeholder text written in one of several languages.

Frame Options

Once inserted onto the page, the shape of your frames can be modified by using the Shape tab in the Properties Palette. Clicking the square button on the right side of the Shape tab will produce the other shapes that you can use as your frame shape.

Using the XYZ tab, you can alter the size and position of your frame. The XYZ tab also includes a tool for rotating the frame around 360 degrees. There are X-Pos and Y-Pos controls that help you to position the left and top page borders. The basepoint control lets you select which corner is used for the coordinates.

The X-Pos and Y-Pos and Basepoint Controls

In Scribus, the shape of the text frame and image frame is, by default, rectangular. However, if you wish, you can create a shape and then convert it into a text frame.

To do this, insert a shape or polygon (Insert ➤ Insert Shape) or (Insert ➤ Insert Polygon) and select Convert to ➤ Text Frame in the Item menu.

Afterwards, you can insert some text. You can even insert text into a large letter shape by creating a large letter, then Convert to ➤ Outlines, then Convert to ➤ Text Frame, and then inserting text.

For the best results, choose the size of the original letter as well as the size of the text carefully. Once you have seen such examples, the possibilities are endless.

Introduction to Nodes

Should you wish to alter the shape of your frame, you can do this in the Shape tab of the Properties Palette. The Shape tab contains two buttons in the upper part of the tab that will help you to edit your shapes.

The button at top left enables you to select another shape, while the **Edit** button on the right enables you to edit the shape. When you click the Edit button, the Nodes dialog will open, as shown in Figure 3-3. The nodes are the little blue dots placed at regular intervals along the perimeter of the frame, and they can be added to the shape by selecting the Add Nodes button. You can move your nodes using the mouse, or you can move them using the X-Pos and Y-Pos spinboxes lower down in the dialog. The button that is second-from-left allows you to add more nodes, and the third-from-left button enables you to delete them.

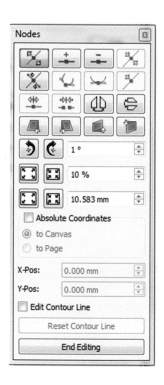

Figure 3-3. *The Node controls in the Nodes dialog box*

In the second row, the first button enables you to edit the control points for the blue nodes. You can edit the control points in order to adjust the line that runs between the nodes. This is useful if you want to adjust the line so that it curves between the nodes.

EXERCISE: CHANGING THE SHAPE OF YOUR TEXT FRAME

Insert a rectangular text frame on your page.

Inside the Shape tab, select the square button, and then select the circle from the menu entitled Default Shapes.

The frame should now be rounded. If you cannot see the rounded frame, use the menu View ➤ Show Frames.

Next, right-click the frame and select Sample Text from the context menu. When you are prompted, choose English as your language.

See how the text adapts to the new shape of the frame. Scribus works best with convex frame shapes. Concave shapes can be a bit troublesome when Scribus tries to fit text into them.

Editing Your Text Frames

The easiest way to edit your text frames is by right-clicking inside them and selecting Edit Text from the context menu. You can also edit your text frames simply by double-clicking them.

It is also possible to edit fonts and styles using the Text tab of the Properties Palette, although the text itself cannot be edited in this way.

You can also select the frame, right-click it, and then copy the frame, so that a copy of it can be pasted into another part of the document, or stored in the scratch space.

Importing Text

You can import text by selecting your text frame, right-clicking it, and selecting Get Text from the context menu. This will throw up a dialog box, which you can use to navigate to the text file that you wish to import. Importing text using the Get Text option will replace any existing text in the text frame.

However, if all you want to do is add some text to the end of the text that is already there in the text frame, you can use the menu option called Append Text (File ➤ Input ➤ Append Text).

Inserting Text Using the Story Editor

Once you have dragged out a text frame, you can begin to insert your text. (You can do this by double-clicking the text frame, or by right-clicking it and selecting Edit Text in the context menu.)

Selecting the Edit Text option will bring up the Story Editor. The Story Editor is a lot like a text editor; it contains all the important text features in one window, as shown in Figure 3-4.

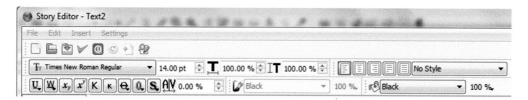

Figure 3-4. *The Story Editor Toolbar*

Once you have selected or highlighted the text you want to work on, you can underline it, center it, or justify it just like you would in a word processor.

However, the Story Editor does not format font faces, so (unless you have some bold or italicized variants contained within your font sets) you will not be able to embolden or italicize your text.

Using Sample Text

Scribus can also import sample text (also known as dummy text or placeholder text) using the context menu. The use of sample text can help you to plan your text layouts if you do not have any written text that you can use. It can also help you make decisions about which font to use, and whether the text should be justified.

The sample text used in Scribus contains the original Latin version, known as Lorem Ipsum. Lorem Ipsum was named after a passage written in Latin by the Roman philosopher Cicero. This passage was often used as sample text in typeface catalogues, and was later adapted for use in Aldus PageMaker.

Importing Files

Ideally, when you import objects using Scribus, you really need those objects to have been formatted so that you are importing fully processed images and fully finished text. Your role, as a designer, is to take the formatted text and modify it to fit your layout.

Scribus will import, with varying degrees of success, text files that are imported as plain text, HTML, CSV, MS Word, and OpenOffice Write files.

Plain Text Files

You can import plain text files from most text editors, although most plain text files have the extension `.txt`.

HTML Files

It is possible to import files as HTML files using Scribus. Scribus will import the whole file, including font faces such as bold and italics. Some of the HTML tags will be converted to paragraph styles, but some of the formatting will be left out. To import the HTML file, use the Get Text command in the context menu.

CSV Files

CSV stands for comma-separated variable or comma-separated value, and CSV files represent the data that is exported from spreadsheets and databases.

Using Scribus, it is possible to import these comma-separated value files into your documents. To import a CSV file into Scribus, you need to select CSV import in the Get Text dialog box and define your field separators. Having established your field separators in the import dialog, Scribus will attempt to convert your CSV data into a default style.

Microsoft Word Files

It is possible to import Microsoft Word files into Scribus, although you will find that they have been stripped of their Word formatting. Word formatting is proprietary (which means that it is owned by a company called Microsoft, and there are major restrictions on its use). A solution to this, which I use regularly, is to open the Word document in OpenOffice Writer, save the Word doc as an ODT file, and then import the ODT file into Scribus. However, some people prefer to use Libre Office. Using either of these seems to work fine for me, though this process does not seem to work with Word tables. It is also possible to save the source document as an HTML file, and export it that way. In theory, it is also possible to save Word tables as OpenOffice Draw files, though I confess that I have not had much success with this method.

ODT Files

As stated above, it is possible to import OpenOffice Writer files into Scribus, and when you do so, you will be given the option of updating the paragraph style or merging the paragraph style. (Note that Scribus cannot handle importing formatting on anything smaller than a paragraph. For example, a word that is italicized will lose its extra italic formatting. The Update Paragraph Styles option means that you are allowing Scribus to alter the style in your Scribus document to follow those in the OpenOffice document.)

The Merge Paragraph Styles option enables Scribus to merge the styles and fonts that it shares with OpenOffice Writer. Basically, it is a way of omitting those styles that are similar but have different names. It is advisable to use your document name as a prefix when naming your styles; this will aid in sorting your styles.

Indenting Text

So you've created a text frame, and you've created, edited, and imported your text. If you are intending to display your text in a frame with a dark background, you will want to think about indenting your text, so that it does not appear to squeeze against the frame boundary, as shown in Figure 3-5.

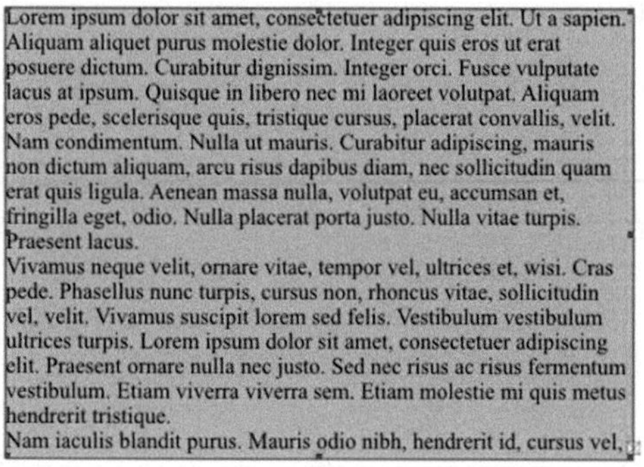

Lorem ipsum dolor sit amet, consectetuer adipiscing elit. Ut a sapien.
Aliquam aliquet purus molestie dolor. Integer quis eros ut erat
posuere dictum. Curabitur dignissim. Integer orci. Fusce vulputate
lacus at ipsum. Quisque in libero nec mi laoreet volutpat. Aliquam
eros pede, scelerisque quis, tristique cursus, placerat convallis, velit.
Nam condimentum. Nulla ut mauris. Curabitur adipiscing, mauris
non dictum aliquam, arcu risus dapibus diam, nec sollicitudin quam
erat quis ligula. Aenean massa nulla, volutpat eu, accumsan et,
fringilla eget, odio. Nulla placerat porta justo. Nulla vitae turpis.
Praesent lacus.
Vivamus neque velit, ornare vitae, tempor vel, ultrices et, wisi. Cras
pede. Phasellus nunc turpis, cursus non, rhoncus vitae, sollicitudin
vel, velit. Vivamus suscipit lorem sed felis. Vestibulum vestibulum
ultrices turpis. Lorem ipsum dolor sit amet, consectetuer adipiscing
elit. Praesent ornare nulla nec justo. Sed nec risus ac risus fermentum
vestibulum. Etiam viverra viverra sem. Etiam molestie mi quis metus
hendrerit tristique.
Nam iaculis blandit purus. Mauris odio nibh, hendrerit id, cursus vel,

Figure 3-5. *Squeezed text on a dark background*

Indenting your text will have the effect of moving it away from the edges of the frame, although this method can cause problems if anything to do with the text or frame changes. Generally, you are better off simply adding some frame margins.

Adding a Frame Margin

To enhance the readability of your text on a dark background, or to move the text away from the frame for any other reason, it is advisable to add a frame margin between the text and the frame border.

To indent your text frame, set up your text frame margin:

- Right-click the text frame
- Go to the Properties Palette
- Select the text frame
- Go to the Text tab
- Click the Column & Text Distances expander (see Figure 3-6)

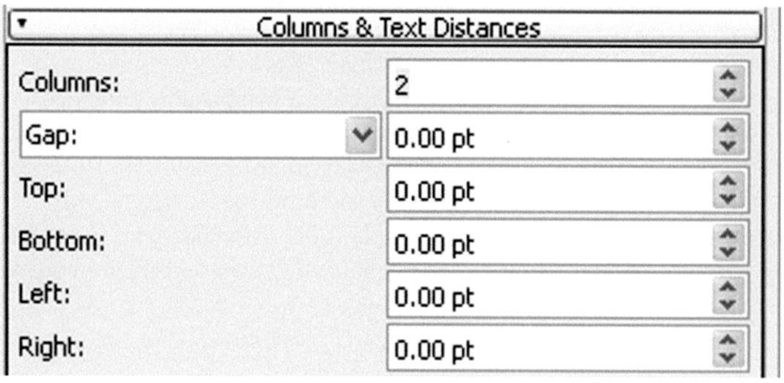

Columns & Text Distances	
Columns:	2
Gap:	0.00 pt
Top:	0.00 pt
Bottom:	0.00 pt
Left:	0.00 pt
Right:	0.00 pt

Figure 3-6. *The spinbox for creating gaps in the Column & Text Distances expander*

Adjust the settings to obtain a left margin by adding/creating a margin, as shown in Figure 3-7.

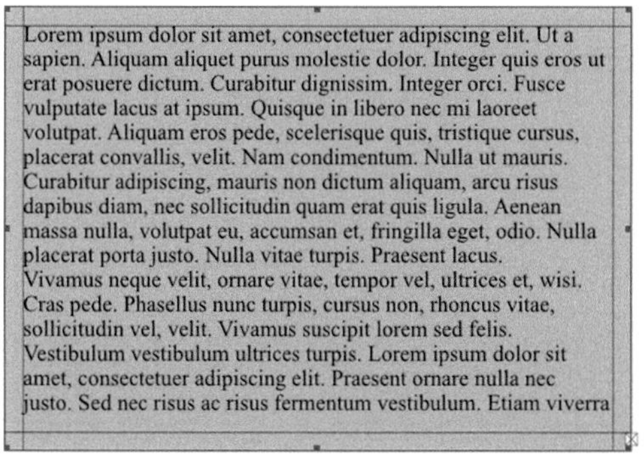

Lorem ipsum dolor sit amet, consectetuer adipiscing elit. Ut a
sapien. Aliquam aliquet purus molestie dolor. Integer quis eros ut
erat posuere dictum. Curabitur dignissim. Integer orci. Fusce
vulputate lacus at ipsum. Quisque in libero nec mi laoreet
volutpat. Aliquam eros pede, scelerisque quis, tristique cursus,
placerat convallis, velit. Nam condimentum. Nulla ut mauris.
Curabitur adipiscing, mauris non dictum aliquam, arcu risus
dapibus diam, nec sollicitudin quam erat quis ligula. Aenean
massa nulla, volutpat eu, accumsan et, fringilla eget, odio. Nulla
placerat porta justo. Nulla vitae turpis. Praesent lacus.
Vivamus neque velit, ornare vitae, tempor vel, ultrices et, wisi.
Cras pede. Phasellus nunc turpis, cursus non, rhoncus vitae,
sollicitudin vel, velit. Vivamus suscipit lorem sed felis.
Vestibulum vestibulum ultrices turpis. Lorem ipsum dolor sit
amet, consectetuer adipiscing elit. Praesent ornare nulla nec
justo. Sed nec risus ac risus fermentum vestibulum. Etiam viverra

Figure 3-7. *The same text frame, but with margins inserted all around the frame and set against a colored background*

A Note About Overflowing Text

If the text starts to overflow the capacity of the text frame, the text overflow indicator **X** will appear. The indicator appears whenever there is too much text to fit into the frame. It appears in the bottom right corner of the text frame, as shown in Figure 3-8.

. Lorem ipsum dolor sit
aesent ornare nulla nec
m vestibulum. Etiam viverra

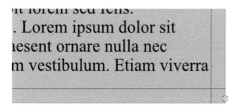

Figure 3-8. *Text overflow in the corner of a text frame*

Whenever it appears, you will know that some of the text in the frame is not visible. This will also show up in the Preflight Verifier.

One solution to the problem of text overflow is to link the text frame to another text frame that follows on from the original one. To do this, highlight your first text frame, click the Link Text Frames icon, and click the text frame that follows after the first.

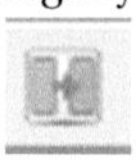

The Story Editor

The Story Editor is the Scribus text editor, in which you will edit and format most of your text. You can use the Story Editor to select font families and apply formatting, such as text underline, spacing, color, and text justification, as shown in Figure 3-9.

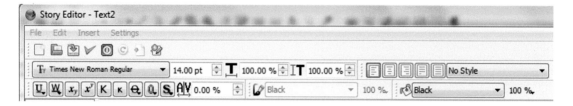

Figure 3-9. *The Story Editor toolbar*

However, whatever editing and formatting you apply to your text frame, you will not be able to see all your changes displayed in the text frame until you update the frame in the Story Editor.

If you want to see the changes applied as you make them, you need to position the Story Editor in the grey scratch space so that you can view it when the document is in full view, as shown in Figure 3-10.

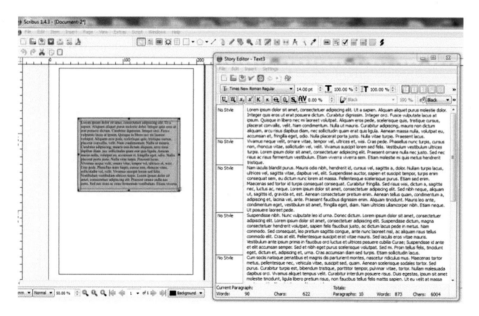

Figure 3-10. *Updating the text with the Story Editor open in the adjacent scratch space*

Having made your changes, you then need to select the Update Text Frame icon on the Story Editor toolbar. This will enable you to view the updated text in the text frame while the Story Editor is still open.

Otherwise, if you wish to update the text frame and close the Story Editor, select the button marked Update Text Frame and Exit on the Story Editor toolbar. ✓ |

The Text Tab

The Text tab can be found on the Properties Palette. It displays the font families that are available in Scribus, as well as two columns of spinboxes for controlling the font size, linespacing, and baseline offset (see Figure 3-11).

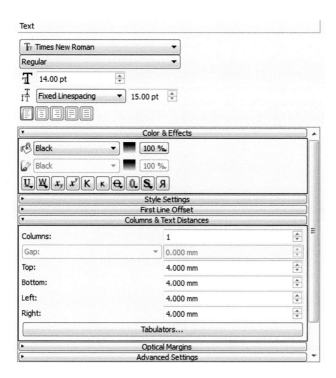

Figure 3-11. *The Text Tab Controls*

Inside the Color & Effects expander are two controls: one for changing the color of selected texts and the other for changing the color of text strokes and drop shadows. Underneath these controls is an array of text formatting buttons for underlines, subscripts, superscripts, and uppercase text. In the Advanced Settings expander, an Offset to Baseline Character spinbox allows you to insert glyphs at a set distance from the baseline grid.

The Tracking spinbox, shown in Figure 3-12, enables you to adjust the space between individual letters.

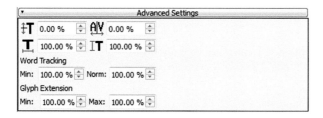

Figure 3-12. *The tracking spinbox can be found in the Advanced Settings expander*

Text Overflow

The term "copyfitting" refers to the process of fitting your text into the proposed layout. There will be occasions when the size of the text will be too large for the frame that you have provided for it. When a text frame is too small for the text that is contained within it, the surplus text will not appear in the text frame, and a red X mark will appear in the lower right corner of the frame.

When this happens, there are a number of different strategies that you can employ in order to make the text fit the frame.

1. **Edit your text**: You can edit the text in the Story Editor, and delete any unnecessary words and characters.

2. **Resize your text frame**: Try increasing the width and height of the text frames so that they include more of the text. You can also try reducing the width of any column gutters. Sometimes, if there are just one or two words overflowing the frame, a slightly wider text frame is all that is required.

3. **Reduce the line spacing**: To do this, use the Text tab in the Properties Palette.

4. **Text threading**: You can link your text frame to another text frame so that the overflowing text is taken up and displayed in the other frame.

5. **Adjust the tracking (the space between a series of characters) on a line**: If you select the paragraph with the least amount of text on the last line, you can use tracking to adjust the spaces so as to take out that line. Be warned, however, that overriding the tracking can produce bad results.

6. **Insert Columns**: Using the columns setting in the Text tab of the Properties Palette, you can replace one column of text with two columns of justified text. This space-saving ploy is often used in the production of newspapers and magazines.

7. **Adjust the size of captions, borders, images and graphics**.

Text Wrapping: Flowing Text Around a Quote

In Scribus, the text wrap facility makes it possible to flow your text around an object that is located on a higher level. It works with layers too. When a text frame is placed behind another text or image frame on a higher layer, the text from your layer can be made to follow the shape of a text frame or graphical object on the higher layer.

There are five options related to text wrapping that are available in the Shape tab in Scribus. You can wrap your text in the following ways.

1. **Use a bounding box**: If you select this option, the text will flow around both sides of a rectangle frame or bounding box.

2. **Use a frame shape**: If you select this option, you can make your text follow the outline of an object contained within a frame. This is highly impressive when used in magazines and newspapers.

3. **Use a contour line**: If you select this option, the text will flow around the contour line of the frame.

4. **Disabled**: There is no text wrap and the text ignores the frame or graphical object.

5. **Use the clipping path of an image**.

EXERCISE

Create a frame for your text and then create a frame containing a quote, one that is smaller in size. Give the text frame containing the quote a colored background (by selecting it and then choosing a color in the Color tab). Then give the larger frame a colored background, choosing a lighter color, as shown in Figure 3-13.

Figure 3-13. *Overlapping frames as they appear with the text wrap disabled*

Position the frame containing the quote on top of the frame containing the main body of text.

Go to the Properties Palette (F2) and expand the Shape tab.

In the Text Flow Around Frame section, select Use Frame Shape.

You will want to have a gap between the quotation and the text, so click the Edit button at the top of the Shape tab.

You will now see the Nodes window displayed. Select the Move Nodes button, and move the blue nodes so that there is a gap between the two text frames, as shown in Figure 3-14.

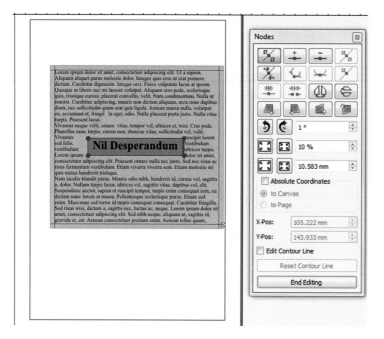

Figure 3-14. *The Nodes dialog appears and four blue nodes are displayed*

The text has now moved away from the frame boundary, as you can see in Figure 3-15.

Figure 3-15. *The finished text wrap, with a margin added to the central quote*

Text Alignment

In the Story Editor (and in the Text tab of the Properties Palette) there are buttons that enable text alignment and justification of text.

The text alignment buttons enable you to align text to the left, right, or center of the page.

Left-Aligned Text

Most of the text you will see is left-aligned, and has a ragged edge along the right side of the column of text. This arrangement of text is determined by the shape of the text along the right edge.

Centered Text

Centered text is text that is aligned centrally so that its sits equidistant from its left and right margins. Centered text is often used as a format for titles, headings, dedications, poetry, verse, and quotations.

Right-Aligned Text

Right-aligned text has a ragged left margin and a flush right margin. It is sometimes used for author's name, for captions, and for marginal notes.

Justified Text

Justified text is text that has been deliberately stretched in order to create a body of text that has both left and right margins. (The process of justification adds space between words so that each line of text aligns at both left and right margin of a column on a page.)

Justified text provides an effective way to save space. It tries to fill up the available space with the existing text.

Forced Justification

If you force justify your text, the last few words of each paragraph will be spaced out across the last line even though there may be too few characters of text to fill the line. The end result can look awful.

One workaround is to force-justify the body of the text, but then use the ordinary justification or left alignment on the last line. (Although this method works as a quick fix, it isn't really advisable as a general rule. If a change was made to the size or the text, you would need to go around altering things again.)

Kerning and Tracking

There are three ways to adjust the spacing of text when using page layout software. You can do it through the use of linespacing, kerning, or tracking.

Linespacing (or leading, as it used to be known) is a way of adjusting the space between lines of text. Kerning (which is set in the font) is a way of adjusting the letterspacing (i.e. the space between characters of text), and tracking is a way of adjusting the space in a line of characters. Scribus can only adjust the tracking by a percentage of the font's internal values).

Properly-designed fonts already have kerning tables in them and shouldn't really be overridden. In Scribus, there is only one tool to handle both kerning and tracking. So you can apply the letterspacing changes to just a pair of characters, or to a wider selection.

We feel that we ought to emphasize here that beginners should be careful when altering tracking values without knowing what they are doing, as it can make for unreadable text.

However, if you really feel that you need to change the manual tracking of some characters, select the frame of text and open the Story Editor. With the Story Editor open, select the line of text that needs adjusting and, using the manual tracking tool, alter the manual tracking configuration to 1% in either direction.

When you are happy with the changes that you have made, click the Update and Exit button in the Story Editor. Then check to see if enough space has been saved with the changes that were made.

Tracking

Processes such as linespacing, kerning, and tracking are handled automatically in a word processor, but in a layout program such as Scribus, you get to assume full control of these processes, making adjustments line by line until everything is to your liking.

Most of the tools you will need for linespacing, kerning, and tracking can be found in the Text tab of the Properties Palette. The Text tab is particularly good at setting or adjusting the individual letter spaces between characters. This is the process known as tracking.

How to Track

To adjust the character spacing in a text frame, select the characters you wish to adjust and then go to the Advanced Settings tab in the Properties Palette ➤ Text tab.

Alternatively, open the Story Editor, select the text, and alter the A/V manual tracking configuration by plus or minus one percentage point.

Text Rotation

The easiest way to rotate your text frame, should you wish to rotate it by 90 degrees, is to right-click the text frame, select the Properties Palette, go the XYZ tab, and enter the value for the required rotation.

Drop Caps

Scribus lets you insert drop caps in your text, but they need to be used sparingly. The use of drop caps goes back to the creation of manuscripts in medieval monasteries, when they were used as a colorful way of ornamenting the first letters of a paragraph. Then the technique got carried over into block printing, and the drop cap became a large letter cast into a block. Then it was carried over into hot metal printing, and today it is a common feature of desktop publishing programs.

In desktop publishing terms, drop caps are the large letters at the start of paragraphs that drop below the baseline. Today, drop caps are used in magazine, journal, and book publishing.

EXERCISE

There is more than one way to create a drop cap in Scribus. The simplest way is to do it manually. Create a text frame for the drop cap. Set the font size to something like 50 points. Set the text fill color and text stroke color in the Properties Palette. Then create another text frame for the rest of your text.

Finally, align the two text frames side by side, as illustrated in Figure 3-16. Use the text wrap facility in the Properties Palette to wrap the body text around the drop cap. You will probably need to alter the line spacing as well in order to get the text to fit flush with the drop cap.

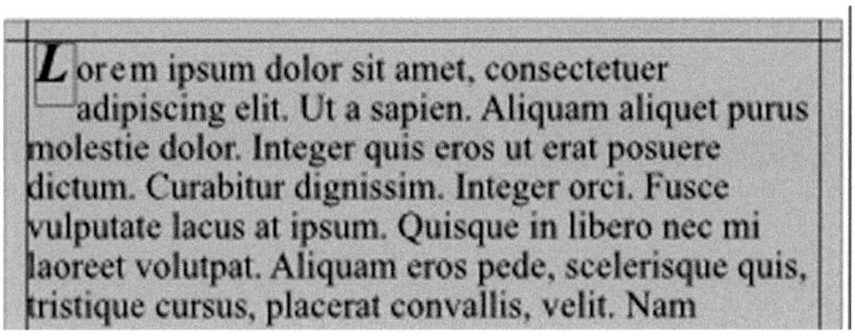

L orem ipsum dolor sit amet, consectetuer adipiscing elit. Ut a sapien. Aliquam aliquet purus molestie dolor. Integer quis eros ut erat posuere dictum. Curabitur dignissim. Integer orci. Fusce vulputate lacus at ipsum. Quisque in libero nec mi laoreet volutpat. Aliquam eros pede, scelerisque quis, tristique cursus, placerat convallis, velit. Nam

Figure 3-16. *A raised cap created manually using two overlapping text frames in a text wrap*

Manipulating the Baseline Grid

Along with guides, grids, and margins, the baseline grid is another handy tool that helps you to position your text. The baseline is the line upon which most characters sit in the text frame, and the baseline grid displays the baselines of text along which the letters and characters run in a text frame (see Figure 3-17). The grid acts as a compositional aid and is essential for professional alignment and page design. It is also useful if you want to raise or lower your lettering relative to other letters on the baseline, and it can be especially useful if you are trying to balance two columns of text frames where the tops of the frames are not aligned.

Figure 3-17. *A blank page in Scribus with the baseline grid turned on*

The baseline grid can be turned on from Preferences ➤ Guides by clicking the checkbox. It can also be turned on by selecting Baseline Grid from the context menu. The baseline grid is global for a whole document; it cannot be changed page by page. The whole point of having one is that it remains the same on every page.

When you have finished using the baseline, you can dismiss it using the context menu, or by using the Guides tab in the Preferences window.

Adding a Text Frame Background

To create a background color, right-click the text frame, select the Properties Palette, and go to the Colors tab. Then choose a color or gradient, as shown in Figure 3-18.

Figure 3-18. *Choosing a background color in the Color tab of the Properties Palette*

If you wish to alter the opacity, go to the Color tab, choose the paint bucket icon, and select a color. Adjust the shade to the desired value. Select the word Normal under the paint bucket and change to one of the gradients. Select a color and change the opacity.

Repeat for the second color if applicable.

Creating Text over a Semi-Transparent Background

Some processes in Scribus, like placing text over a busy image with lots of contrasting colors, can be a real problem. Light-colored text will be barely visible if placed over a light background image; dark text will disappear over a dark background. It can also be difficult to highlight text when its background image contains many contrasting colors. One solution to this problem is to create a semi-transparent text frame so that the text appears clearly on your image. Here is how you do it:

Create your text frame, but place it over a shape with a colored fill with the opacity set to 60%.

Change the opacity in the Color tab of the Properties Palette, as shown in Figure 3-19.

Figure 3-19. *Text displayed on a semi-opaque white background, so that the text is still visible over dark colors*

Creating Text on a Path

Scribus can attach a line of text to a path. To create a text on a path, you need to follow these steps:

- Create a text frame and enter your text.

- Create a line or a shape and right-click it to convert it into a Bezier curve.

- Select both the text frame and the curve.

- Select Attach Text to Path from the Item menu.

And that is pretty much all there is to it. You could also create a curve by inserting a Bezier Curve from the Insert menu (Insert ➤ Insert Bezier Curve) and drawing your curve that way.

So, to begin with, create a text frame and enter you text, and then insert a shape alongside it, as shown in Figure 3-20.

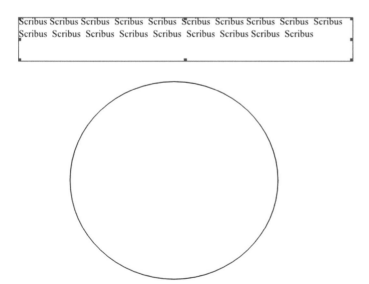

Figure 3-20. *The text and a circular shape representing the curved path on which you wish to flow the text*

Next, select both the text frame and the shape, using the Shift key, and then select Attach Text to Path from the Item menu, as shown in Figure 3-21.

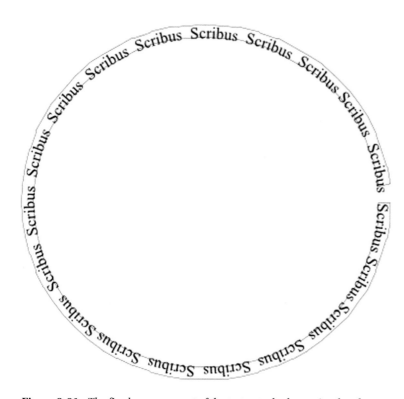

Figure 3-21. *The final arrangement of the text attached to a circular shape*

Paragraph Alignment and Formatting

In Scribus, to create a new paragraph, all you have to do is open the Story Editor, enter your text, and press the Enter key. You can also do this by double-clicking the text frame and using the Enter key while in Edit mode.

Having said that, there are some paragraph alignment and formatting tools available in the Text Tab of the Properties Palette.

Making Tabs

Tab stops are the location that the cursor stops at after the tab key has been pressed. Pressing the tab stop helps you to align the text.

To create some tab stops for your text frame, go to the Text area of the Properties Palette, select the Column & Text Distances expander, and then scroll down to the Tabulations control, as shown in Figure 3-22.

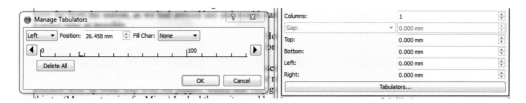

Figure 3-22. *The tabulation ruler, and the tabulator controls found in the Columns & Text Distances expender, in Properties ➤ Text*

If you click on the ruler, you will create by default a left tab stop. Once you've created the tab, you can move it and place it more precisely with the mouse or the spinbox locators.

To delete your tab stops, drag them off the ruler in the Manage Tabulators dialog box.

With Scribus, it is also possible to assign a character other than the tab stop's default empty space. You can do this by using the Tabulator button in the Columns & Text Distances expander to open the Manage Tabulators dialog box, as shown in Figure 3-23.

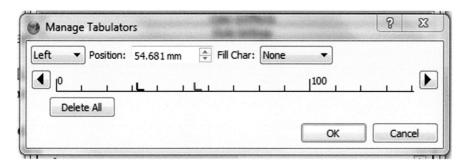

Figure 3-23. *The Manage Tabulators dialog box*

The Manage Tabulators dialog box has a field that enables you to swap the default empty space of the tabulator for characters such as dot, hyphen, or underscore. It will also let you choose your own custom tab fill character.

The Manage Tabulators dialog box also contains a ruler for your frame in the appropriate units.

Scaling the Text Size

At some point you have probably been resizing your text frames by using the mouse to drag the frame handles. However, if you try pressing the Alt button when you do it, you will find that the text will be resized with the frame. (And if you press Alt+Ctrl, you can preserve the aspect ratio of the frame and of the text.) It's striking how the text frame can be resized to the same size and yet produces three slightly different results, shown in Figure 3-24.

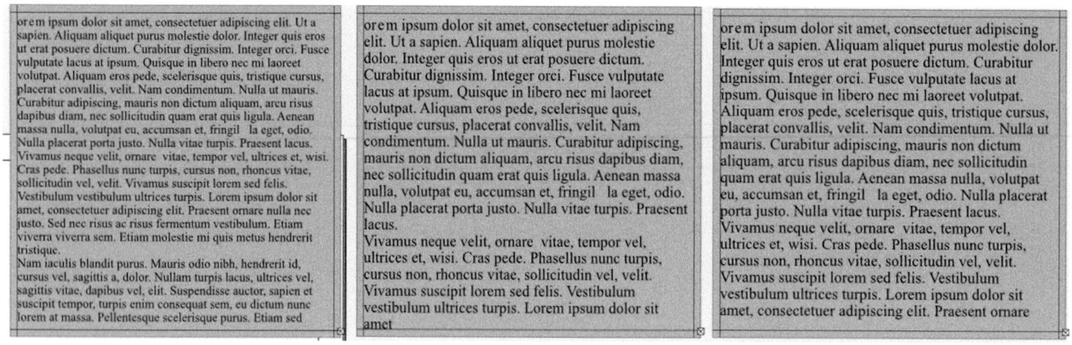

orem ipsum dolor sit amet, consectetuer adipiscing elit. Ut a sapien. Aliquam aliquet purus molestie dolor. Integer quis eros ut erat posuere dictum. Curabitur dignissim. Integer orci. Fusce vulputate lacus at ipsum. Quisque in libero nec mi laoreet volutpat. Aliquam eros pede, scelerisque quis, tristique cursus, placerat convallis, velit. Nam condimentum. Nulla ut mauris. Curabitur adipiscing, mauris non dictum aliquam, arcu risus dapibus diam, nec sollicitudin quam erat quis ligula. Aenean massa nulla, volutpat eu, accumsan et, fringil la eget, odio. Nulla placerat porta justo. Nulla vitae turpis. Praesent lacus. Vivamus neque velit, ornare vitae, tempor vel, ultrices et, wisi. Cras pede. Phasellus nunc turpis, cursus non, rhoncus vitae, sollicitudin vel, velit. Vivamus suscipit lorem sed felis. Vestibulum vestibulum ultrices turpis. Lorem ipsum dolor sit amet, consectetuer adipiscing elit. Praesent ornare nulla nec justo. Sed nec risus ac risus fermentum vestibulum. Etiam viverra viverra sem. Etiam molestie mi quis metus hendrerit tristique. Nam iaculis blandit purus. Mauris odio nibh, hendrerit id, cursus vel, sagittis a, dolor. Nullam turpis lacus, ultrices vel, sagittis vitae, dapibus vel, elit. Suspendisse auctor, sapien et suscipit tempor, turpis enim consequat sem, eu dictum nunc lorem at massa. Pellentesque scelerisque purus. Etiam sed

orem ipsum dolor sit amet, consectetuer adipiscing elit. Ut a sapien. Aliquam aliquet purus molestie dolor. Integer quis eros ut erat posuere dictum. Curabitur dignissim. Integer orci. Fusce vulputate lacus at ipsum. Quisque in libero nec mi laoreet volutpat. Aliquam eros pede, scelerisque quis, tristique cursus, placerat convallis, velit. Nam condimentum. Nulla ut mauris. Curabitur adipiscing, mauris non dictum aliquam, arcu risus dapibus diam, nec sollicitudin quam erat quis ligula. Aenean massa nulla, volutpat eu, accumsan et, fringil la eget, odio. Nulla placerat porta justo. Nulla vitae turpis. Praesent lacus. Vivamus neque velit, ornare vitae, tempor vel, ultrices et, wisi. Cras pede. Phasellus nunc turpis, cursus non, rhoncus vitae, sollicitudin vel, velit. Vivamus suscipit lorem sed felis. Vestibulum vestibulum ultrices turpis. Lorem ipsum dolor sit amet

orem ipsum dolor sit amet, consectetuer adipiscing elit. Ut a sapien. Aliquam aliquet purus molestie dolor. Integer quis eros ut erat posuere dictum. Curabitur dignissim. Integer orci. Fusce vulputate lacus at ipsum. Quisque in libero nec mi laoreet volutpat. Aliquam eros pede, scelerisque quis, tristique cursus, placerat convallis, velit. Nam condimentum. Nulla ut mauris. Curabitur adipiscing, mauris non dictum aliquam, arcu risus dapibus diam, nec sollicitudin quam erat quis ligula. Aenean massa nulla, volutpat eu, accumsan et, fringil la eget, odio. Nulla placerat porta justo. Nulla vitae turpis. Praesent lacus. Vivamus neque velit, ornare vitae, tempor vel, ultrices et, wisi. Cras pede. Phasellus nunc turpis, cursus non, rhoncus vitae, sollicitudin vel, velit. Vivamus suscipit lorem sed felis. Vestibulum vestibulum ultrices turpis. Lorem ipsum dolor sit amet, consectetuer adipiscing elit. Praesent ornare

Figure 3-24. *Three text frames dragged out to a similar size, but with different scaling*

The first frame was enlarged manually, the second was enlarged using the Alt key, and in the third, the text was enlarged using Alt+Ctrl. There is a noticeable difference. Some scaling will have occurred: you will have resized your text frame, but in doing so you will have applied some rescaling to your font.

This need not be a problem. All vector fonts support scaling, and if you are using TrueType or OpenType fonts they support scaling. Scaling is only a problem if you use bitmap fonts, which do not support scaling.

We ought to say, at this point, that scaling is an advanced topic and it should be used sparingly.

Inline Objects

It is a little known fact that Scribus is capable of inserting small graphics files into the baselines of its text frames, in a way similar to inserting a special character like a wingding. In fact, it is possible to add a small image frame, line, shape, or Bezier curve; copy it; and paste it into your text frame at the point where you have positioned the cursor.

These miniature graphics files, which need be no larger than the characters in your text frame, are known as inline objects or inline graphics.

For the insertion of inline objects to work, the object needs to be roughly the same scale as the font size. To insert an object, you first need to copy it to a location outside the text frame (such as the scratch space). You can do this by pressing Ctrl+C. Then you need to place the cursor inside the text frame at the exact place where you intend to insert the graphic.

So double-click the text frame to position the cursor, but do not open the Story Editor, because that will not work.

Once you have found the correct place in the text frame, edit and paste the graphic into the text.

Use the Text tab controls in the Properties Palette to resize the object (using Offset to Baseline for vertical placement and Word Tracking for horizontal placement).

If you want to delete the object, position the cursor in front of it and press the Delete key.

Fonts in Scribus

A sound knowledge of fonts and their uses is a prerequisite for a good document design. The use of fonts goes back to the days of hot metal printing, when fonts were known as typefaces and were made by pouring molten lead into a caste.

Today, however, the desktop publishing revolution has popularized the use of the term "font" to describe what was once called a "typeface," and lead fonts have been replaced by computerized fonts that can be made in any size or style.

Traditionally, what we term a "font" was considered to be a particular form of font family. So, for example, the popular Times New Roman was considered to be an example of a font family, but Times New Roman Bold at 12 points was seen as an example of a font.

Font Preview

There are thousands of fonts that you can obtain, but matching a particular type of font to the look that you are aiming for in your document is very much a process of trial and error. Initially, it is probably best to create a mock-up of your document so that you can experiment with a variety of fonts, and see what works best.

An easy way of assessing how different fonts will look in your document is to make use of the Font Preview tool, which can be loaded from the Extras menu, as shown in Figure 3-25.

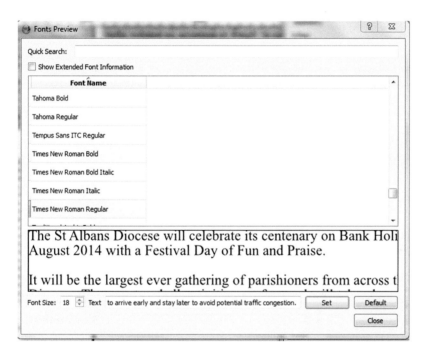

Figure 3-25. *The Font Preview*

Use the Quick Search facility at the top of the Font List to search the names of fonts.

The Font List contains the name of the font, the font type, and the fonts used in the document you are working on.

There is also a field that enables you to preview the font in the lower part of the dialog box, using some sample text. The Font List contains a list of all the available fonts. Selecting a font will result in a preview in the lower part of the window.

The Quick Search facility is a useful feature that enables you to search for both fonts and font styles.

Unfortunately, when it comes to composing the document proper, it is only possible to view a single document at a time in the Story Editor. However, if you position the Story Editor window in the scratch space, so that you can also view the document, you can use the Update Without Exiting button to try out a range of fonts on the page.

In order to achieve a reliable output, Scribus is very selective about the fonts that it recognizes, and will disable any font that it sees as defective, and whose glyphs cannot be accessed consistently.

Font Families

Here is a list of the main font families in common use today:

- Serif
- Sans-Serif
- Monospaced
- Cursive or Script
- Ornamental or Decorative
- Symbols

Serif Fonts

A serif typeface has small strokes or appendages, called serifs that extend from the edges of the character. They are designed to make the letters look more distinctive, whereas a sans-serif font does not have these appendages.

Elements of a Typeface

The following is a set of standard terms to describe the elements that go to make up a typeface. Figure 3-26 displays some of them.

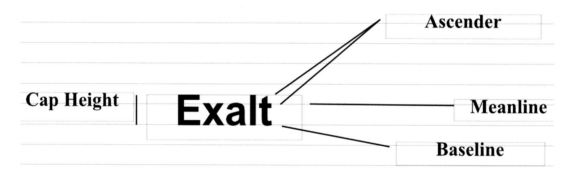

Figure 3-26. *Basic diagram of the anatomy of a typeface*

- **Cap Height**: The cap height is the height of the average uppercase letter, such as the letter E in Figure 3-26.
- **Serif**: Serif fonts have an extra horizontal stroke at the end of the letter or symbol.
- **Ascender**: The ascender is the part of a letter that extends above the meanline or x-height.
- **Descender**: The descender is the part of a letter that extends below the baseline.

- **X-Height**: The x-height is the distance between the meanline and the baseline. It is also the height of the average lowercase letter based on the letter x.

- **Baseline**: The baseline is an invisible line at the base of most characters, on which they all sit.

Italic and Roman fonts

The difference between italic fonts and Roman fonts appears to lie in their history. Italic fonts are based on handwritten letter shapes, and are usually slanted in appearance. They are often used as a way of emphasizing a word or phrase in a body of text, and are often combined with a heavier typeface (e.g. Times New Roman Italic Bold).

By contrast, Roman fonts were supposed, originally, to have been chiseled in stone and are usually typeset upright. Text set in Roman is generally considered to be more legible than text set in italic.

Font Management in Scribus

Fonts in Scribus are managed in the Fonts dialog, which can be found in Preferences or in Document Setup. Contained within the fonts dialog are three tabs: Available Fonts, Font Substitution, and Additional Fonts, shown in Figure 3-27.

Figure 3-27. *The three tabs in the Font Substitution Dialog*

Available Fonts lists the fonts included on your computer that are available to Scribus when it fires up. You may not see all the fonts that are listed on your computer because Scribus is selective about the fonts it uses.

The Available Fonts tab consists of 12 columns: one for the names of the fonts available to Scribus; a column called Use Font that enables you to deselect a font that has been listed as being available; a column that says whether the font will be embedded when the document is exported as Postscript; and a Subset column that tells Scribus to limit the character glyphs in the font when exporting to only those actually used in the document, which also prevents them from being embedded in Postscript and PDF files. Finally, there is a column showing the Path to Font File.

The Font Substitutions Tab displays a list of fonts that are available on your installation of Scribus, and which you can use to substitute for those that have been used in a document, but which you do not have.

Font Managers

If you are really serious about managing your fonts, you might want to consider installing a font manager. Most computer operating systems possess basic font management capabilities. However, if like me, you collect a lot of fonts, you can end up with hundreds of fonts on your system, and you will need an effective and reliable way to manage them.

This is where the font manager comes in. Font management software makes it easier to browse, install, preview, organize, and group your fonts.

The use of a font manager will save you time, will be economical with disc space, and might well provide you with layout ideas as well.

One of the most popular and reliable font managers available on the Internet is Font Matrix, especially if you are looking for advanced font management features. Font Matrix started out as a Linux-based system but there are now versions available for Windows and Mac user as well.

Letter Spacing: Proportional and Monospaced Fonts

Just to confuse things a bit further, fonts can also be divided into two systems according to their letter spacing, or the spacing between the individual letters.

The two designs in question are monospaced and proportional fonts. These days, in the wake of the desktop publishing revolution, proportionally-spaced fonts seem to be very popular; Steve Jobs boasted about using them when he was promoting the Macintosh.

Proportionally-spaced fonts have a variable spacing between the letters, and are generally considered to be more beautiful and more legible than monospaced fonts.

In monospaced fonts, on the other hand, each character occupies the same amount of space. For example, the letter i takes up as much space as the capital letter W. As a result, some monospaced letters will look too cramped, while other will have too much space. The end result looks similar to what may be produced by a typewriter.

Having characters of equal width makes monospaced fonts unsuitable for anything much other than the field of computer programming, where it is important to make individual characters discernible as an aid to debugging.

Superscript and Subscript

Superscripts and subscripts are characters that have been formatted so that they appear smaller than the normal line of type. Subscripts appear at or below the baseline, whereas superscripts (which were a feature of medieval manuscripts) are set slightly above the baseline. They are commonly used for footnotes, as well as in math and science papers.

Drop Shadow

The effect known as drop shadow is commonly used in headings. The text itself is duplicated and the two copies are moved slightly apart so as to create the effect of a 3D shadow.

TrueType, OpenType, and PostScript

Traditionally, there are three makes of fonts: Postscript, TrueType, and OpenType. The fonts that you have stored on your computer will usually be from these three types.

Postscript fonts use the Postscript programming language and played an important part in the desktop publishing revolution. For many years, Postscript fonts were the standard fonts used in professional printing, but their popularity declined after Microsoft and Apple introduced TrueType fonts. TrueType fonts had the advantage of being standalone and of not requiring separate screen and printer components, whereas PostScript fonts consisted of two files and could not be switched between operating systems.

Furthermore, a TrueType font can contain up to 60,000 glyphs, where an old-fashioned PostScript font is limited to 256 glyphs per file.

Having said all that, Scribus is able to use PostScript, TrueType, and OpenType fonts.

OpenType is an extension of the TrueType specification. It combines the properties of TrueType and Postscript fonts and provides some additional features as well. The OpenType format was the result of collaboration between Adobe and Microsoft. Both companies wanted to end what had become known as the "font format war" between the two vendors.

Font Installation

Generally, it is recommended that users install fonts on their machines in the usual manner. Then they can use Preferences ➤ Fonts to tell Scribus which fonts they don't want to use at all.

For individual documents, they can use Document Setup ➤ Fonts to limit the number of fonts that can be used in that document (which also helps to keep the font selection drop-downs nice and small).

If, like me, you collect any free fonts that you happen to come across on the Internet, you should be aware that they might not load in Scribus. The emphasis, in Scribus, is on preserving the integrity of the tools used in the publishing process, so if you do not see your new font in the font list, there is every chance that Scribus has rejected it on the grounds of quality control.

When you first start collecting fonts, it is tempting to show them off by using as many of them as possible in your new documents. It is best to avoid this temptation. As a general rule, only three fonts are needed in order to make a document look attractive: one font for the main headings or titles, a second font for sub-headings, and a third font for the body text.

If you have amassed a large collection of fonts, you will want to make them available to Scribus. You can install fonts in almost any location on your computer, but you need to make Scribus aware of them first.

Adding a New Font

To add a new font in Scribus, you need to set a path that tells Scribus where it can find it. Open Scribus, and close all you documents so that you can only see the scratch space.

Place all you fonts in one folder or directory.

Go to the Preferences ➤ Fonts option (File ➤ Preferences ➤ Fonts ➤ Additional paths).

In the Additional Paths column, click the Add option.

Browse to the folder containing the fonts that you want to add.

Click Apply and then click OK.

Your new font files should now have been detected in Scribus, but you will need to restart Scribus in order to use them.

Now that you have installed your new fonts, you will want to preview them. You can do this using the Font Preview facility in the Extras menu.

Font Sample

The Font Preview is a handy device, but a limited one. If you want to compare different fonts in more detail, you should try the Font Sample script in the Scripts menu (Scripts ➤ Font Sample). (You will be learning how to use scripts in a later chapter.) Font Sample lets you compare the look of different fonts at different weights, until you find one that is more suitable for your layout.

Special Characters

Special characters are characters that you won't find on your keyboard, characters such as typographic symbols, ligatures, and foreign language characters. In Scribus, you can use the Insert menu to insert characters such as page numbers, copyright symbols, registered trademark symbols, bullets, and dashes.

Ligatures are specially designed characters consisting of multiple letters that are used to replace poorly-spaced letter combinations.

A glyph is a symbol that provides the appearance or form for a character; basically each character of a font is a glyph.

To insert a special character in a text frame, open the Story Editor, position the cursor at the place in the text frame where you wish to insert the character, go to the Insert menu, and select the character.

Hyphenator

To produce a text that looks readable and attractive to the reader, it is important to be able to hyphenate properly. Word processors tend to do this automatically, but in a page layout system such as Scribus, you are given much more control over the procedure.

The process of hyphenating your text is probably best left until last, when the text frame and its contents have been organized, edited, and formatted. When you've reached that stage, and you wish to hyphenate your text, select the text frame followed by Hyphenate Text in the Extras menu.

If the results are not what you had in mind, you can tweak the hyphenator in File ➤ Document Setup ➤ Hyphenator (shown in Figure 3-28). Using this dialog, it is possible to specify whether you want your words hyphenated and how they should be hyphenated.

Hyphenation and Spelling

Hyphenation	Spelling		
General Options		Behaviour	
☐ Hyphenation Suggestions		Language:	English ▾
☐ Hyphenate Text Automatically During Typing		Smallest Word:	3 ⬍ Chars
		Consecutive Hyphenations Allowed:	2 ⬍
Exceptions		Ignore List	

Figure 3-28. The Hyphenation settings as they appear in the Preferences window

Once you have finished hyphenating your text, you can check to see if you would prefer to revert to an unhyphenated version by selecting Extras ➤ Dehyphenate Text. Alternately, you can switch your hyphens back on by using Extras ➤ Hyphenate Text.

EXERCISE: TEXT COLUMNS AND GUTTERING

A particularly effective way of saving space if you want to squeeze a lot of text into a frame is to have it running in two parallel columns.

To divide a text into two parallel columns, go to the Text tab of the Properties Palette, and increase the number of columns to 2, as shown in Figure 3-29.

Figure 3-29. *Splitting the text frame into two columns using the Properties Palette*

You will note that the text frame is now split in two, but the text from one runs right up to the edge of another. The result looks unattractive and is likely to confuse the reader.

To remedy this, you need to create a gap.

It is advisable not to make the gap too narrow. If you do make it too narrow, the columns of text will converge and become difficult to read.

In the Properties Palette, go to the Text expander for Columns & Text Distances, and enter 8.00 mm in the spinbox to the right of the drop-down box that currently shows a gap. The results are shown in Figure 3-30.

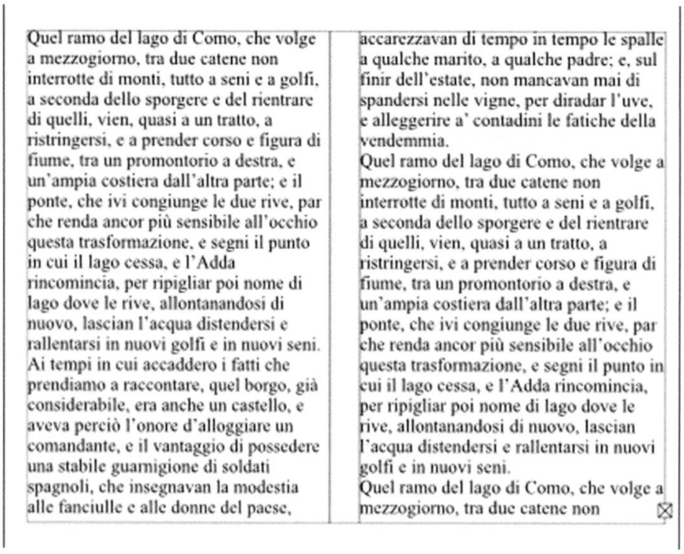

Quel ramo del lago di Como, che volge a mezzogiorno, tra due catene non interrotte di monti, tutto a seni e a golfi, a seconda dello sporgere e del rientrare di quelli, vien, quasi a un tratto, a ristringersi, e a prender corso e figura di fiume, tra un promontorio a destra, e un'ampia costiera dall'altra parte; e il ponte, che ivi congiunge le due rive, par che renda ancor più sensibile all'occhio questa trasformazione, e segni il punto in cui il lago cessa, e l'Adda rincomincia, per ripigliar poi nome di lago dove le rive, allontanandosi di nuovo, lascian l'acqua distendersi e rallentarsi in nuovi golfi e in nuovi seni. Ai tempi in cui accaddero i fatti che prendiamo a raccontare, quel borgo, già considerabile, era anche un castello, e aveva perciò l'onore d'alloggiare un comandante, e il vantaggio di possedere una stabile guarnigione di soldati spagnoli, che insegnavan la modestia alle fanciulle e alle donne del paese,

accarezzavan di tempo in tempo le spalle a qualche marito, a qualche padre; e, sul finir dell'estate, non mancavan mai di spandersi nelle vigne, per diradar l'uve, e alleggerire a' contadini le fatiche della vendemmia. Quel ramo del lago di Como, che volge a mezzogiorno, tra due catene non interrotte di monti, tutto a seni e a golfi, a seconda dello sporgere e del rientrare di quelli, vien, quasi a un tratto, a ristringersi, e a prender corso e figura di fiume, tra un promontorio a destra, e un'ampia costiera dall'altra parte; e il ponte, che ivi congiunge le due rive, par che renda ancor più sensibile all'occhio questa trasformazione, e segni il punto in cui il lago cessa, e l'Adda rincomincia, per ripigliar poi nome di lago dove le rive, allontanandosi di nuovo, lascian l'acqua distendersi e rallentarsi in nuovi golfi e in nuovi seni. Quel ramo del lago di Como, che volge a mezzogiorno, tra due catene non ⊠

Figure 3-30. *The two columns with an 8mm gap separating them*

The text frame columns are now separated by a white gutter space and are now easier to read.

Summary

If you use a word processor such as Microsoft Word, much of the decision-making work required to format your text is done for you. However, in a professional page-layout system such as Scribus, you are given the freedom to manage your own indents, linespaces, tabulations, and hyphenations. This freedom to manipulate the appearance of your text can sometimes appear daunting, but it means that you get to arrange the appearance of your pages in exactly the way that you want them.

In this chapter, you learned how to manipulate your text frames, how to manage your text overflows, how to wrap your text around an image or a quote, and how to arrange your text frames using margins and gutters. You also learned how to insert a drop cap, how to vary the opacity of your text frames and how to select, install, and manage your fonts.

In the next chapter, you shall take a more detailed look at the image frame and the things that can be done with it.

CHAPTER 4

■ ■ ■

Working with Graphics

In Chapter 3, you looked at typography, and at how to manipulate text in a text frame. In this chapter, you will be looking at the graphical capabilities of Scribus. You will learn how to manipulate imported pictures, how to work with bitmapped images, and how to work with lines and shapes.

In this chapter, you will learn the following:

- How to create an image frame

- How to import, modify, and scale your images in the image frame

- How to make changes to the size and proportion of the image frame

- The types of image formats that Scribus can handle

- How to insert and modify lines and shapes

- How to use shapes to define text wraps on a path

- How to create a Bezier Curve

Working with Graphics Files

We live in an increasingly visual world in which visual imagery plays an important part. In print publishing, graphical images are often the most attractive part of a document; they help to convey meaning and they help to catch the reader's attention.

So it is vitally important that you treat your handling of graphical images with the same degree of planning and attention to workflow that you did with your text files. As with text files, the graphical images are often created outside Scribus using image editors such as Gimp, Photoshop, and Inkscape. You are generally better off creating your image files in these image editing programs, but the good news is that Scribus also contains a set of graphics tools that will allow you to import, edit, and lay out your pictures. As with text files, the trick is to think ahead, and develop a carefully considered workflow; this will save you time and effort, and disk space.

In the first half of this chapter, I will show you how to insert an image frame onto the page, how to import images into Scribus, and how to edit things in it. After that, I will explain the various image formats that are supported by Scribus, and finally, I will show you how to draw straight lines and how to create shapes.

There are basically two kinds of image formats that you can add to your page layout: bitmap images and vector drawings. Most of the shapes and the line art that you will be importing into Scribus come in the form of vector graphics. The advantage here is that vector images can be scaled to any size without suffering distortion or loss of detail.

However, if you are importing photos into Scribus from a digital camera, these are likely to have been stored in another bitmap format called JPEG. Bitmap images are composed of little square dots, or picture cells, hence the term *pixels.*

If you wish to position these bitmap images in your document, the first thing you will need to do is insert an image frame.

Working with Image Frames

To place an image onto a page in Scribus, you first have to insert an image frame. There are three ways to insert an image frame in Scribus:

1.   You can select Insert Image Frame from the Insert menu.

2.   You can press the I key on your keyboard for a shortcut.

3.   You can click the Insert Image Frame icon in the toolbar.

Once you have clicked the image frame icon so that it is selected, you can insert it in the same way that you did with your text frame. You go to the place on the top left of the page where you want the image to start. You then hold down the left mouse button and click-drag the frame onto the page, releasing the mouse button when you reach the place where you want to position the lower right-hand corner of the frame. See Figure 4-1.

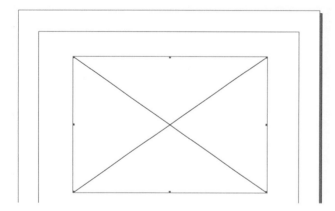

Figure 4-1. Placing an image frame on a blank page

You can adjust the size of the frame by selecting the control points on its red border lines, and then dragging them with the mouse. You can move the frame around the page by selecting the entire rectangular frame and dragging it with the mouse.

You will notice that there is a black X in the center of the frame. This indicates that the image frame is empty.

In Scribus, there are other ways to import an image. You can use the DirectImageImport script in the Script menu. This creates an image frame and loads an image. Or you can use the Manage Images window in the Extras menu. If you try loading the DirectImageImport script, it will ask you to select an image to import. It will then create a default frame size and import the image.

Loading an Image

To load an image in the image frame, make sure that the relevant frame is selected and then select File ➤ Import ➤ Get Image.

However, to save time, it is easier and quicker to right-click the image and select Get Image from the context menu. The Open window will appear, giving you the opportunity to select an image. When you have selected an image, it should then appear in the image frame, but it is likely that it will be oversized, and will need adjusting in order to make it more compatible with the image frame. What you will usually see in your frame is the upper left portion of a much larger image, as shown in Figure 4-2.

Figure 4-2. *A newly inserted image in its native size can often appear too large for the image frame*

You can move the image within the frame by double-clicking the image frame. The frame will then go into content-editing mode. This will enable you to move your image manually within the frame and to center the image more effectively, as you can see in Figure 4-3.

Figure 4-3. *The imported image after it has been moved while in content editing mode*

As soon as you click outside the frame with your mouse, you will find yourself back in frame-resizing mode again, and you will no longer be able to move the image inside the image frame.

It is important to be clear about the difference between resizing the frame and rescaling an image. Resizing is when you alter the width or the height of the frame, whereas scaling means changing the size of the image. It is likely, at this point, that you will want to adjust the scaling. You can adjust the scaling manually using the context menu, or you can adjust it using the Properties Palette. To rescale the image size using the context menu, right-click the frame and select Adjust Frame to Image or Adjust Image to Frame Size.

You can resize and rescale the image to the frame in one of three ways:

1. In the Properties Palette, under the Image tab, you can try scaling the image numerically in percentages. X-Pos and Y-Pos refer to the offset of the image (upper left corner) inside the frame. You can also change the DPI settings to change the size of the image on the page.

2. In the same Image tab, there is an option to Scale to Frame Size, which will adjust the image to the proportions of the frame. (This option fulfills the same function as the Adjust Frame to Image command in the context menu.) There is also a checkbox for preserving the proportions of the image. However, if you are not worried about preserving the image proportions, unchecking the checkbox marked Proportional will enable you to change the scaling of the image and crop the edges.

3. It is possible to perform the same functions in the context menu, by right-clicking on an image frame, and selecting Adjust Frame to Image. This will resize the frame so that the image fits perfectly into it. The context menu also provides the Adjust Image to Frame option.

EXERCISE: FRAMING YOUR PICTURES

Some of the smaller A5 glossy magazines tend to frame their photographs to give them a more three-dimensional effect. You can do this is Scribus.

Method 1

The first method involves placing a shape around the perimeter of the image. So open a new document, click the toolbar, insert an image frame, and then right-click the frame to get an image, as shown in Figure 4-4.

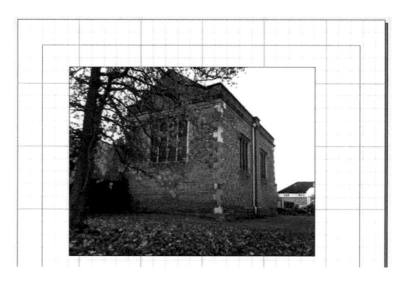

Figure 4-4. *Showing image frame and photo*

Now click the Insert Shapes icon on the Toolbar.

You can then draw a shape around the perimeter of the picture frame, as shown in Figure 4-5.

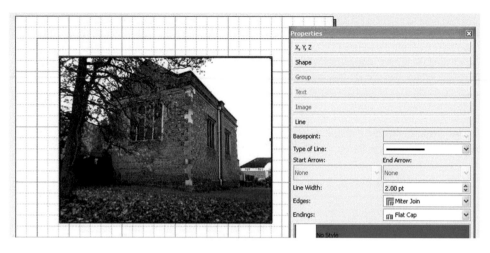

Figure 4-5. *Showing the photo with a shape drawn around its perimeter*

The advantage of this method is that it is quick and easy, and you can go into the Line tab of the Properties Palette if you need to increase the line width of the border. However, there is another way.

<u>Method 2</u>

Select the image frame and photo. Go into the Image tab of the Properties Palette and select Free Scaling. Increase the vertical offset of the image by increasing the Y-Pos setting to 5 points, as shown in Figure 4-6.

Figure 4-6. *Showing the border created by increasing X-Pos and Y-Pos*

Now increase the horizontal offset by increasing the X-Pos setting to 5 points. To give you an idea of the overall effect, I have added a cyan background for the image frame, and created a white background inside the image frame, by selecting the objects individually and then selecting a color in the Color tab of the Properties Palette.

Collecting for Output

At some point you will probably want to transfer your Scribus files to another computer. Scribus has its own built-in way to do this, using the Collect for Output window, displayed in Figure 4-7.

Figure 4-7. *The Collect for Output window*

If you select File ➤ Collect for Output, you will be prompted to create a new folder (and given the option of compressing the file). When Scribus duplicates the SLA file and copies the images into the new folder, it adjusts the relative paths in the duplicated SLA to point to the copied files (which are all put in the same folder regardless of their position on your storage device). There are checkboxes for including fonts and color profiles and for compressing files. This is the recommended way to transfer projects between systems.

However, I must admit that I generally save my image files in the Documents folder and then save the folder to a flash pen drive. I then install the folder onto another computer that also has Scribus installed. It seems to work okay.

Missing Files

Moving image files in Scribus can be a problem (and I should know). When you import an image into an image frame, Scribus adds a reference to the file's location, so each time you load the document, Scribus will search for the location of its images. Scribus will look for the file each time it needs it, and if the file is not there, you will get a warning message.

If you move your image files to another folder, the image will no longer appear in the image frame. Instead of an image you will see an image frame containing a red diagonal cross. This indicates that the image is missing from its original location (a black diagonal cross would merely indicate an empty image frame).

In order to find out what happened to the image, you need to open the Manage Images window, shown in Figure 4-8.

117

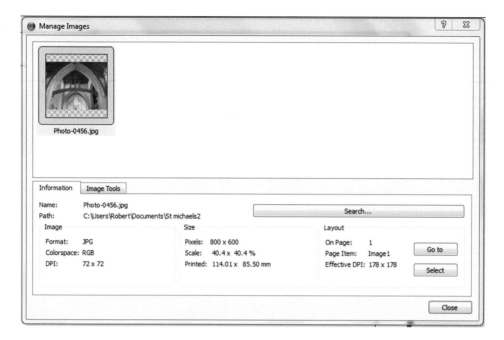

Figure 4-8. *The Manage Images window*

The Manage Images window displays the image path, the scale factor, the size and resolution of the image, and the name of the frame in which it is imported.

If you have lost an image file, click the Search button in order to locate it, as shown in Figure 4-9. The Manage Images window will help you to locate the image.

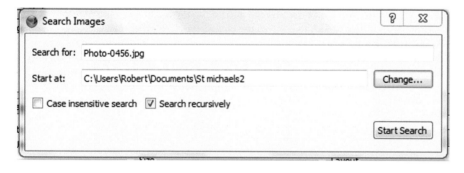

Figure 4-9. *The Search Images dialog in the Manage Images window*

Sometimes images go missing because they cannot be found, or because the file has been renamed, and in these cases you can relink them using the steps above. However, if you delete the file by mistake, you might still be able to retrieve it from the trash can. Otherwise it will be lost for good.

The Info Box

It is also possible to obtain information about an image by using the Info option in the context menu. The Info box provides information about the file name, the resolution in pixels per inch, the type of colorspace used, and whether it is possible to print the image (it's possible to save memory by disabling the printer icon in the XYZ tab).

Working with Image Effects

When you import an image into an image frame, it is possible to apply some basic graphic effects to the image. This type of operation is best done in a dedicated image editing program such as Gimp or Photoshop, but the effects in Scribus are actually quite impressive, and they are non-intrusive, so there's no danger of destroying your favorite photo. I ought to point out, however, that the process of adding effects to your images in Scribus can also slow the program down a bit.

The easiest way to apply effects to an image is by right-clicking the image and selecting Image Effects from the context menu. You can apply an effect by selecting it in the left column and then clicking the >> button, as shown in Figure 4-10. Applied effects are listed in the right column.

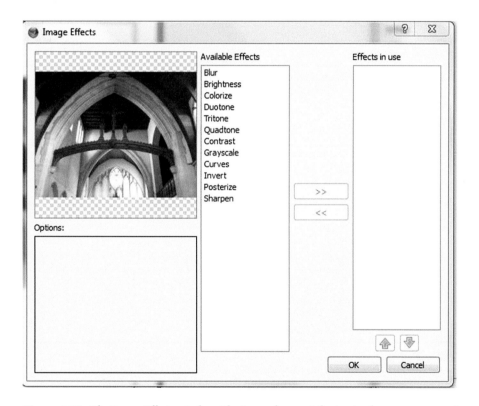

Figure 4-10. *The Image Effects window. The image frame at the top is where you can preview you image effects*

The effects available in Scribus are as follows:

- **Blur**: Use this effect to reduce the sharpness of your image.

- **Brightness**: Use this effect to increase or decrease the brightness of an image.

- **Colorize**: Use this effect to replace dark or bright tones with another color.

- **Contrast**: Use this effect to increase or decrease the bright and dark areas of your image.

- **Greyscale**: Use this to convert your colors to grey tones.

- **Invert**: Use this to invert your image colors.

- **Posterize**: Use this to reduce the number of colors in your image.

- **Sharpen**: This effect sharpens the contours and details of an image.

- **Duotone**: Use this to embrace an image's midtones using two halftones.

- **Tritone**: Use this to embrace an image's midtones using three halftones.

- **Quadtone**: Use this to reproduce an image using four specific colors.

Flipping Your Image

It is also possible to flip your image in Scribus, so that the original image is mirrored (but not copied) from left to right or from top to bottom. This is useful if you want to change the direction of a person or object in a photograph.

To flip an image, open the XYX tab of the Properties Palette and click the Flip Horizontally button.

Flipping is not only applicable to images. However, the effect of flipping a non-image varies depending on what is being flipped, as you can see in Figure 4-11.

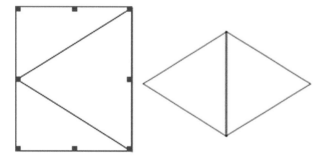

Figure 4-11. *The shape on the right has been copied and then flipped to mirror the one on the left*

IMAGE EFFECTS EXERCISE

Load a TIFF file that has some strong, clearly defined colors, such as the hexagon in Figure 4-12.

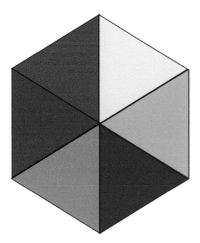

Figure 4-12. *A shape with clearly defined colors that has been converted into an image*

Display the Image Effects window by selecting the image and right-clicking to select Image Effects (or follow the path: Properties ➤ Image ➤ Image Effects), as shown in Figure 4-13.

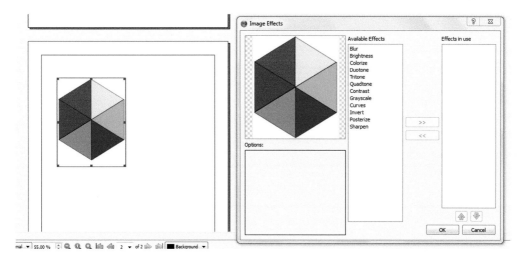

Figure 4-13. *The image as it appears in the Image Effects window*

Select and apply the Invert button by clicking the >> arrows. The result is shown in Figure 4-14.

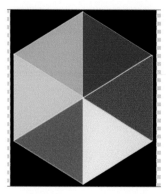

Figure 4-14. *An inverted version of the image should appear in the preview window*

If you try the same exercise with the greyscale, duotone, and blur settings, you get the results shown in Figure 4-15.

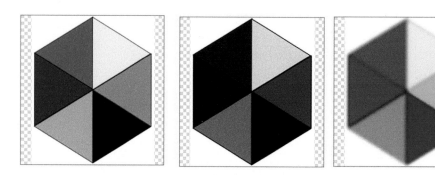

Figure 4-15. *The same exercise with the greyscale, duotone, and blur settings*

When you select the duotone effect, you'll be able to set the colors you want (I've chosen red as my first color and dark slate blue as my second color), as well as the amount of color.

If you have the time, you can try varying the intensity of the colors. I will go into the subject of color management in more detail in the next chapter.

Image Formats

There are, essentially, two kinds of images that can be imported into Scribus: bitmap images and vector drawings.

Vector drawings are often used to make line art and shapes because their images can be resized without suffering any distortion or loss of detail. Bitmap images (such as JPEG photos) need to be imported into a Scribus image frame via a link to its source file.

Bitmap images are made up of grids of tiny colored cells, or pixels, and any attempt to resize them can result in distortion of the image and loss of detail. We refer to the level of detail in a bitmap image as its *resolution*, or the number of pixels per inch of an image.

You can find out the resolution of an image by accessing the Properties of the image file (in Windows, you can do this by right-clicking the image).

Where the resolution of a bitmap image is concerned, the greater the number of dots, the clearer the image will be, and the easier it will be to reproduce the image on paper. However, you also need to factor in the size of the intended reproduction on the page. If you submit a Scribus PDF to a commercial printer, they will usually require an image resolution of at least 300 dots per inch (dpi).

Bitmap Images

As mentioned, bitmap images are made up of grids of tiny colored squares called pixels. A bitmap image can be displayed in a Scribus document by first inserting an image frame.

Common bitmap formats are GIF, TIFF, JPEG, PNG, and PSD. However, it is generally recommended that you use TIFF and PNG for Scribus documents and not the popular web format known as JPEG. JPEG images use what is known as *lossy compression*. This means that every time you save a JPEG image you lose some information in that image. TIFF files use a *lossless compression*. This means that they can be edited and saved as often as you like without losing any of their detail. This makes them much more suitable for graphic design work, and for working in Scribus. Having said all that, the use of JPEGs is fine as long as you know the limitations and understand that the image might not be at its best if printed.

The bitmap images that you view on your computer are created in what is known as the RGB color space. The RGB acronym stands for Red, Green, and Blue. And every pixel in your bitmapped image is created using these colors.

Scribus is able to import TIFF, JPEG, PNG, and GIF files. It can also import EPS files (EPS files are not bitmaps, but they do contain a bitmap preview which Scribus displays, though the vectors are what is exported at the end of the process).

JPEG

JPEG is a very popular image format, named after the group that developed it: the Joint Photographic Expert Group. Most digital cameras now seem to support this format and use it as their image default, because JPEG files are lightweight. The compression of images using the JPEG format makes for efficient use of memory in the camera, so that many more images can be stored on a flash storage card. Thus, the use of JPEG images has become widespread, both in photography and in web design.

The ubiquitous and lightweight nature of JPEG files means that you will probably end up using them in your publishing workflow at some point. There is no real problem with this in Scribus (I use them myself for publishing PDF files on the Web) but the Scribus user should be aware of two important drawbacks when using JPEGs in their workflow.

Firstly, JPEG files are *lossy* images. This means that JPEG images degrade slightly each time they're opened and resaved in an image editor. So don't use JPEG images if you plan to edit them repeatedly. It's better to convert an existing JPEG file to a TIFF before you consider editing it. However, as a format for exchanging photos with other people, JPEG is excellent. And if you are not planning to edit the image, Scribus will display the data as it is, so no detail will have been lost.

It is also useful to use JPEG in publishing workflows if you want to lighten your Scribus file, because JPEG files are light. However, when printing a JPEG, it is best to use a resolution of 300 dpi, if possible.

The second drawback to using JPEG files in Scribus is that the JPEG format does not support transparency. So you cannot create translucent or transparent backgrounds with JPEG (to create a transparent background in a JPEG file you need to put the image on a layer with opacity less than 100%).

TIFF

If you are interested in using a popular but non-lossy format in Scribus, you should use TIFF files. TIFF stands for Tagged Image File Format. It is one of the oldest image file formats in computer graphics. It was created by the Aldus Corporation (the company that developed the first page layout program known as PageMaker) in 1986.

If you intend to print your documents commercially, you are well advised to use TIFF files whenever possible because this format is well tested in print workflows. TIFF is a popular bitmap format for many publishers. It has an option for lossless compression and is used for extremely high quality printed images. However, this quality comes at a price: some TIFF images can also be very large files.

Another drawback is that TIFF images come in many different types, and some of them are of inferior quality. The TIFF format is not a single standard, but a set of standards with differing interpretations. Furthermore, a TIFF file written by one program may not read particularly well in another program. For example, Photoshop has its own version of the TIFF format. These proprietary versions differ from the free format in that they can handle some alpha channels, and they can handle layers (alpha channels are used to produce transparencies and a collection of objects can be stored as a layer).

Using TIFFs in Scribus

However, TIFFS are excellent for keeping originals of images that you might want to edit again, and most image graphics programs can use them.

Because it has a long history of use, it has an interesting feature that is not possible with PNG, namely *clipping paths*. These are vector paths that are used to mask parts of an image in order to isolate particular areas for special effects purposes. TIFFs can display color up to 24 bits (or 16.7 million colors) in the RGB model.

PNG Files

PNG is pronounced "PING." It originally stood as a recursive acronym for "PNGs not GIFs," but it is now used as an acronym for Portable Graphics Network. It was developed by Adobe in the mid-nineties as a replacement for GIF (which had encountered a lot of legal problems) and as an alternative to the more complex TIFF format.

PNG has certain advantages over its rivals. Unlike JPEG, it is lossless. This means that whatever compression ratio you use, your image will still look as good as the first time you opened it. But, like JPEG, it can also reproduce full color images, although the file sizes will be larger than if it had been saved as a JPEG. This makes PNG ideal for storing original copies of your images. It doesn't support the CMYK color space, which might be important if you need proper color management.

Scribus can load PNGs without trouble, and GIMP and Inkscape support the format as well. One big advantage that PNG has over other formats is that it supports both full and partial transparencies. This makes it an ideal image format for creating translucent background effects.

GIF Files

GIF stands for Graphics Interchange Format and is widely used on the Internet. However, it possesses one big drawback that makes it quite unsuitable for most forms of commercial printing. The format is indexed and limited to 256 colors, so saving a photo in this format will result in a very poor quality image.

On the plus side, though, it offers full transparency. This means that you can use it to isolate graphical objects in a photo against a clear background. This is useful for making icons intended for use in programming or the Web. But Scribus cannot handle animated GIFs; only the first frame will be used.

PSD Files

PSD stands for Photoshop Document. Photoshop is the world's most popular commercial graphics editing program, and its file format has become the standard format for graphic design work. It has a number of advantages over other formats. It can handle more information than other formats, and its files contain such diverse data sources as text, vector artwork, and metadata. But it poses problems for Scribus users.

Firstly, its format is closed and proprietary. It is owned by Adobe, and they have kept some of the specifications of the format secret since Version 7 of the software. So PSD files will have a limited functionality in Scribus.

It should be possible to load PSD files in Scribus, and you should be able to access its layers and transparencies, although you will have to use the Extended Image Properties dialog (accessed via the context menu) in order to do this.

Working with Vector Images

As you are already aware, bitmap images are made up of grids of tiny colored dots (pixels) and can only be displayed in a Scribus document if an image frame has been inserted beforehand. The big problem with bitmap files is that when they need to be resized, they lose their quality, especially when they are scaled up.

Vector drawings are composed using mathematical descriptions of the lines that make up their shapes. Like shapes, they can be imported directly into Scribus, and like shapes, they can be manipulated in Scribus.

The advantage of using vector drawings in Scribus is that you can scale them to any size you like without blurring or distorting them. They retain their clarity when enlarged, and they can be rescaled to any size without suffering a loss of detail. Vector drawings are therefore ideal for creating things like logos, maps, and various forms of line art.

The most popular vector file formats are SVG, EPS, and AI. Inkscape uses SVG as its native format, and Adobe Illustrator uses AI (Scribus supports most SVG features but some effects or parts of the drawing might not be imported). It can also support other vector formats like EPS, OpenOffice Draw files (.SXD), and Macintosh Picture files (PICT).

Importing a Vector Image

You can import a vector image directly into Scribus by clicking the page (so that no item is selected) and then going to File ➤ Import ➤ Get Vector File. You can then select a vector file (and a vector format) from the choices available. Click the place on the page where you want to place the upper left corner of the vector drawing and then insert the image. If the vector drawing is badly positioned, or too large or too small, you can easily resize it and adjust its positioning afterwards.

SVG

SVG stands for Scalable Vector Graphics. It is very much seen as the open source alternative to Encapsulated Postscript and is the vector format of choice in Scribus. It comes recommended by the World Wide Web Consortium and is the default format in Inkscape.

EPS

Encapsulated Postscript represents a development of the Postscript language. The Postscript language was created by Adobe in 1982 as a way of describing pages to a printing device. It used to be the default file format for print offices but its popularity has declined due to the emergence of quicker, more user-friendly ways of printing.

Using File ➤ Export, you can export your Scribus documents in a vector format either as EPS or SVG files.

Although vector files can be imported directly into Scribus, it is also possible to import EPS and PDF files into an image frame. And although the vector image is shown on-screen as being rasterized, you will be able to export it as vector file. In fact, PDF files in Scribus can only be displayed using an image file, and they can only import one page: the page that will be imported is displayed in the Page Number selection in the Properties ➤ Image tab. If you are mixing your color models, the final rasterized image will look small and rather bleached compared to the original PDF.

Once a vector file has been imported into Scribus, you can resize it by using the handles around its select box.

All this talk of bitmaps, vector drawings, and image resolutions can be confusing for the beginner. So it is worth remembering that when you export your documents to PDF, Scribus will be doing some of the calibration for you.

The bitmap images that you use will always require an image frame, but your vector drawings and polygons can be click-dragged directly onto the page.

Shapes, Lines, and Paths

Scribus has a selection of shapes that can be inserted directly onto the page. The Insert Shape tool is the icon represented by the white rectangle on the Toolbar.

If you click the arrow next to the Insert Shape tool, it will display a list of predefined shapes, organized into default shapes, arrows, flow chart, jigsaw, and special categories. When you select the default rectangle shape on the toolbar, you'll notice an arrow with a drop-down list of shapes that you can choose from. The selections are illustrated in Figure 4-16.

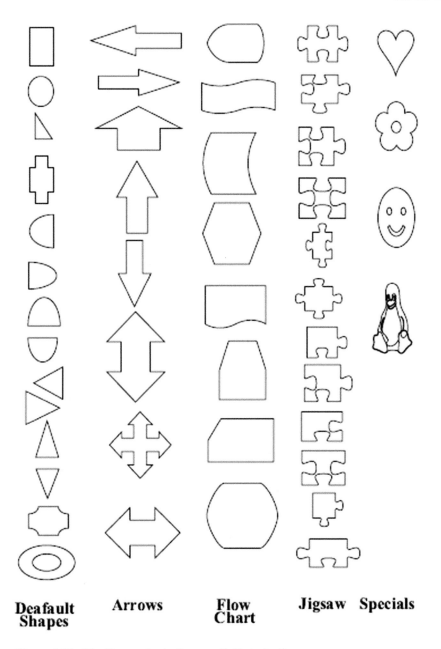

Figure 4-16. *The Shape subselections available in Scribus*

Furthermore, if you insert a rectangle, Scribus contains a rather nifty tool for rounding the corners off, as shown in Figure 4-17. You can find it in the Shape tab of the Properties Palette.

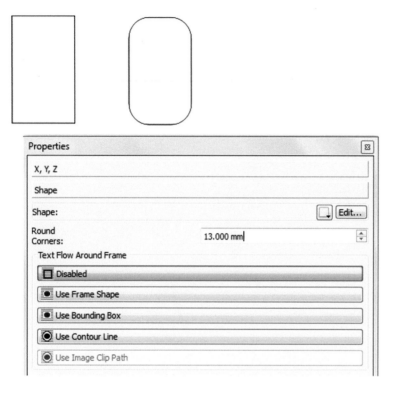

Figure 4-17. *It's possible to round the corners of a rectangular frame using the Rounded Corners tool in the Shape tab*

Drawing Polygons

It is also possible to create shapes with the Insert Polygon Tool, which is situated to the right of the Insert Shapes tool on the Toolbar (see Figure 4-18). However, where the Insert Shapes tool offers you a selection of predefined elements, this tool allows you to create your own.

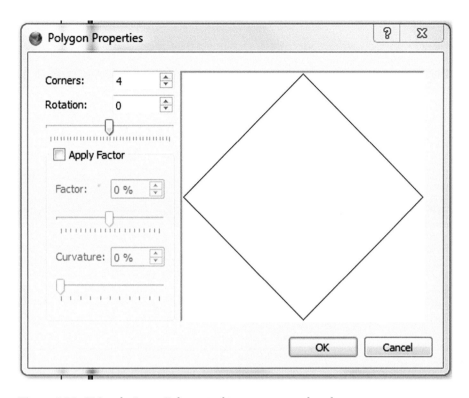

Figure 4-18. *Using the Insert Polygon tool to create a sample polygon*

Polygons can be defined using the polygon properties of the Insert Polygon tool. Click the arrow to the right of the Insert Polygon Tool icon, and then choose Properties in the menu that appears. You can then choose your angle of rotation and the number of sides that you want.

Having created your shape, it is now possible to convert it into a text or image frame. To do this, right-click the shape and select Convert to Text Frame (or Convert to Image Frame) in the context menu.

CREATING A SIMPLE SIGNPOST USING SHAPES

With Scribus, it's actually really easy to create interesting shapes in very little time. Figure 4-19 shows a signpost I made.

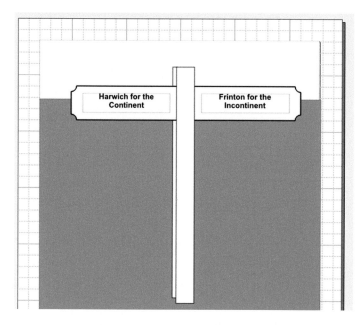

Figure 4-19. A simple signpost made from rectangular shapes and a couple of text frames

First, click the rectangular polygon shape on the Toolbar and draw it out into the shape of a post, as shown in Figure 4-20. Then draw out a second horizontal rectangle to make it into the form of a cross.

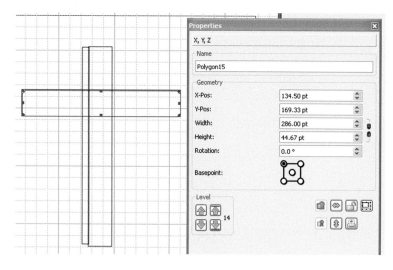

Figure 4-20. Composing the cross from shapes and editing the horizontal rectangular shape in the Properties Shape tab

Edit this shape by decreasing the round corners by -5 in the Shape tab of the Properties Palette, as shown in Figure 4-21.

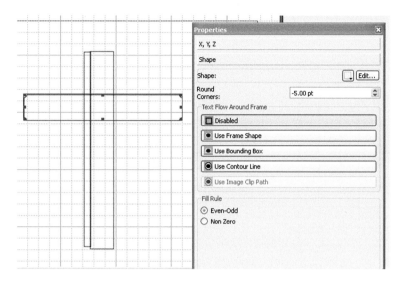

Figure 4-21. *The shape tab settings for the round corner of the horizontal shape. Round corners set to -5 to make the shape look more like a signpost*

Add a small vertical shape at the back to give the post a three-dimensional look.

Then add a white background to your shapes by selecting white for each shape in the Properties Color tab.

Finally, add some background frames, and push them into the background by selecting Levels from the context menu and selecting Lower to Bottom. Then add the text frames for your signs.

Mesh Distortion

It is possible to modify your shape using a process called mesh distortion, shown in Figure 4-22.

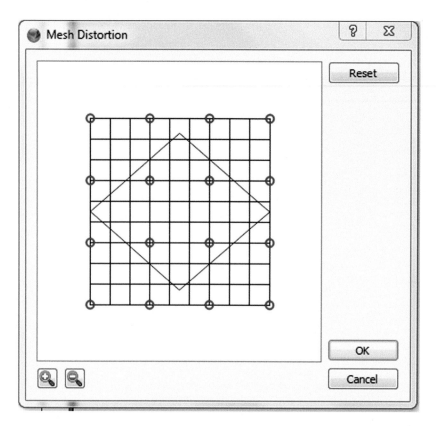

Figure 4-22. *The above polygon as it appears in the Mesh Distortion window*

To modify your frame or shape, select it and go to Item ➤ Path tools ➤ Mesh Distortion. A window will appear, and the selected frame or shape will be displayed inside a grid containing circular handles, as shown in Figure 4-23. (There is no "snap to grid" option available with this tool. Also, note that the process of Mesh Distortion is not easy to undo. In fact, undoing a mesh distortion can be a rather hit-or-miss operation.)

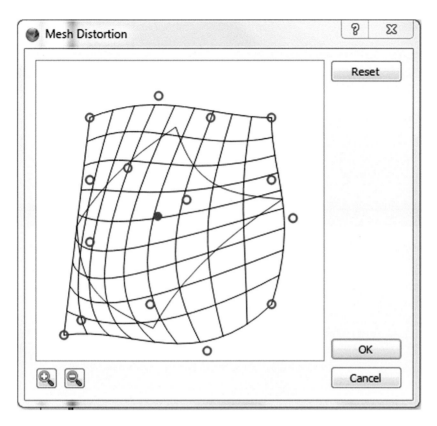

Figure 4-23. *Playing with the control points on the grid enables you to add curves and alter the shape of the polygon*

Working with Lines

A common requirement in desktop publishing is the need to create straight lines, for use either as borders or as a form of demarcation. You can draw straight lines in Scribus by using the Insert Line tool on the toolbar or by going to Insert ➤ Line in the Menubar.

Once you have selected the Insert line icon, you can click the line with the mouse in order to bring up a dialog box. Here, you can specify how the line will be drawn.

It is also possible to rotate the line incrementally on the page by pressing the Ctrl key (in Windows) while you are dragging/drawing the line. This will have the effect of snapping the line's rotation in 15 degree increments.

To draw lines on the page, press the left mouse button to start a line, then drag the mouse along the page in the direction you want, and release the mouse button when you reach the point where you want the line to end.

Arrows

Arrows are available from the drop-down menu by the Shapes icon on the main Toolbar.

This category contains both single-ended and double-ended arrows.

Using Arrows in Scribus

I have been using the default arrows that can be found in the default collection of Shapes, but I find them rather chunky for professional work. It's actually easier to create an arrow by inserting a thin line and then adding an arrow shape on the end of the line.

EXERCISE: CREATING AN ARROW

Insert an arrow from the Toolbar by clicking the drop-down list next to the Shapes icon.

The arrow that is created is a bit thick and chunky and it is difficult to alter the width of the line without affecting the shape of the arrow as a whole.

You could try to edit it in the Shape tab, but instead insert a line and add an arrow shape on the end.

Add a line, and set it to a 2-point line width in the Line tab of the Properties Palette.

All that remains is to insert a default arrow shape, and reduce its width so that it can be placed on the end of the line.

And there's your arrow!

Clipping Paths

Scribus can read the clipping paths on image frames that are generated in Gimp. A clipping path is an invisible boundary that you can use to mask the part of a picture that you want to hide, such as a background, while isolating another part, such as a foreground object. It's a technique that is used to cut out images for use as icons. But this feature is only available for images made using the TIFF file format.

You used a clipping path in previous chapters in order to flow some text around an image.

If your image has extended properties, you can locate a clipping path by using the External Image Properties window in the Image tab of the properties palette.

The Bezier Tool

You can use the Bezier tool on your Toolbar to create what is known as a Bezier curve.

On the toolbar, select the Bezier curve icon, and click the page to create a starting point for your curve.

Now move the mouse to the next point in your curve, and click and hold, and then drag the mouse in order to shape the curve (or draw a straight line, depending on what you did before).

Finally, move the mouse in order to create the end point of your curve, and left-click the mouse to complete the curve. Your curve might look like the one in Figure 4-24.

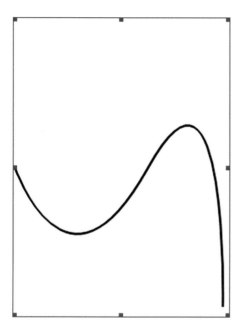

Figure 4-24. *An impromptu Bezier Curve*

Using the Pen Tool

The pen tool is designed to imitate the action of a pen on paper. However, it is probably more suited to those who use a pen tablet regularly in their design work. If all you are doing is manipulating the pen tool with your mouse, the end results can be rather wobbly, and depend to a large extent on your ability to control the mouse.

To use the Pen tool, click the Insert Freehand Line icon on the Toolbar, or use the Insert ➤ Freehand line menu. Then click your document, hold down the left mouse button, and move the mouse to draw a line. Release the mouse button when you want to stop drawing.

To use the pen tool, follow these steps:

- Select Insert ➤ Freehand Tool to activate the pen tool.

- Press the left mouse button and drag the mouse, relaxing the button when you want the line to stop.

- If you need to modify the line you have drawn, use the Line tab or the Colors tab in the Properties Palette.

135

Summary

Managing your images in Scribus can seem like a daunting task. When inserting a bitmap file, you need to balance the desire to enlarge an image with the need to achieve the right level of dpi for your printer.

I generally restrict myself to using TIFF and PNG images in my documents, and it's a system that's worked well for me, although there have been occasions when I've used JPEGS and GIFS without encountering any problems. So don't rule out their use, by any means; just be aware of their limitations.

I hope that this chapter has given you some idea of how to go about managing your colors, and how to get the best out of your photos and drawings.

In Chapter 5, I will show you how to calibrate your monitor's RGB color palettes so that they are compatible with the CMYK system of your printer.

■ ■ ■

CHAPTER 5

Working with Colors

In Chapter 4, you looked at the graphical capabilities of Scribus. You learned how to manipulate imported pictures, how to work with bitmapped images, and how to work with lines and shapes. In this chapter, you will be looking at how Scribus handles color.

There will be quite a lot of information to take in because it is important to understand the concept of color models. The incompatibility of different color models is an important issue in desktop publishing. If you are planning to print in color, it is good to know a bit about color theory, about additive and subtractive colors, and about primary and secondary colors.

Scribus comes with a fairly basic set of RGB colors, but you can add to these colors quite easily. You can even create your own custom colors, and introduce some flashy background effects.

In this chapter you will learn the following:

- The difference between the two main color models, RGB and CMYK

- How to choose a color scheme using the color wheel

- How to embellish yours texts and shapes with fill and stroke colors

- How to add colors to your RGB color palettes

- How to create color gradients

- How to use the Eyedropper tool to capture on-screen colors

Color Theory

The ability to perceive color in everyday objects is an important part of our life experience. Yet, for the desktop publisher, the accurate application of on-screen colors to paper documents can seem like a daunting task.

First, there is the color generated by your computer monitor, which uses three primary colors. Then there are the colors generated by your professional printer, which uses four process colors. These primary colors (cyan, magenta, and yellow) when added together make a muddy brown that is interpreted as black. They are known as *subtractive colors* because as you add more and more of them to a reflective surface such as paper, the ink absorbs more color and this subtracts from the color that reflects back into your eye, making it appear darker.

If you are planning to use Scribus to design a document that uses various shades of black (or greyscale), then the issue of color might not appear significant. But there will probably come a time when you will want to use vibrant colors to help enliven the look of your documents, and there are a number of color palettes in Scribus that can help you to do this. Scribus will also let you edit your colors and add more colors to your palettes.

If you decide to use color in your documents, you will need to make some fairly informed decisions.

- First, you need to define your intended audience and select a format that is guaranteed to reach them. Is your document going to be web-based or print-based? It is going to be a poster that attracts crowds or a brochure that addresses individual readers?

- Then you need to decide how to produce your colors by choosing a color model. Will you be using spot colors or process colors in order to produce your document? Will you be using a CMYK color set, or will your color set be defined by Pantone? Or are you going to use web-safe RGB colors?

Color Models and Color Space

You will find the terms *color model* and *color space* being used a lot in this chapter. The terms have become so interchangeable within mainstream literature on the subject that they have lost much of their meaning. For the purposes of this book, however, a color model is a mathematical way of defining the way that color can be represented, whereas a color space is a specific way of mapping colors using the values described by a model. So RYB and RGB are both examples of color models, but sRGB and AdobeRGB are examples of color spaces that use RGB as their color model. sRGB (or Standard RGB) was developed by Hewlett Packard and Microsoft in 1977, and Adobe RGB is the standard color gamut from Adobe.

In desktop publishing, there are two main types of color model in use: RGB and CMYK.

The RYB Color Model

Red, yellow, and blue are generally thought of as our three basic primary colors, and we can mix these primary colors to get secondary colors. So mixing red and yellow makes orange, and mixing yellow and blue makes green. Then you can mix primary colors with secondary colors to get *tertiary colors*. These three sets make up the color wheel, shown in Figure 5-1. If we split the wheel in half, we can see that it is divided into warm colors and cool colors.

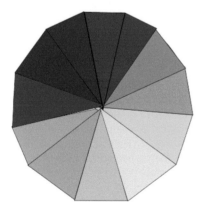

Figure 5-1. *The Color Wheel*

The RGB Color Model

Another example of a color model is RGB, which is used to produce the colors on a computer screen. Each pixel in a computer screen is a combination of red, green, and blue lights. The colors are produced by varying the amount of the red, green, and blue lights that are used to light up the pixels on the screen. These three colors can be mixed in different ratios to produce other colors, as shown in Figure 5-2. A total of 16,777,216 colors can be produced in this way.

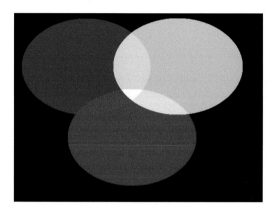

Figure 5-2. *The primary and secondary colors of the RGB color model*

RGB colors are also known as *additive colors*. In an additive color system, the colors are illuminated from a source like the light from a television or computer screen. The color is transmitted by mixing different color lights, with red, green, and blue being the primary colors.

If you keep adding additive light colors to each other, eventually you will end up with the color white. But the colors used in printing are known as subtractive colors. In subtractive color theory, all colors mix to produce black. If you add subtractive ink colors to a white surface, essentially you are subtracting or removing brightness from the white surface of the paper, and you will end up with a muddy brown that is close to black. You can see the primary and secondary subtractive colors in Figure 5-3.

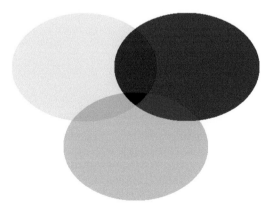

Figure 5-3. *Primary and secondary subtractive colors*

139

The Color Compatibility Issue at the Heart of Desktop Publishing

Each image that appears on your computer screen is generated using a mixture of red, green, and blue, but it has to be converted into CMYK color in order to get professionally printed. So the additive colors used to produce colors on your computer screen are, in a sense, the exact opposite of the subtractive colors used in professional four-color printing. In order to accurately reproduce your original additive colors on paper, a printer will require the use of subtractive CMYK/process colors.

And the problem here is that these subtractive process colors do not always reproduce the additive colors of the computer screen at the same hue. So there is no guarantee that the color you see on your computer screen is what you will see when your document is printed.

■ **Note**   It would be tempting to illustrate the issue of the color model incompatibility that lies at the heart of desktop publishing by using the example of the commercially-produced office/home inkjet printer. These printers often use cartridges that are a combination of the four process colors (cyan, magenta, yellow, and black). However, although this is often the case, most inkjet printers actually seem to conform to the RGB color model and use RGB drivers to reproduce the colors.

If all this talk of color incompatibility seems rather daunting, the good news is that Scribus takes care of it all for you; you can work in RGB colors on your computer, and Scribus will export your color-rich documents in a CMYK-friendly format.

■ **Note**   In Scribus, it is also possible to calibrate the RGB colors of your monitor using a colorimeter and some software. I will talk about this process in more detail at the end of the chapter. I ought to warn you, however, that tampering with your monitor's color space is a highly specialized task and not one that should be attempted by someone who is learning about desktop publishing for the first time.

Ink Types

The two main ink types that are used in commercial printing are designated as either spot colors or process colors.

Process Colors: CMYK

CMYK is the color model used in professional printing. It represents colors in terms of combinations of cyan, magenta, yellow, and black. It is possible to produce a large range of colors by combining cyan, magenta, and yellow color plates, but the key (black) plate is added in order to improve the reproduction of some dark colors.

Collectively, CMYK represents the four primary colors of publishing, but they are known individually as *process colors*. These four basic colors can be mixed to produce most of the colors that the human eye can see.

Spot Colors

Spot colors, on the other hand, are single ink colors that the print shop mixes up separately in order to color specific elements within a document. Spot colors are sometimes referred to as second colors. They are used when few colors are required and color accuracy is essential. Spot colors are often used in the production of stickers and posters, where a bright color like red is added to a basic design in black. You can, though, use more than one spot color in a document. A popular spot color is red, which can be added to a black and white poster in order to highlight a product or service.

Scribus is able to include proprietary spot color palettes in its color collection, though they need to be designated as spot colors first. To designate a spot color, simply select the Is Spot Color checkbox in the Edit Color dialog box, as shown in Figure 5-4.

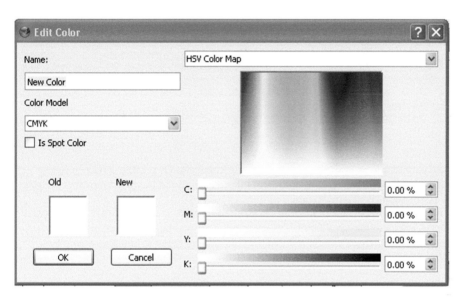

Figure 5-4. *A color can be designated as a spot color in the Edit Colors dialog box*

To identify a spot color in Scribus, go to the color list and look for a color accompanied by a red circle.

To print a document using a spot color, export it as a PDF file (using the Save As PDF dialog box), select the Color tab, choose Printer as the Intended Output, and uncheck the option to Convert Spot Colors to Process Colors, as shown in Figure 5-5.

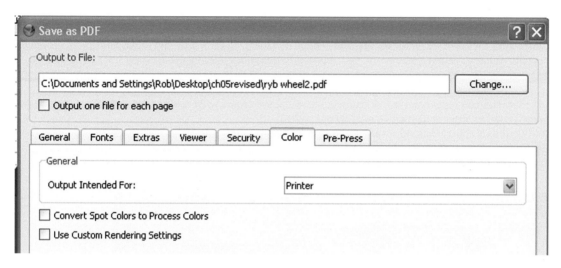

Figure 5-5. *Exporting a PDF with spot colors*

PANTONE

There are several industry standards for spot colors, but the most widely used is produced by a company called Pantone. If you decide to use a spot color manufacturer like Pantone, you ought to know that Scribus cannot integrate these colors because of legal issues.

Pantone is the company responsible for producing the Pantone Matching System, which was intended to provide an international standard for color. Pantone is responsible for producing a standardized set of thousands of colored inks, all of which are numbered. Pantone also makes metallic and fluorescent inks.

Choosing Colors: The Color Wheel

Learning about color theory can seem like a daunting prospect for beginners to desktop publishing. If, like me, you find it difficult to select the right colors for your documents, there is a rather useful tool in Scribus that can help you make the right selection. It is called the color wheel, and you can launch it from the Extras menu (Extras ➤ Color Wheel), shown in Figure 5-6.

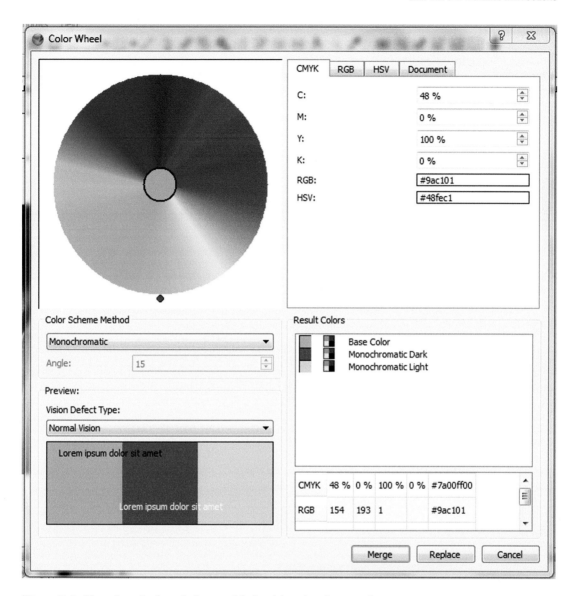

Figure 5-6. *The color wheel can help you pick the right colors for your document*

Before you choose a color scheme, you need to select your basic color. This will be the main color that you intend using in your document. You can pick your base color using the color wheel in the top left corner. Directly under the wheel is the Color Scheme Method selection area where you can choose how Scribus selects other colors. And under that is the Preview area, where you can see how your chosen colors will look together under different circumstances.

Color Schemes

The color wheel provides various color schemes for you to choose from, such as Monochromatic, Analogous, Complementary, Split Complementary, Triadic, and Tetradic.

The monochromatic color scheme, shown in Figure 5-7, takes a single color as its base color and then varies it to create variant shades and tones of that color. The overall effect is said to be soothing and easy on the eye.

Figure 5-7. *A typical monochromatic color scheme featuring a base color and two variants*

The analogous color scheme, shown in Figure 5-8, uses colors that are adjacent to each other on the color wheel, with one color dominating and the others enriching the scheme.

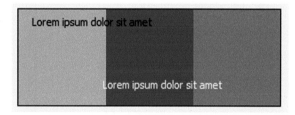

Figure 5-8. *An analogous color scheme featuring three adjacent colors*

The complimentary color scheme, shown in Figure 5-9, is made of two colors that are opposite each other on the color wheel.

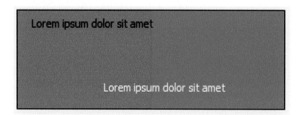

Figure 5-9. *A complimentary color scheme featuring two opposing colors*

Two colors that are of the same value but opposite hues are known as complements. The split complimentary color scheme uses a main (often warm) color against two complementary (and often cooler) colors, as you can see in Figure 5-10.

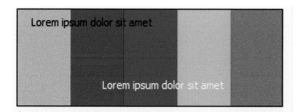

Figure 5-10. *The Split Complementary Color Scheme*

The triadic color scheme uses three colors equally spaced around the color wheel, as shown in Figure 5-11.

Figure 5-11. *The Triadic Color Scheme*

The tetradic color scheme uses four colors arranged in two complementary color pairs, as shown in Figure 5-12.

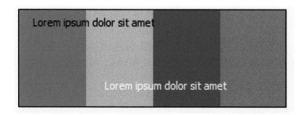

Figure 5-12. *The Tetradic Color Scheme*

Composing Your Palette

If you follow the menu selection Edit ➤ Colors, you will be presented with a dialog showing the colors currently available for use in your document, as shown in Figure 5-13.

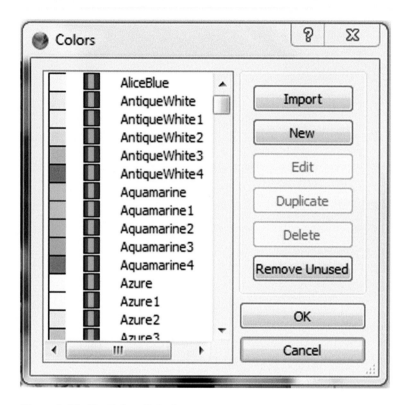

Figure 5-13. *The Colors dialog box*

If you select the Edit button in the Colors window, you will be presented with the Edit Colors dialog, which displays the name of you color and the color model used, as shown in Figure 5-14.

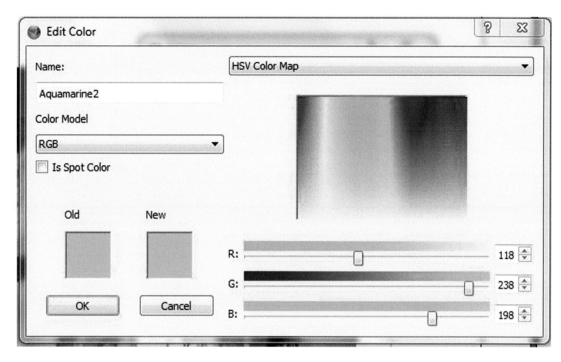

Figure 5-14. *The Edit Color dialog box*

The color models listed on the left are CMYK, RGB, Greyscale, and Web-safe RGB. As mentioned, RGB is the model used by your computer monitor. Web-safe RGB is a set of colors that are designed so that they can be reproduced accurately in a web browser, greyscale translates color content into shades of black, and CMYK represents how your colors would look in print if the color management function was activated.

The color spaces listed at the top of the Edit Color box are all based on RGB. Scribus Basic is the simplest of the color sets and is also the default color set in Scribus. As its name suggests, it is rather basic.

The HSV Color map, which is shown at the top of the Edit Color dialog box, uses three numbers to represent color, but it represents color in terms of the color properties Hue, Saturation, and Value (or Lightness). HSV was developed by computer graphics researchers in the 1970s as an alternative representation of RGB, so the HSV Color Map provides a rearranged version of the RGB color model. The Hue property is a measure of where each color is located within the spectrum, the Saturation property is a measure of how intense each color is, and the Value property is a measure of how bright each pixel is, based on a scale of 0 to 100.

Applying Colors

In Scribus, colors are usually applied via the Color and Text tabs in the Properties Palette.

To apply color to your text, highlight the text in the frame, open the Text tab of the Properties palette, and then open the Color & Effects Expander, shown in Figure 5-15.

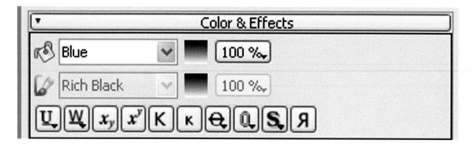

Figure 5-15. *Applying color with the Color & Effects expander*

You can then select a color for your text.

Text colors can also be set from within the Story Editor, as shown in Figure 5-16, although this feature only seems to become activated when shadow text is applied to the text inside the Story Editor. Although the resulting selections will not be displayed in the editor, they will be seen when the layout is updated.

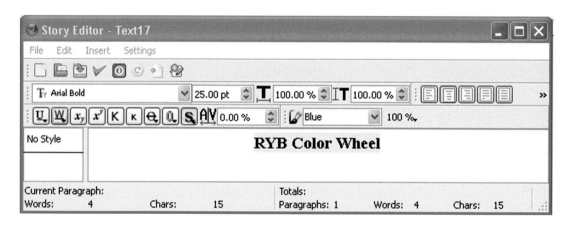

Figure 5-16. *Setting the text color from within the Story Editor*

It is also possible to change the background color of the Story Editor by opening it up and selecting a different color in the Select Color box. To open this box, follow the Setting ➤ Background path in the Story Editor.

Fill Color

If you want to add color to the background of a shape or a frame, you can do so using the color tab of the Properties palette, as shown in Figure 5-17.

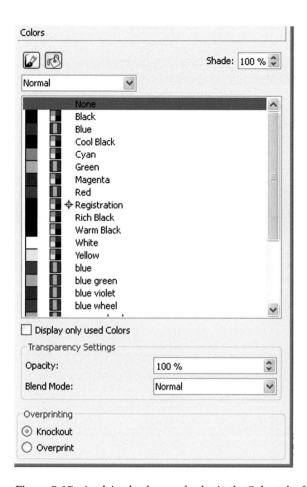

Figure 5-17. Applying background color in the Color tab of the Properties Palette

You can also change the line color (the color of an image or text frame's border, or the outline of a shape). To change a border's line color, check that the frame border's line width is greater than 0. Then select your chosen color in the Color tab of the Properties Palette by nominating a stroke color. Line color can also be applied to straight lines and freehand lines.

Setting Stroke Color in Scribus

Note that when you first format your text in a text frame, it will possess no actual stroke color because the text has no outline. To apply a stroke color to your text, you need to highlight the text and then select the Stroke tab in the Color & Effects expander, and then choose your color.

Background Color

To apply a background color to a frame, you need to use the Color tab of the Properties Palette. Highlight your shape or frame, and then select your fill color.

Shade and Transparency

You can control the application of your colors more precisely by using your Shade and Transparency controls, shown in Figure 5-18.

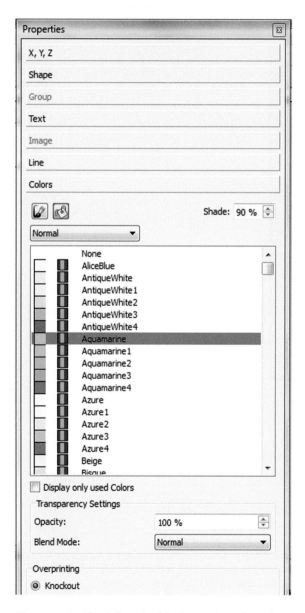

Figure 5-18. *The Color tab of the Properties Palette, featuring spinbox controls for varying the shade and opacity of your images*

The Shade setting can be used to lighten a color. Every color that you select has a shade value, as you can see in Figure 5-19.

Figure 5-19. *The Shade setting*

The default shade level is 100% and this represents the full saturation level for that color. As this shade level is reduced, the color will lighten, and when it reaches a measurement level of 0%, it effectively becomes a shade of white.

The Transparency setting (Figure 5-20), on the other hand, can be used to control a color's visual solidity.

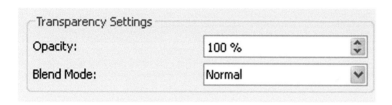

Figure 5-20. *The Transparency setting*

At the default level of 100%, the color of the selected object will be opaque, but when it is reduced to 0%, it will become invisible. It is also possible to reduce the opacity of an object on a top level relative to the objects below it in order to reveal those underlying objects.

Creating Custom Colors

You can create your own colors in Scribus by following the Edit ➤ Color menu, selecting the New button, and using the Color Preview pane to select a color map. See Figure 5-21.

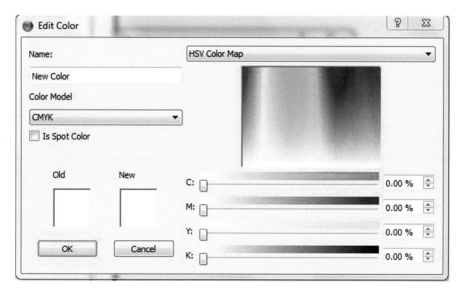

Figure 5-21. *Selecting a new CMYK color on the HSV Color Map*

151

CREATE YOU OWN RGB COLOR IN SCRIBUS

Follow these steps to create your own custom color in Scribus.

Go to the Edit menu and select Colors to open the Edit Color dialog box.

Select the New button and use the Color Preview pane to select a Color map.

Once you have selected your map, use the Preview pane in the lower left of the dialog box to select the shade of color that you want, and, when prompted, name it.

Color Sampling with the Eyedropper Tool

Choosing a custom color from one of your color spaces is an effective way to create a custom color. However, the most fun way of collecting colors in Scribus is to use the Scribus Eyedropper.

The Eyedropper icon can be found on the Toolbar. The Eyedropper lets you capture any color that you can display on your computer screen. Simply click the Eyedropper Tool icon, click a screen color, and name that color. Enter a name and the color will be added to the list of RGB colors that are available for use in your Properties Palette.

■ **Note**   As of this writing, the Eyedropper tool does not currently work on images in Mac OSX.

Gradients

The Gradients tool in Scribus is really quite fun! A gradient provides a smooth transition from one fill color to another. What you see when you print a gradient is two or more colors blending gradually from one to the other across a set distance. If used sparingly, gradients can look quite impressive; I sometimes use them as a background for the headlines in my magazine. Gradients are eye-catching and add a touch of vibrancy to your documents.

There are two specific kinds of gradients, namely radial and linear gradients. Linear color gradients are specified by two points of color, whereas a radial gradient is specified by a circle that has one color at the edge and another at the center.

In order to produce a gradient, you have to select a frame or shape and then open the Colors tab of the Properties Palette. Gradients can then be added by selecting Gradient instead of Normal from the option list. The drop-down list above the list of colors in the middle of the Colors tab offers several kinds of gradients: horizontal (see Figure 5-22), vertical (see Figure 5-23), diagonal, cross-diagonal, radial (see Figure 5-24), free linear, and free radial.

Figure 5-22. *A horizontal gradient made with two shades of blue*

Figure 5-23. *A vertical gradient made with two shades of blue. This time the lighter shades flows into the darker shade running from top to bottom*

Figure 5-24. *A radial gradiant with the lighter shade flowing out in a circular shape from the centre*

Using the Properties Palette, select a color, and then click your gradient inside the Colors tab to insert your triangular gradient stops, as shown in Figure 5-25.

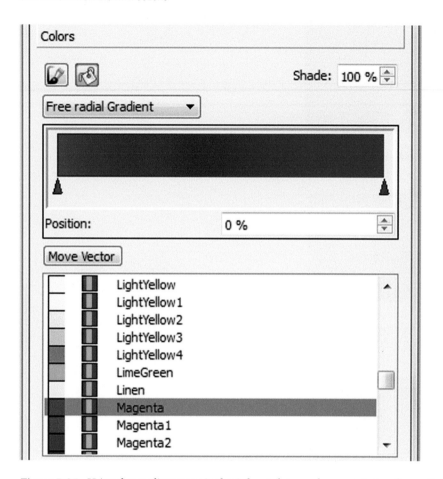

Figure 5-25. *Using the gradient stops in the Colors tab to apply magenta to a free radial gradient*

The red triangular stops can be moved away from the start or the end point with the mouse pointer. Each time you select a color and add a stop you are introducing the gradient stop to a new color.

A gradient always has at least two stops. If you have more than two, you can delete them by dragging the stops away from the gradient box.

CREATING GRADIENTS

Open a new page in Scribus and insert a text frame onto that page. Then right-click the text frame and open the Properties Palette.

Now open the Color tab of the palette and select the bucket-fill icon to the right of the paint brush icon, as shown in Figure 5-26.

Figure 5-26. *The Color tab*

Go to the drop-down box that is set to Normal and change it to Horizontal Gradient, as shown in Figure 5-27.

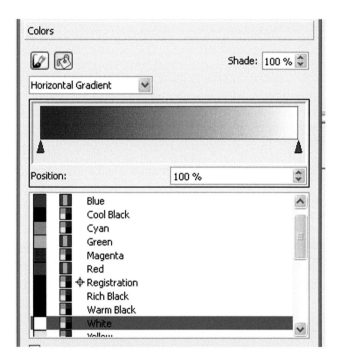

Figure 5-27. *Selecting a Horizontal Gradient from the Normal or Gradient Fill list*

It should now be possible to create a two-color gradient that moves from magenta through to white. You can do this by clicking the left triangle and selecting the color magenta, and then clicking the right triangle and clicking the color white. If you wish, you can create a three-color gradient by clicking in the middle of the Gradient box, inserting another gradient stop, and selecting another color. I have chosen to stay with two colors, but I have moved the color white to the central gradient stop, as shown in Figure 5-28.

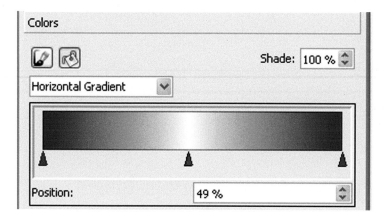

Figure 5-28. *A two-color gradient with three stops*

Working with Patterns

As well as using gradients for fills in Scribus, it is possible to use patterns too. Unfortunately, Scribus does not come with its own selection of patterns, so you will have to start collecting them yourself. The good news is that there are plenty of free patterns and textured backgrounds available for download on the Web.

When you see a pattern that you like, check to see if there are any licensing conditions, and then download it as a bitmap file to your computer.

If you have a pattern that you like, you can save it by right-clicking for the context menu, and then choosing Send to patterns.

Use the Edit ➤ Patterns menu to manage your patterns.

To insert a pattern, open the Colors tab in the Properties Palette, and select the drop-down button below the fill selector. This will open a drop-down list of gradients. If any patterns have been saved, you will see an entry for Pattern at the bottom of the gradient list. When you select the Pattern option, you will see a list of all saved patterns and you can select one to apply to the currently selected item.

Select your pattern, and if required, make adjustments to its scale, position, and opacity. Patterns should be used sparingly. Used as background fills they can overwhelm the reader and reduce the readability of the document

SAVING AND USING A PATTERN

Insert your version of the three-stop gradient that you just made into a text frame background. Then right-click the text frame and select Send to Patterns from the context menu.

Now lay out a set of text frames around the border of the page. Right-click in each text frame, open the Color tab of the Properties Palette, and select Pattern from the Normal or Gradient fill drop-down box, as illustrated in Figure 5-29.

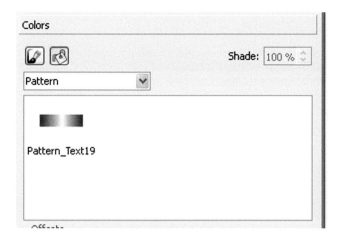

Figure 5-29. *Selecting a pattern in the Normal or Gradient Fill box*

You should end up with a patterned border like the one in Figure 5-30.

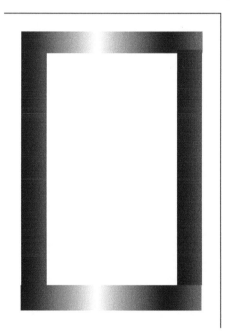

Figure 5-30. *The Finished border pattern*

Calibrating Colors in Your Computer's Monitor

In order to make the colors you see on your screen match the colors you place on your paper, you need to configure your monitor using a calibrator and some color-matching software.

First, you need to create a color profile of your monitor using a calibration device known as a colorimeter. Some popular colorimeters are

- Datacolor's Snyder

- Datacolor's Spyder5 PRO

- Datacolor's Sypder5 Lite

- X-Rite's Colormunki

- X-Rite's i1Display

- X-Rite's iDisplay 2

When you have obtained a color profile of your monitor, you need to install some color management software. The favorite among Scribus users is Little CMS, which you can download from www.littlecms.com. Argyll and DispcalGUI are also popular (www.argyllcms.com and http://dispcalgui.hoech.net/).

Once you have everything ready, you can go into the Document Setup window and scroll down to the Color Management section. Here you can enable color management and set up the correct profile for your monitor. You can also set the output profile for your own printer, or to the details that your print shop has provided. Remember to also check your color management settings when exporting PDFs.

■ **Warning**   Tampering with your monitor's color profile is a highly specialized task, and not one that is suitable for those who are learning about desktop publishing for the first time.

Summary

Color handling and color models are rather daunting concepts for the beginner, but it is important to understand the difference between the RGB and CMYK color models if you are planning on getting your documents printed professionally, as this could impact the colors that you use and the printing that you do.

However, Scribus can take much of that responsibility off your shoulders because it produces print-friendly colors in its exported PDF files.

In the next chapter, I will demonstrate how to compile and export you documents as PDF files.

■ ■ ■

CHAPTER 6

Exporting and Printing Your Documents

In Chapter 5, you looked at the color-handling capabilities of Scribus. You also looked at the issue of color management, and you discovered the differing methods by which Scribus manages color in its image input files and in its PDF output files.

In this chapter, you will be learning how to check your document layouts for errors, and how to go about exporting your documents for printing.

In this chapter, you will learn the following:

- How to preview your document layouts using the Preview Mode

- How to run a check for layout errors using the Preflight Verifier

- How to export your documents as images

- How to export your documents using Adobe's Portable Document Format

- How to manage your PDF exports

- How to create lightweight versions of your PDFs

- How to create a simple flyer using color sampling and color gradients

Copy Editing and Proofreading

In the previous chapters, you learned how to compile a document in Scribus. You also saw how to set your preferences, and how to control your text frames. However, as part of an effective workflow, and before you begin the layout of your documents in Scribus, it is a good idea to subject your source documents to a process known as copy editing.

Copy editing refers to the process of checking your documents for accuracy, style, punctuation, and grammar. It is a process that is best done before you attempt to lay out your document in any detail, as this will prevent any later issues that can affect your layout.

However, once you have finished laying out your materials in Scribus, the final, completed document will need to be proofread. The word "proofreading" comes from the era of hot-metal typesetting, in which a typeset version of the manuscript (or proof) was read and checked for typesetting errors. Today we use the term to refer to the process of checking an electronic version of a document for production errors.

It is quite possible that you will want to make significant changes to your document during the proofreading stage. When checking the layout of my magazine, my proofreaders often spot errors in grammar and syntax that have crept in, and having thought about the layout, I often end up moving some articles and changing the layout in order to achieve more of a visual balance, and a more effective flow of text.

Squeezed or missing text is a common problem. All that is required at this stage is to move some frames around and then go into the Story Editor to correct any text or formatting errors. As a rule of thumb, and based on personal experience, I feel that the time you spend on proofreading is never wasted.

Quality Control

Scribus is, at its core, a PDF editor, and in order to export your document as a PDF file, you need to establish that it is free from errors. This requires a high degree of quality control.

Checking Your Documents for Errors

If it helps, you can think of your Scribus program as a graphic design and layout system for designing PDF files. In order to produce a PDF to your exacting requirements, certain checks need to be carried out so that the finished document looks as good as possible and is free from errors.

So when you come to do a final check of your document, you need to pay particular attention to the number of pages, and check for any signs of missing text. It's also a good idea to check that your layout does not exceed the boundaries set by your margins, and to look for spelling mistakes.

Spell Checking

If you need to check the spelling of words in a text frame, you should use the built-in Spell Checker. All you have to do is select the text frame and then select Check Spelling in the Item menu.

When you run the Spell Checker, a dialog box will appear notifying you of the language that the Spell Checker is searching. It will then run through the entire text frame searching for errors; when an error is found, it will be highlighted in red.

To use the Spell Checker, illustrated in Figure 6-1, select the text frame that you wish to check, and then select Check Spelling from the Item menu.

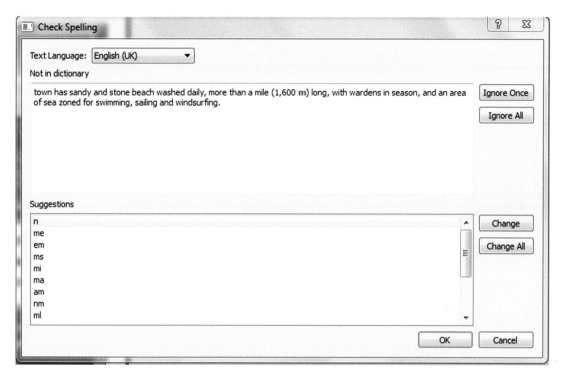

Figure 6-1. *Scribus offers a Spell Checker, which you can access from the Item menu*

SPELL-CHECKER EXERCISE

As a way of showing you how the Spell Checker works, I have made a purposefully clumsy attempt to reproduce a poem by "Mrs Leo Hunter" that appears in the novel *The Pickwick Papers*, by Charles Dickens. The poem is entitled "An Expiring Frog."

Can I view thee pantting, lying

On thy stomach, without sigghing;

Can I unmoved see thee dying

On a log,

Expiring frog!'

Say have fiends in shape of boys

With wild halloo, and brutal noise

Hunted thee from marshy joys,

With a dog,

Expiring frog!

(Charles Dickens, *The Pickwick Papers*)

It's a poem consisting of two stanzas with an A.A.A.B.B rhythm. Unfortunately, my transcription of the poem has been rather clumsy, and I need to check the spelling.

Start this exercise by typing my version of the poem into a text frame, as shown in Figure 6-2.

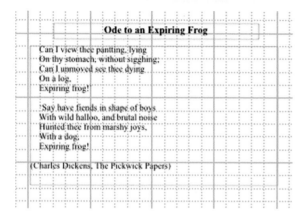

Figure 6-2. *"An Expiring Frog," as it appears in the text frame*

The spelling in some of the text does not look right, so select the text frame and then select Check Spelling from the Item menu. After a few seconds, the Check Spelling window should appear, as shown in Figure 6-3.

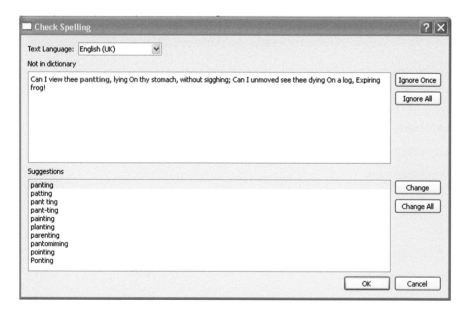

Figure 6-3. *The Check Spelling Window*

The Check Spelling window shows that my spelling of the word "panting" is not in the dictionary. It also suggests some alternative spellings.

The Check Spelling window contains two panes. The upper pane has the word "pantting" from the first line of the first stanza highlighted in red, indicating that it has found a spelling that is not in the dictionary. You are given the option to Ignore Once or Ignore All, or you can choose one of the alternative spellings in the lower pane and select Change. Select the correct and originally intended spelling of the word ("panting") from the lower pane of the Check Spelling window, and click the Change button.

Having clicked the button to change the spelling, the Spell Checker now moves to the word "sighing," which it highlights in red in the upper pane as being not in the dictionary. This is illustrated in Figure 6-4.

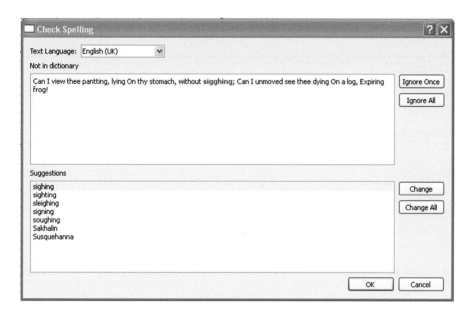

Figure 6-4. *The Spell Checker window querying the spelling of the word "sigghing"*

The lower pane of the Check Spelling window displays seven alternative spelling suggestions. Opt for the first suggestion, which is "sighing," spelled with one g, as this is the intended spelling. Highlight the word "sighing" in the lower pane and click the Change button again.

The Spell Checker goes on to highlight the word "halloo" and the word "Pickwick" in red, but as these spellings were the ones originally intended by Dickens, click Ignore All. When the Spell Checker ends, both panes are left empty, and the words "Spelling check complete" appear at the bottom of the window, as in Figure 6-5.

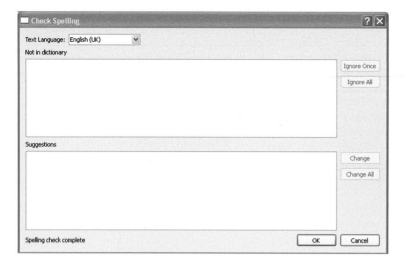

Figure 6-5. *The Spell Check window indicates the spell check is complete*

Search and Replace

The Search/Replace tool will help you search for texts, fonts, fill colors, and stroke colors in your documents, and then replace them.

To search for text, select the relevant text frame, and then select Search/Replace in the Edit menu. The Search/Replace tool will then appear, as shown in Figure 6-6.

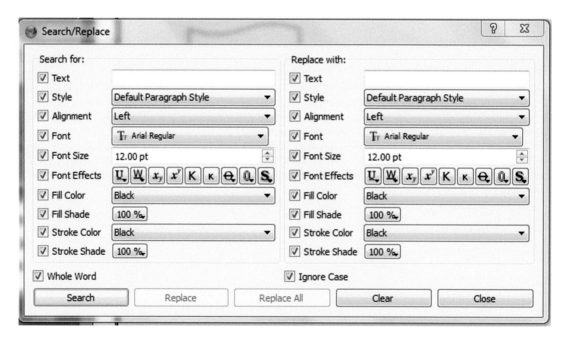

Figure 6-6. *The Search/Replace Tool Options*

This tool will prove useful if you have repeated a mistake in your text frames and you need to correct them quickly. To locate the errors, you simply enter the text that you wish to search for, and then click the Search button.

When an instance of this word has been found, you simply enter a replacement word, and then choose whether you wish to repeat the procedure for the rest of the text frame. The Search/Replace window gives you the option of enabling searches that can handle font size, shade, effects, and color as well as text.

SEARCH/REPLACE EXERCISE

The Search/Replace tool is located in the Edit menu. The Search/Replace dialog box in Scribus 1.4.5 is really quite impressive, as can be seen in Figure 6-7.

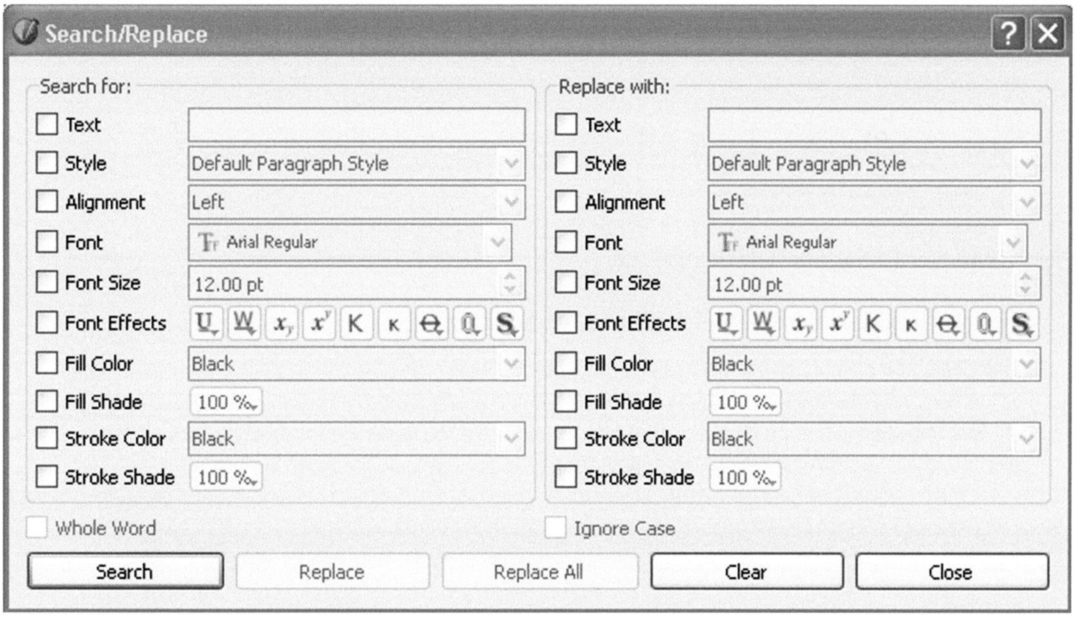

Figure 6-7. *The Search/Replace Tool*

This tool not only allows you to search and replace text, it also allows you to search and replace styles, alignments, fonts, font sizes, font effects, fill color, fill shade, stroke color, and stroke shade. I think you will agree that it has developed into quite a formidable editing tool.

To begin the exercise, insert a text frame that covers most of the page up to the margins, then right-click the frame, and insert some sample text into it (in English), as shown in Figure 6-8.

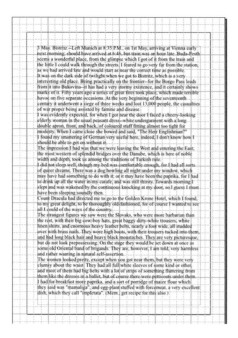

Figure 6-8. *A text frame filled with sample text*

Select the frame, and then select Search/Replace in the Edit menu.

In the Search for column, check the Text box and enter the word "dog." In the Replace with column, check the text box and enter the word "canary." Check the font box and enter Comic Sans MS Bold; check the Font Size and change it to 14 pt; check Font Effects and press the Underline text button. Check the Fill Color box and select the color Red. Your search terms should now look like those in Figure 6-9.

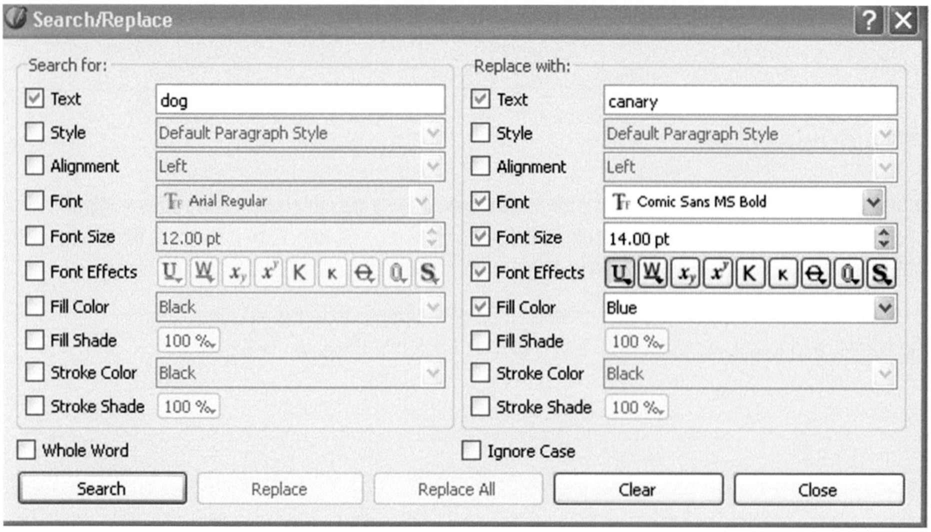

Figure 6-9. *The Search/Replace dialog box with search and replace options checked*

Then click the Search button. You should end up with a text frame like the one in Figure 6-10.

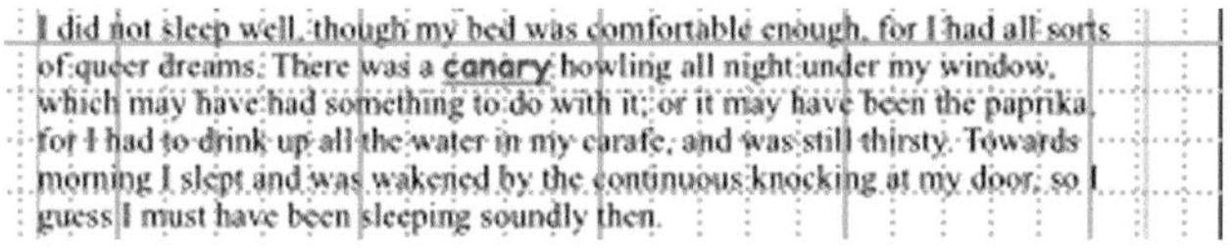

Figure 6-10. Sample text with replacement options added

The Preflight Verifier

At this point, it is important to introduce you to the tool known as the Preflight Verifier. The term "preflighting" was appropriated from the aeronautical industry by the printing industry, and originally refers to the preflight checks that were carried out by aircraft pilots prior to take-off. In the printing world, the term is used to describe the process of pre-press checks prior to printing.

In Scribus, the Preflight Verifier is set to run automatically when you select File ➤ Print or when you select the option to Export As PDF from the File menu (you can, however, prevent it from appearing at all by deselecting the checkbox for Automatic Check before Printing & Exporting in the Preflight Verifier section of Preferences).

When working in Scribus, you can use the Preflight Verifier any time in order to check your Scribus documents. Think of it as part of your proofreading process. It's useful to be able to call on the Preflight Verifier before your document is exported to PDF. The Verifier is designed to track errors and cut down on problems during the export process. It will list the errors that it finds in a document, including those that you may have missed during proofreading, though it will not detect errors in spelling or grammar. It then provides you with an opportunity to correct those errors. You can use the Preflight Verifier to check for overflowing text in text frames, or missing text, or the use of images with low image resolutions.

To launch the Preflight Verifier, click the button on the Scribus toolbar, or select Preflight Verifier from the Windows menu. The Verifier window will then appear, as shown in Figure 6-11, and it will list the errors on each page in the document in the order that they appear.

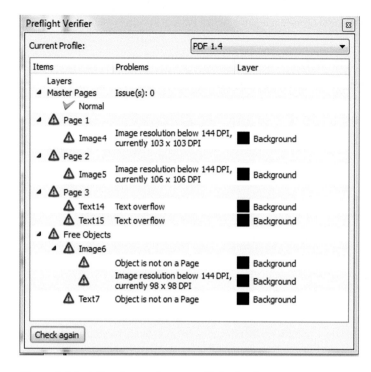

Figure 6-11. *A list of errors from a preflight check*

The errors that are listed will be related to the default profiles in the Verifier's Preferences tab. It is possible to set the parameters for the Preflight verifier in the Preflight Verifier tab of the Preferences window. Here, you can run checks for such things as missing images, missing glyphs, items not on page, text overflow, the use of transparencies, the use of GIF images, and the highest and lowest image allowable resolution settings.

One of the most common errors to appear (in my experience) is text overflow. A text overflow indicates that there is too much text contained within a text frame, and as a result, some of that text is not being displayed in the document.

Setting Up the Preflight Verifier

To make the Preflight Verifier run to your requirements, you will need to configure it in the Preferences tab (File ➤ Preferences ➤ Preflight Verifier).

The checking that the Preflight Verifier does will depend on the profile that you select in Preferences. For instance, you can use Preferences to designate the minimum level of image resolution for images that can be included in your documents.

The Preflight Verifier will check for overflowing text, objects that are off the page, and incompatible images, transparencies, and layers.

Corrections

In Figure 6-11, you can see a line of errors that have been listed in the Preflight Verifier. In order to clean them up, you need to double-click their entries in the Verifier window. Double-clicking each error that is listed will take you to the relevant page and the relevant object in Scribus.

So if you have a text overflow, double-click the object's name next to the red triangle, and this will take you to the offending text frame. You can then think about linking your text frame to a follow-up frame, or you might consider reducing the font size.

For objects that are listed as being Free Objects that are off the page, it is simplest to double-click the entry in the Verifier and then delete them if they are not needed.

PREFLIGHT EXERCISE

Select the text frame full of sample text that you created in the previous exercise, and then select the Preflight Verifier from the Windows menu. You will then be presented with the Preflight Verifier window, as shown in Figure 6-12.

Figure 6-12. *The Preflight Verifier Current Profile Box*

As you can see from Figure 6-12, there are green ticks against the Master Page Normal and against Page 1, indicating that there are no issues with these items. If you try clicking the entry for Normal, the Edit Master Page dialog box will open, and if you click the entry for Page 1, it will take you straight to Page 1.

Unfortunately, I have two Scribus objects that I moved onto the grey scratch space in order to make some space. These objects were the text frames from Mrs. Leo Hunter's poem "Ode to an Expiring Frog." The error messages relating to these text frames have been included under the column marked Problems. The problem reads as "Object is not on a page." If I move the objects onto a page and click the Check Again button, the Preflight Verifier issues the message "No Problems Found," as shown in Figure 6-13.

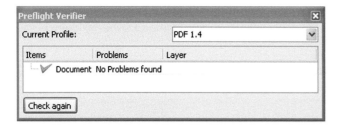

Figure 6-13. *After the initial errors were corrected and the document was checked again, no problems were found*

Print Preview

By default, the text frames and image frames that you use in your layouts will (when exported to PDF) display no visible boundaries. But with so many frames on the Scribus page, this can sometimes make for an appearance that is confusing. However, View ➤ Show Frames will show or remove the frames.

One solution (if you want to see what your current layout will look like when compiled) is to use the Print Preview tool, as shown in Figure 6-14.

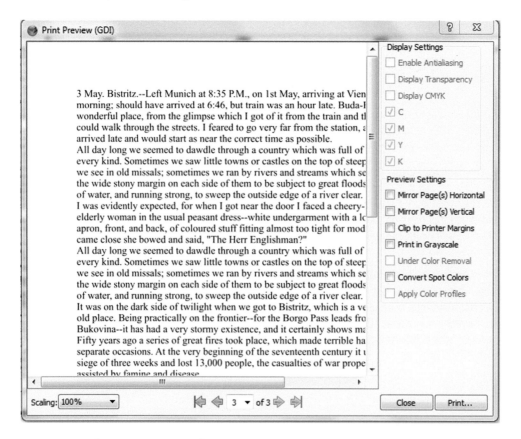

Figure 6-14. *The Print Preview Window*

The Print Preview tool is available in the File menu. It is easy to confuse the Print Previewer with the Preflight Verifier (particularly as the Verifier itself appears automatically when you select the Print Previewer) but whereas the Verifier exists to detect problems in the documents before they are exported as PDF files, the Print Preview tool enables you to see what your layout will look like before it is printed.

The Print Preview tool can help you to detect those objects and images that might provide trouble with your print setup, particularly objects such as gradients and transparencies. It can also help to give you an idea of the changes to expect when you move from viewing color images on-screen in the RGB mode to printing them in the print-based CMYK mode.

When the Print Preview window appears, it appears at a default level of magnification (usually 100%). You will probably want to resize it to display the full height of the page.

Use the Scaling controls at the bottom of the page to magnify the details of your document, and use the green arrows in the middle to navigate through your document pages.

On the right side of the Preview window are options for mirroring the page vertically and horizontally, as well as for printing in greyscale and converting to spot colors. Mirroring the page will flip the page horizontally or vertically, so that you have an inverted version of the original page. But you can always flip the page back to its original state if you don't like it.

Printing in greyscale will show you what your document will look like if everything in it is converted to various shades of black ink, which results in a grey tone visual appearance. This is useful if you have produced a document in color and want to see what it will look like if printed in black and white. The Print Preview also gives you the opportunity to see what your colors might look like in the CMYK color mode.

Note that the Print Preview mode is not totally reliable. It is generally recommended that you use the Preview Mode instead. Having said that, Print Preview does have some extra options that are not available in the Preview Mode.

PREVIEW MODE

If you have loaded a page and you would like to get a quick and accurate look at how the page will look when finished, you need to enable the Preview Mode. To do this, simply click the eye icon in the lower right-hand corner of the Scribus workspace.

If you have grown accustomed to using the Print Preview tool, I think you will find the change to Preview Mode to be quite extraordinary. In the Preview Mode, the color wheel that you created looks positively vibrant! The pages that you created in Chapters 5 and 6 have come out a treat, as you can see in Figure 6-15.

5 May. Bistritz.--Left Munich at 8:35 P.M., on 1st May, arriving at Vienna early next morning; should have arrived at 6:46, but train was an hour late. Buda-Pesth seems a wonderful place, from the glimpse which I got of it from the train and the little I could walk through the streets. I feared to go very far from the station, as we had arrived late and would start as near the correct time as possible. It was on the dark side of twilight when we got to Bistritz, which is a very interesting old place. Being practically on the frontier--for the Borgo Pass leads from it into Bukovina--it has had a very stormy existence, and it certainly shows marks of it. Fifty years ago a series of great fires took place, which made terrible havoc on five separate occasions. At the very beginning of the seventeenth century it underwent a siege of three weeks and lost 13,000 people, the casualties of war proper being assisted by famine and disease. I was evidently expected, for when I got near the door I faced a cheery-looking elderly woman in the usual peasant dress--white undergarment with a long double apron, front, and back, of coloured stuff fitting almost too tight for modesty. When I came close she bowed and said, "The Herr Englishman?" I found my smattering of German very useful here, indeed, I don't know how I should be able to get on without it. The impression I had was that we were leaving the West and entering the East; the most western of splendid bridges over the Danube, which is here of noble width and depth, took us among the traditions of Turkish rule. I did not sleep well, though my bed was comfortable enough, for I had all sorts of queer dreams. There was a canary howling all night under my window, which may have had something to do with it; or it may have been the paprika, for I had to drink up all the water in my carafe, and was still thirsty. Towards morning I slept and was wakened by the continuous knocking at my door, so I guess I must have been sleeping soundly then. Count Dracula had directed me to go to the Golden Krone Hotel, which I found, to my great delight, to be thoroughly old-fashioned, for of course I wanted to see all I could of the ways of the country. The strangest figures we saw were the Slovaks, who were more barbarian than the rest, with their big cow-boy hats, great baggy dirty-white trousers, white linen shirts, and enormous heavy leather belts, nearly a foot wide, all studded over with brass nails. They wore high boots, with their trousers tucked into them, and had long black hair and heavy black moustaches. They are very picturesque, but do not look prepossessing. On the stage they would be set down at once as some old Oriental band of brigands. They are, however, I am told, very harmless and rather wanting in natural self-assertion. The women looked pretty, except when you got near them, but they were very clumsy about the waist. They had all full white sleeves of some kind or other, and most of them had big belts with a lot of strips of something fluttering from them like the dresses in a ballet, but of course there were petticoats under them. I had for breakfast more paprika, and a sort of porridge of maize flour which they said was "mamaliga", and egg-plant stuffed with forcemeat, a very excellent dish, which they call "impletata". (Mem., get recipe for this also.)

Ode to an Expiring Frog

Can I view thee panting, lying
On thy stomach, without sighing;
Can I unmoved see thee dying
On a log,
Expiring frog!'

'Say have fiends in shape of boys
With wild halloo, and brutal noise
Hunted thee from marshy joys,
With a dog,
Expiring frog!'

(Charles Dickens, The Pickwick Papers)

Figure 6-15. *The color wheel and text as displayed using Preview Mode*

Exporting to EPS or SVG

Most Scribus users will want to export their documents as PDF files, because this format has been widely adopted by commercial printers as a sort of de facto standard for digital printing. However, as well as exporting you documents in PDF, Scribus lets you export them in vector formats such as Postscript (EPS) and Scalable Vector Graphics (SVG).

To export as an EPS or SVG file, select Export from the File menu. When the Save As dialog appears, choose a suitable file name and directory in which the file can be saved. The Scribus page can then be saved as a vector image, and the results are quite impressive.

SAVING YOUR OBJECTS AS VECTOR FILES

Insert a blank page in Scribus, insert an image file on the page, and then load it with one of your favorite raster images, one that you would like to save as a vector file. Try the makeshift color wheel TIFF file that you created in Scribus for use in Chapter 5, as shown in Figure 6-16.

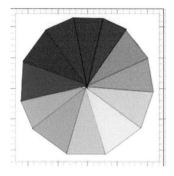

Figure 6-16. *Loading the color wheel TIFF from Chapter 5*

Now select File ➤ Export ➤ Save As SVG. When the export has finished, insert another blank page and select File ➤ Import ➤ Get Vector File. Then select the SVG file that you have just created. The color wheel is now a scalable vector graphic (see Figure 6-17).

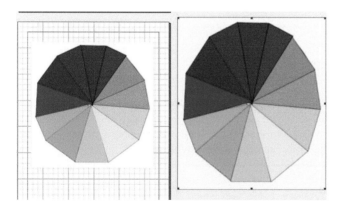

Figure 6-17. *Loading the color wheel as a scalable vector graphic*

When you insert it on a new page, you will not need to create an image frame for it; you can simply insert it as it is, and you can move it around and rescale it without the image being subject to distortion.

Save as Image

Scribus will also let you export your document to a bitmap format such as JPEG and PNG, again with quite impressive results. You can save your Scribus pages as images by using the path File ➤ Export ➤ Save As Image.

1. Choose a directory to save to (File ➤ Save As Image).

2. Choose a group of pages to export.

3. Choose the format of the image (e.g. BMP, JPEG, TIFF, PNG).

4. Choose the quality of the image.

5. Choose the resolution of the image.

When you do this, you end up exporting the entire page as an image, as shown in Figure 6-18.

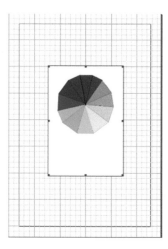

Figure 6-18. *The color wheel exported as an image*

For a computer monitor, a screen resolution of 72 dpi works best, but if you are using a printer, most printers will need an image resolution of 300 dpi to provide a good image reproduction.

Introduction to Adobe Portable Document Format

However, in all likelihood, you will want to export your Scribus documents to a print shop or desktop printer using Adobe's Portable Document Format (or PDF), as this is the most popular format for print shops.

The Portable Document Format was developed by Adobe so that its users could view and manage their documents on-screen irrespective of the type of computer or software that they were using. It is platform-independent, and is now widely available on almost every platform, so you can view your PDF files in Windows, Mac, Linux, and Android.

Although the Portable Document Format is proprietary, it has become the industry standard for document distribution. It lets you store all your text, fonts, and graphical content in one file, ready for printing. PDFs are generally recognized as final products that are not intended for further editing.

PDF Versions

When you export your documents to PDF, you will be given a choice of PDF versions. This can be really confusing for the first-time user.

When I was producing the first copy of my magazine, I thought it would be really clever if I exported my magazine using the latest version of a PDF that I could find, so I exported the magazine using PDF/X-3. The finished product was, to be frank, a bit of a disaster, though not a complete disaster. PDF/X-3 is a version of PDF 1.3 and is really only intended as a pre-press format for those who know what they are doing (and at that time I really didn't).

In fact, the oldest versions of PDF are probably the safest to use. Certainly, for most documents that do not require layering or transparencies, PDF 1.4 will do nicely. Most commercial printers will print from it without trouble, but if you want to include layers in your Scribus document, you are better off using PDF 1.5.

Exporting a PDF: The Quick Export Method

If, like me, you like to export your documents to PDF quickly, so that you can check the design and layout of your documents, here are the steps you need to follow:

Select File ➤ Export ➤ Save As PDF from the File menu.

Ignore all the errors in the Preflight Verifier (you can worry about them later).

In the General tab, name your file, select a folder in which to save it, and (as long as you're not using layers) select PDF 1.4.

In the Fonts tab, check that the fonts that you have used in the document are embedded with the document.

In the Color tab, you are given a choice of three color export formats: Screen/Web, Printer, and Greyscale. For PDFs that are intended for viewing on the Web or on other computers, select Screen/Web. For high-quality color PDFs that are good enough to send to a print shop, select Printer. Choosing the Printer option will produce a high-quality color PDF file that is suitable for commercial printing. (Note that exporting for Printer can produce a very large PDF file. The reader is advised to check with their print shop first.) For PDFs that are intended to be printed in black-and-white, choose the Greyscale option.

Click the Save button.

Exporting to PDF: The PDF Tabs

The Save As PDF dialog box contains seven tabs, and it looks quite complicated when you view them for the first time. But fear not. For beginners, it's only really necessary to know about three out of the seven tabs.

Exporting your documents to PDF is actually quite straightforward when you know how, but it is important to know your PDF tabs, so that you can make the right choices in order to create the document that you want.

The PDF Export window is divided into seven tabs: General, Fonts, Security, Viewer, Color, Extras, and Pre-press.

Three of the above tabs (Extras, Viewer, and Security) contain advanced settings aimed at the specialist user, or those wishing to create interactive PDFs. These tabs are useful if you want to create a PDF for the Web and need to control the way it will appear when viewed in a PDF reader. However, for the more general user, these tabs can be safely left on their default settings.

Exporting a PDF: The Longer Method

From the File menu, select Export ➤ Save As PDF. This will open the Preflight Verifier. Each page will be listed under the column marked Items, along with a brief description of the errors in the column marked Problems.

Examine the list, and look out for any entries that are marked by a red triangle rather than a green tick. If one of your entries has a red triangle with an exclamation mark on it, this indicates that there is a problem with this item, and you need to correct it. Double-click the item and it will display the problem page and object.

Try to resolve the errors, and then click the Check Again button in the Preflight Verifier window and confirm that all the red triangles have been removed. If not, double-click the listed items and remove them, and check again until you receive the message "Document No Problems Found."

Finally, click the OK button so that the Save As PDF window opens.

The PDF General Tab

The General tab (displayed in Figure 6-19) is the tab that first appears after you have dismissed the Preflight Verifier, and it is where you will choose most of your settings. Scribus will assign a default name to your document, but you can name the file yourself and select an output path to your destination folder.

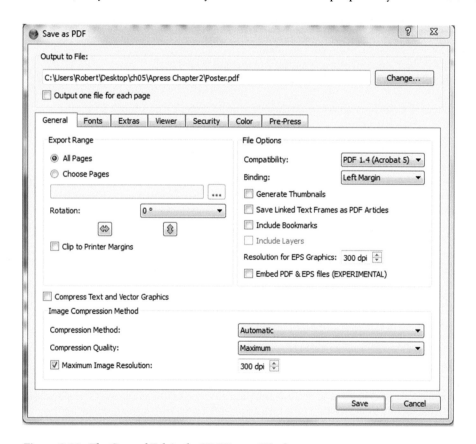

Figure 6-19. *The General Tab in the PDF Export Window*

The General tab is where you get to choose the version of PDF output that you wish to use, the image compression level that you require for your images, and a further option of compressing your text and vector files. It also gives you the option of producing one PDF file for each page of your document.

Choosing a PDF Version: File Compatibility

The first option you will see in the General tab is the Compatibility option (se Figure 6-19). This option enables you to select which version of the Adobe Portable Document Format you want to use to export your Scribus document. It is an important decision in your document design; there are several versions of the PDF specification, and each version has different capabilities. It is useful to have some basic knowledge of the Portable Document Format so that you can make an informed choice about the version that is most compatible with your proposed layout.

Scribus supports PDF versions 1.3, 1.4, 1.5, and X-3 (although in order to choose the X-3 version, you need to have Scribus Color Management enabled). In deciding which version of PDF is best for your needs, you should ask yourself whether you are planning to print the document on your home or office desktop printer, or whether you are planning to have it printed commercially. If you are planning to have it printed commercially, you need to ask your high street printer which version of the PDF they would prefer.

Secondly, if you plan to include transparencies in your document, you should use PDF 1.4 or 1.5.

Thirdly, you need to think about the recipients of your finished document. If the PDF is intended for email distribution, you probably want to use PDF version 1.4.

Finally, if you intend to include layers in your document, you need to use PDF version 1.5.

In theory, the lower the version of PDF that you choose, the more compatible it is likely to be with your local high street printers. The downside to using an earlier version is that you will lose some of the innovations that come with the later versions.

A good way of checking to see that your choice of PDF is compatible with your document is to run the Preflight Verifier. This will confirm if the export is compatible.

PDF 1.4

PDF 1.4 was introduced when Adobe launched Illustrator Version 9, and its main innovation was its ability to handle transparency and alpha transparency; something that had not been possible with PDF 1.3. This makes it a popular choice for direct printing, and it is a must if you use transparencies in your documents.

PDF 1.5

The next release, PDF 1.5, has much that will be of interest to Scribus users. As well as supporting transparencies, PDF 1.5 supports the use of layers as well. So if you are using layers in your Scribus documents, and you want to retain them in your PDF file, you should use PDF 1.5. PDF 1.5 comes with features that can be used in the creation of PDFs, such as annotations (annotations provide the ability to add notes and comments to your PDF documents).

PDF/X-3

PDF/X-3 is a subset of the PDF 1.3 version in which a lot of restrictions have been added. It is intended for use in pre-press work, and is really only for use by advanced users and professional printers.

In order to use PDF/X-3, you need to activate Scribus Color Management, which you can do by selecting it in the Document Setup. This will enable you to select PDF/X-3 in the General tab of the PDF export dialog. However, Color Management is a very advanced exercise and not really suitable for the beginner.

Unlike PDF 1.4 and PDF 1.5, PDF/X-3 does not handle CMYK color conversion, which makes it unsuitable for many Scribus users. Instead, PDF/X-3 tags its Scribus images with ICC color profiles (which you can get from your printer), and the process of conversion to CMYK is left to the color experts in the print shop.

Binding

There is an option for changing the Binding, located in the right column under PDF Compatibility.

Binding refers to the place where you insert the stitching or stapling when you create a publication. It is the place where Scribus adds some space along the spine in order to allow for the binding of your document. By default, the binding is on the left side, in accordance with languages that are written left to right, and it is better left alone.

Thumbnails

The Generate Thumbnails checkbox refers to the thumbnail images that can be made to appear in a PDF file in order to help the reader navigate the document. Check this box if you want to add thumbnails to your PDF file.

Bookmarks

A bookmark is a link that you can add to your PDF files in order to help the reader navigate through a large document. They are often used in place of a table of contents to help the reader access other parts of a book. Use the checkbox for bookmarks if you are planning on using them in your PDF file. To set a text frame as a bookmark, right-click the text frame and select PDF Options ➤ Is PDF Bookmark.

Include Layers

The Include Layers option is for use with PDF version 1.5 or later. If you use layers in your Scribus document, you need to check this box if you want to retain them in your PDF file. Use layers if you wish to edit an object without adversely affecting other objects, or if you need to separate printable from non-printable items.

Image and Text Compression

The Scribus General tab includes an option for reducing your PDF file size by compressing the text and vector graphics. This is a sensible option if you plan to distribute your documents by email, but it is to be avoided if you plan having them printed professionally, as the results will be disappointing.

Many commercial high street printers will insist that PDFs are submitted with an image resolution of at least 300 dpi. If you were to submit vector images smaller than that, it might cause problems.

The General tab also includes a control for setting the maximum resolution of the images exported in your PDF. If you plan to distribute the document by email, then you can select a maximum image resolution of 72 dpi. However, as already stated, most commercial printers require a minimum resolution of 300 dpi.

The PDF Viewer Tab

The Viewer tab (shown in Figure 6-20) enables you to control the look of your document when it is viewed through a compatible PDF reader. You can select default preset actions, or, if you know how to add JavaScript functions, Scribus allows you to define your own custom actions.

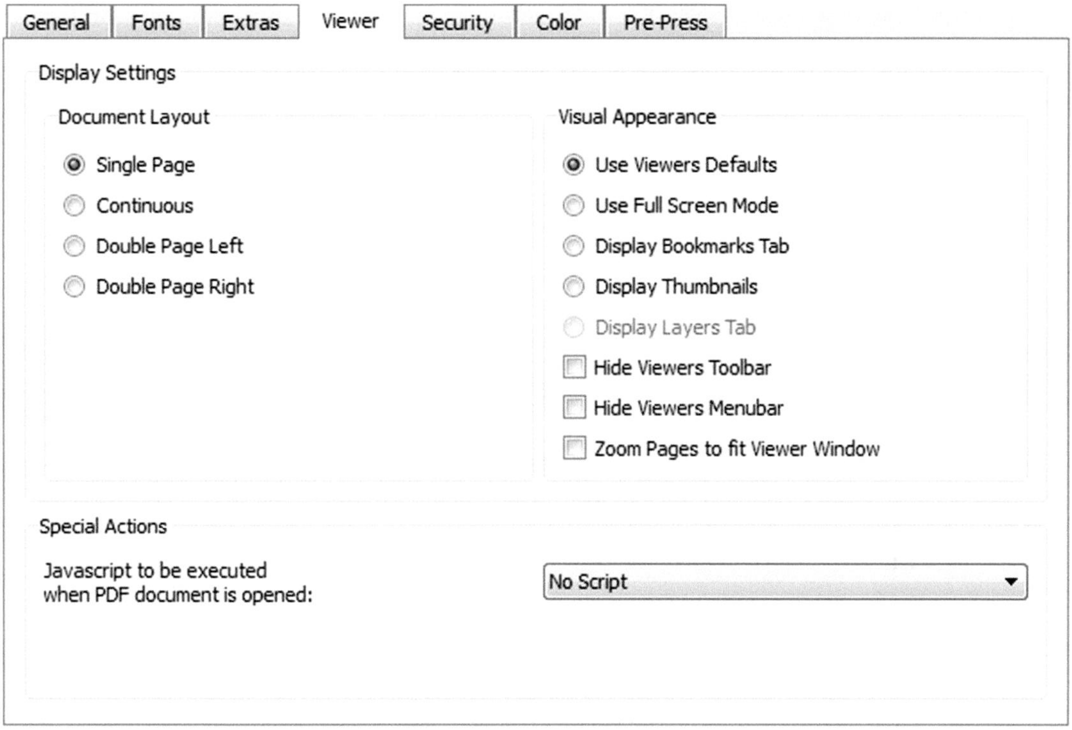

Figure 6-20. *The Viewer Tab*

On the left side of the tab is the Document Layout column. Use this group to control how your pages will look in a PDF reader. The default setting is for a single page, which is the easiest on the eye for the reader. Clicking Double Page Right will produce a double page format with a single first page. This is a really useful layout if you are producing a booklet or magazine and you want to balance the content on both pages so that the titles, headings, texts, and page numbers are all level.

The Visual Appearance column enables you to adopt a full-screen mode for your PDF file, which is very useful if you are producing a presentation. And if you have defined some bookmarks in your document, it also lets you display those bookmarks in order to help the reader navigate the document. Note that the document reader's PDF reader may be set up to override these options.

The PDF Security Tab

It is possible to add PDF passwords to your documents if you wish to prevent people from having unauthorized access to them. If you want to format your document in such a way that a password is required in order to open it, you can do that in the Security tab. In this tab, you can set a password for the Owner (yourself) and for the User (your reader).

The PDF Extras Tab

The Extras tab of the PDF Export window contains settings that will enable you to turn your Scribus PDF export into a slide presentation that is viewable in your PDF reader. While it's not quite up to the standard of Microsoft PowerPoint, it's a useful set of effects for those who wish to use their documents in a conference presentation or seminar.

To add transitions to your document, select Enable Presentation Effects and then select the effects for each page on the right side. Scribus lets you set a range of settings connected with page transition effects. You can set the display duration, effects type, and effects duration. Then you can choose the Apply Effects to All Pages option or to just apply them to a single page.

It is best not to be over-ambitious in your use of page effects and transitions, and you are advised to limit yourself to one effect or transition per document wherever possible; too many effects can be distracting for the viewer, and all of the options in that tab might prove pointless if all you are intending to do is print your documents.

The PDF Fonts Tab

The Fonts tab is the second tab that you need to check. Failure to do so will mean that some of your text could go missing in the finished PDF file.

The Fonts tab, shown in Figure 6-21, provides a list of all the fonts that you have used in your document, together with a section listing those that have been embedded in your PDF file. If you intend to export your PDF file to a commercial printer, it is very important that you embed your fonts within the PDF file using the arrows provided. It is the practice to embed as many fonts as possible in a document just in case the print shop does not possess a copy of the fonts being used. However, Scribus will be unable to embed every font, due to copyright and licensing restrictions. When this happens, Scribus will outline the font, and the text will be converted into an image. Outlining works just as well for most fonts, but the file may be larger if the outlined font is used extensively.

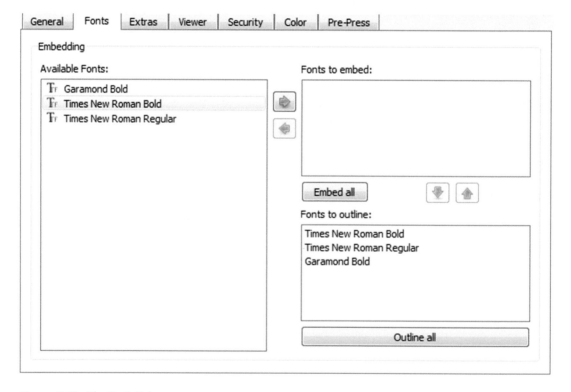

Figure 6-21. *The Fonts Tab*

This is a precautionary measure in case the recipient of your document does not have the font on their system. If you take the precaution of adding your fonts to your PDF, your recipients, be they fellow readers or a commercial print shop, will get to view your text in exactly the way that you intended it to be viewed.

The PDF Color Tab

The Color tab (shown in Figure 6-22) provides three choices regarding the use of color space in your PDF file. These choices are Screen/Web, Printer, and Greyscale.

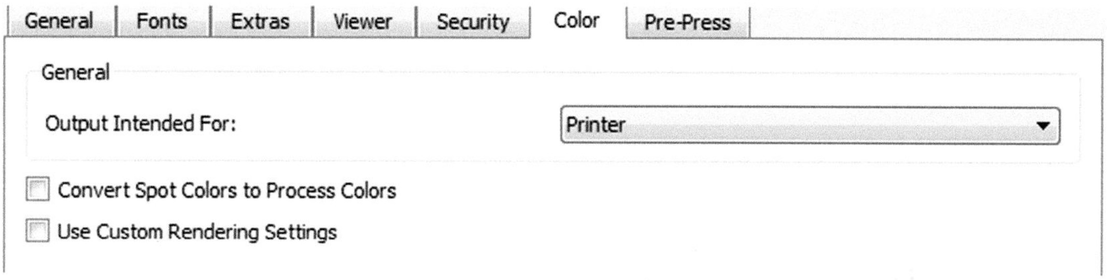

Figure 6-22. *The Color Tab*

If you intend the PDF to be viewed on screen, or are planning to distribute it by email or upload it onto a website, you should use the Screen/Web option. Selecting this option, Scribus will export your document to PDF using on-screen RGB colors.

Select the Printer setting if you intend getting your document printed professionally. If you wish to ensure that any spot colors you may have accidentally used are converted to CMYK, you can select the option to Convert Spot Colors to Process Colors. The document will then be color-separated, and the exported PDF file will use the CMYK mode. This option is sometimes used for documents that contain Pantone colors.

Select Greyscale if you want to display your PDF document in black and white. This setting can produce some impressive black and white PDF files, but you need to check its handling of photographs and text frame background colors, as it does not reproduce dark or dimly lit photographs particularly well.

Custom Rendering

There are some advanced settings that you can use as well, but unless you know what you are doing, these are best left to the professional printer.

Select the Use Custom Rendering Settings option and use the Spot Function if you wish to change the shape of the printed dots. You have a choice of Simple Dot, Line, Round, and Ellipse.

The PDF Pre-Press Tab

The Pre-Press tab enables the user to control advanced pre-press settings, such as bleeds, as shown in Figure 6-23.

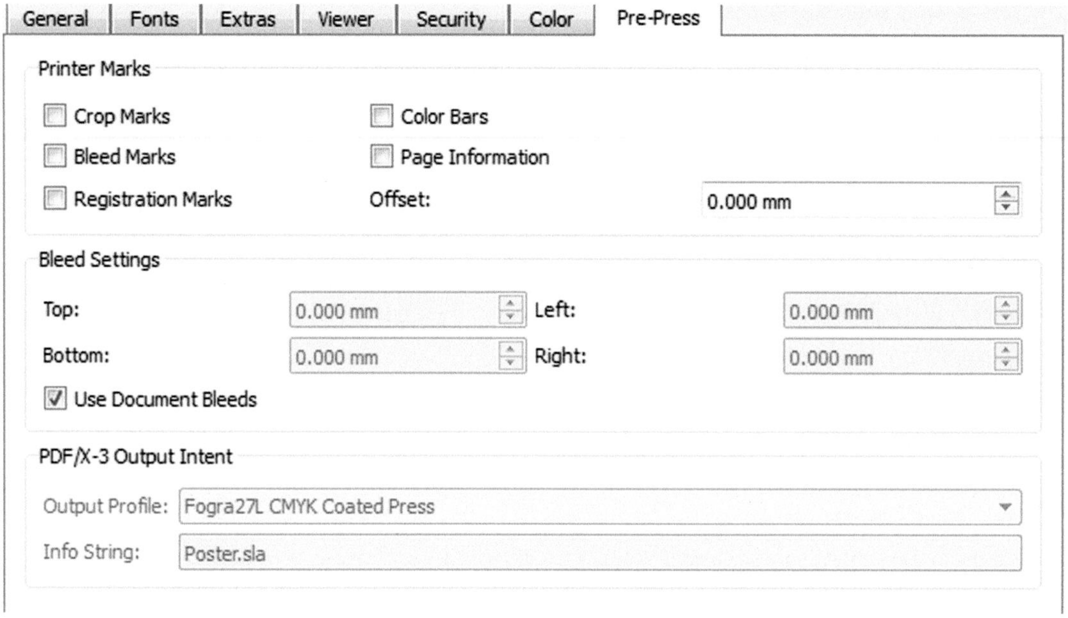

Figure 6-23. *The Pre-Press Tab*

Bleed Marks

The Pre-Press tab contains a box for bleed marks, as shown in Figure 6-23. A bleed is an extra area of paper outside the page size that is used as a grip by the printing machine. Printing machines require some space on either side of the page in order to grip the page so that it can be fed through the printer. So, to get a full page print, paper of larger size than the final print is used, and an extra margin is added. After printing, the finished page can then be cut to the required size.

However, if you really need to print to the edge of the paper, you need to get your document professionally printed, and you might need to set what are known as bleed marks. The print shop should be able to advise you on this.

Bleed marks are marks that show where these bleeds can be cut. If you are using an inkjet or laser printer to print your documents, you are unlikely to be able to print to the edge of the paper, as these printers produce a narrow margin at the edges where the grip holds the paper.

You can set up a default bleed in the Preferences dialog, or you can set up your bleed values when creating a Scribus document in the New Document dialog, and you can change your bleed settings in the Document Setup dialog.

Remember to check the Use Document Bleeds checkbox in the Save as PDF window if you need to use bleeds.

Note that if you are going to use bleeds, you might need to extend some objects (with background color, etc.) over the edge of the page in order to make sure that (when the page is cut) there is no gap between the object and the edge of the cut paper.

Printer Marks

If you are planning on having your finished document cut, folded, or bound, remember to check the box for placing printer marks on the document. It is very important to check with your print shop first.

Save and Export

Once you have completed all the settings you need to make in the PDF Export dialog, click the Save button to generate your PDF file.

Viewing Your Document in a PDF Reader

Once you click the Save button in the PDF Export dialog, a PDF file will appear in your designated document folder. If you are still in the process of compiling your document in Scribus, you can view this PDF as a form of soft proof, as it will give you an idea of how the finished document will look on your computer monitor.

Open up the PDF file in an Adobe Reader so that you can check that it looks just how you want it, while bearing in mind the difference in color spaces between the monitor (RGB) and the printed product (CMYK). Although other PDF readers are available for viewing PDF files, Adobe Reader is the one that Scribus functionality is tested against.

A soft proof of your document in PDF will enable you to see layouts that need changing, images that need moving, and text frames and borders that need modifying. Once you make your changes, you can export again and recheck the document.

EXERCISE: EXPORTING TO PDF

Start a new document in Scribus made up of one page in A4 portrait format. Insert a text frame across the length and width of the page, right-click it, and select Sample Text. When the Lorem Ipsum window opens, select the English language version, and choose at least 10 random paragraphs of text.

When you have completed the insertion of your sample text, it should look like the text in Figure 6-24.

Figure 6-24. *An A4 page full of sample text*

Select the text frame, select Page ➤ Copy, and add a further seven copies of this page to the document. You should now have eight pages of A4 filled with sample text.

Now, using the navigation arrows at the bottom of the page, return to Page 1, and move your text frame halfway down the page. Then add a text frame to act as a working title for the document, and then add an image frame in the remaining area of white space.

You should end up with a page that looks structurally similar to the one in Figure 6-25.

Figure 6-25. *Page 1 with a title frame and image frame added to the sample text*

Now let's export the document as a PDF file. Select File ➤ Export ➤ Save As PDF. The Preflight Verifier window will open, showing the current profile, listing the items in the document, and listing the problems it has found with the document, as shown in Figure 6-26.

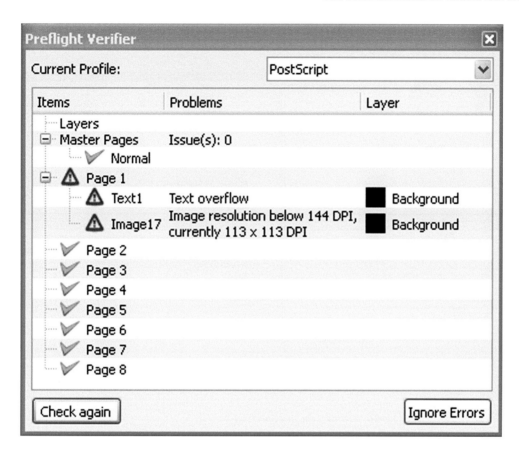

Figure 6-26. *The Preflight verifier diagnostic listing*

As you can see, Pages 2-8 look fine, but the current profile is set in Postscript, and the image resolution on my portrait is below 144 dpi. There is also a text overflow on Page 1. I am not worried about the image resolution, as I will be exporting the document as a web-friendly PDF at 72 dpi, but I do want to fix the text overflow, as some of the sample text is obviously hidden from view, and does not appear on Page 1.

So, if I position the mouse over the error message for "Text 1 Text overflow" and click it, Scribus will move back to Page 1 and highlight the offending text frame (see Figure 6-27).

If you wish, you can open the Story Editor to remove the text overflow (or you could link up your text frames using the Link Text Frames tool on the Toolbar [icon]).

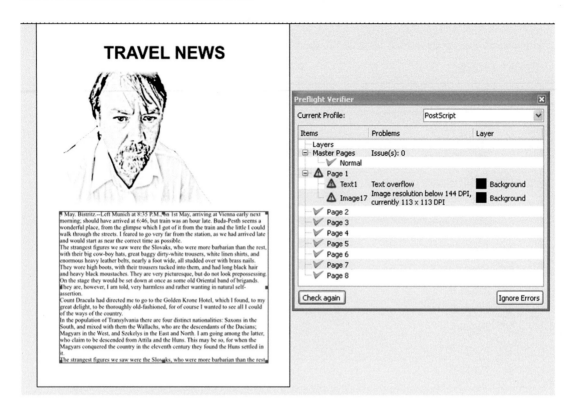

Figure 6-27. *Using the Preflight Verifier to locate the text overflow*

The end result should look like Figure 6-28, in which the text overflow has been removed.

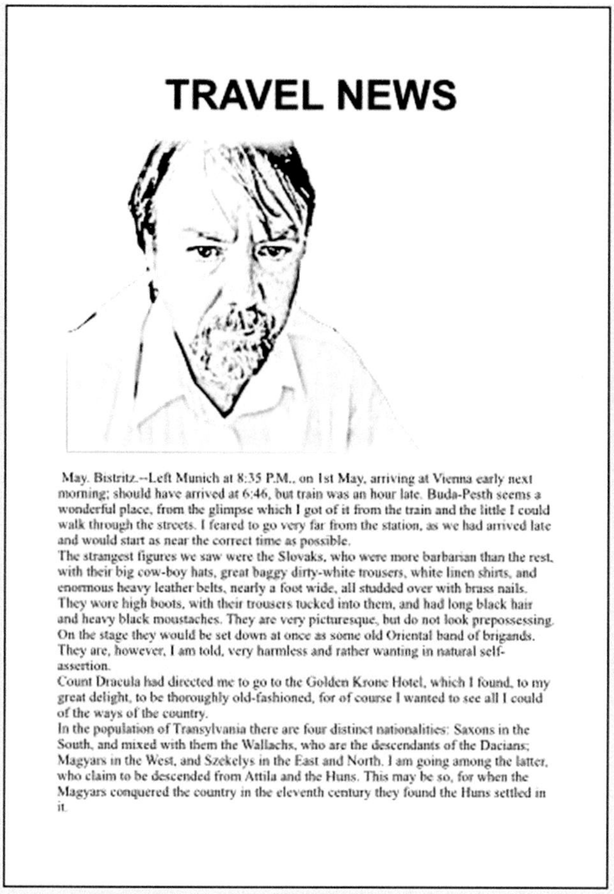

Figure 6-28. *The text frame for Page 1 with text overflow removed*

Exporting As PDF

Now you need to export the document as a PDF file. In the Preflight Verifier, select PDF 1.4 as your current profile. Then you can either click Ignore Errors, or you can run the Verifier again by selecting File ➤ Export ➤ Save as PDF.

If you opt to ignore the errors, the Save as PDF dialog will open, as shown in Figure 6-29.

Figure 6-29. *The General tab of the Save as PDF dialog box*

Name your document and establish your directory path using the Output to File field and the Change button at the top of the dialog box.

In the section marked Export Range, select All Pages.

In the section marked File Options, set the resolution to 72 dpi, and in the section headed Image Compression Method, check the box marked Maximum Image Resolution and ensure that it reads 72 dpi. Your settings should look like those in Figure 6-30.

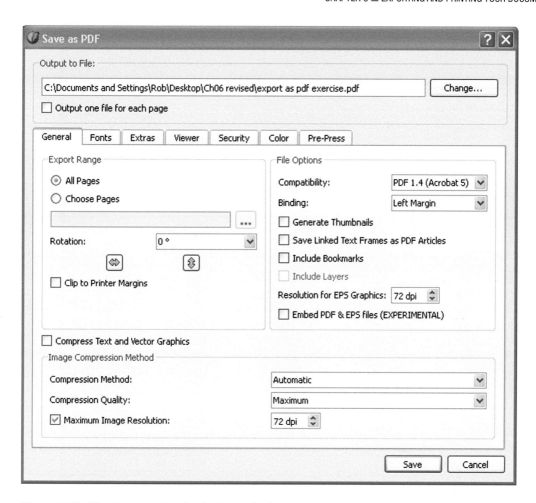

Figure 6-30. *The Export settings for the General tab*

Now select the Fonts tab next to the General tab. The Fonts tab is illustrated in Figure 6-31.

Figure 6-31. *The Fonts Tab*

There are only two fonts to embed in this document, and they look like they have been outlined.

Moving on to the Color tab, shown in Figure 6-32, select Screen/Web as the Intended Output, as you will only be viewing the finished document on a computer screen.

General	Fonts	Extras	Viewer	Security	Color	Pre-Press

General

Output Intended For: Screen / Web

Figure 6-32. *In the Color tab, set the color to Screen/Web and click the Save button*

Finally, click the Save button.

When you go to the relevant folder that was listed in the Output to File field, you should find your newly created PDF file, as shown in Figure 6-33.

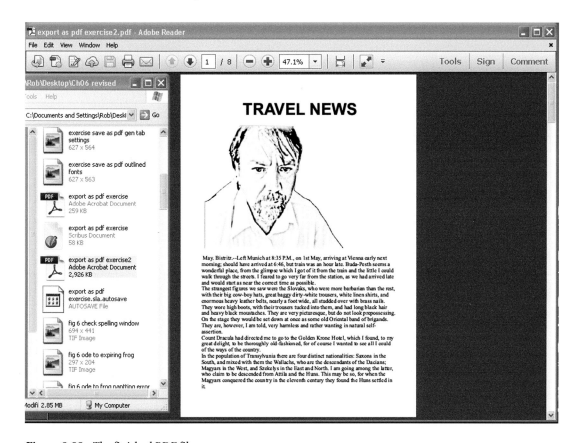

Figure 6-33. *The finished PDF file*

Printing from within Scribus

It is possible to print a document from within Scribus, to give you an idea of how your layout is progressing. In professional printing, this sort of thing is known as a proof print or a hard proof. However, the Print function in Scribus is not recommended. It is buggy and does not always produce nice results. It is generally recommended instead that you export a PDF first and then print from there.

To obtain a print of your Scribus layout, select Print from the File menu. This action will produce the Preflight Verifier window. Click the Ignore Errors option and the Setup Printer window will appear, as shown in Figure 6-34.

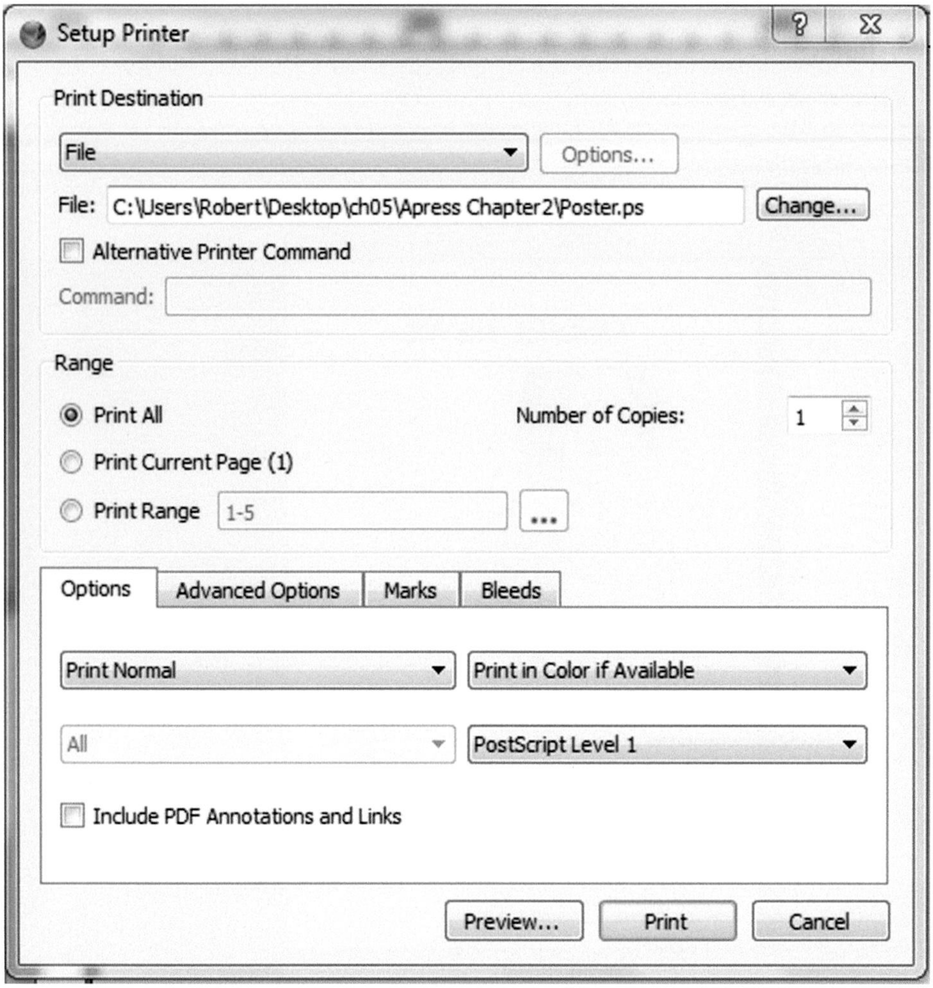

Figure 6-34. *The Setup Printer Window*

After you have dismissed the Preflight Verifier window, Scribus will open the Setup Printer window.

The Setup Printer window gives you the option of sending your file to a printer that is installed on your computer, or printing it to a (Postscript) file.

If you want to print a selection of pages, you can specify a range of consecutive pages (e.g. 1–10) or you can specify a comma-separated range of selected pages (e.g. 1, 5, 8, 10).

The Options tab provides options for setting your page orientation as either portrait or landscape. The Advanced Options tab provides options for mirroring your pages horizontally or vertically, and for converting spot colors to process colors.

The Marks tab is there if you want to add crop marks, bleed marks, or registration marks. These are options for the advanced user: crop marks are added if you want to show where your pages should be trimmed before binding, and bleed marks show where the printed page needs to be cut in order to dispose of the extra margin that has been added.

When you come to print the document, the end result will be dependent on the quality of your printer, and, though not perfect, it should give you some idea of how your layout is shaping up.

Printing Booklets: Imposition

When you compile a booklet in Scribus, you work from the first page to the last in a linear fashion. But if you try to print it out from the PDF in a booklet format, you will discover that the sequence for printing in booklet form is a little more complicated than that.

Magazines and booklets have a codex format in which each page is printed double-sided, with two pages facing each other, with the first page facing the last page. So to print this booklet on a desktop printer, the pages would have to be rearranged in a process known as imposition.

Thankfully, many desktop printers today can handle duplex printing and they include software that enables you to organize your linear PDF files especially for printing as booklets. And if you are taking the PDF to a commercial printer, they will already be able to produce the imposition for a booklet from the linear format of your PDF.

It is also possible to print from PDF using the order of pages you require, such as 12, 1, 2, 11, 10, 3, 4, 9, 8, 5, 6, 7

There are various imposition software tools that are available to assist with booklet printing, particularly Bookbinder, PDFedit, and PDFbook. However, Adobe Readers 8 and 9 are able to handle booklet printing, and I use them to print an A5 magazine.

Creating Lightweight PDFs

At some point, you will produce a beautiful-looking PDF file of which you are immensely proud, and you will want to share it with others via email or a website. It is at this point that you may discover to your horror that the file size is too large to send as an email attachment, and you will look for ways of deleting as much excess weight from the file as possible. There are a number of strategies that you can employ in order to reduce your PDF file size.

Firstly, I recommend deleting any unwanted objects that you have stored off the page or in the grey scratch space. Then check to see if you have any pages containing unwanted content in your Scribus document, and delete them as well. Blank pages can be left in, as they will not add to the file size.

The next thing is to reduce the image resolution for the images in your document. Use the image compression tool on the General tab of the PDF Export window. You might also consider the use of lightweight, lossy JPEG files with a setting of 72 dpi.

Next, make sure that you are using the Screen/Web setting in the Colors tab. One good way to reduce the size of a file is to go through each image and check the scale and DPI. You can obtain a reading of the scale and DPI of an image by opening the Image tab of the Properties Palette. If the scale is small and the DPI is large, then you will need to edit the images in GIMP. Cropping an image before importing it into Scribus can also save on space.

Finally, reduce the number of fonts in Scribus. For the purpose of readability, it is advisable to restrict yourself to using two or three fonts at most. Fonts can be heavy and their over-use tends to confuse the reader.

DESIGNING A SIMPLE FLYER

Let's create a very basic flyer on your computer using a simple holiday snap. I have designed this exercise as a way of practicing some of the color selection and text manipulation techniques that you looked at in previous chapters. And it includes the use of the eyedropper tool, which will enable you to add the RGB colors on your computer screen to your Scribus palette so that you can use them again later in your documents.

First of all, I'd like to give you an idea of what the finished product will look like. So, in the best traditions of British daytime television, Figure 6-35 shows one I made earlier.

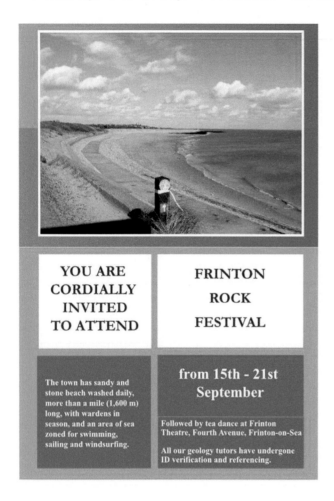

Figure 6-35. *A simple poster designed in Scribus using color sampling and gradient tools*

It's really just a bit of nonsense, but this flyer shows you what can be done in Scribus in less than 20 minutes. I've used a holiday snap that I took on the East coast of England, mainly because it looks quite picturesque, but also because it contains some RGB colors that I'd like to capture and use in the flyer.

So open your installation of Scribus, and create a single A4 portrait-oriented document. Then right-click the page and select Manage Page Properties from the context menu. The margins are a bit big for what I have in mind, so click the chain at the side of the Margin Guide selectors, and then reduce the margins to 10mm all round, as shown in Figure 6-36.

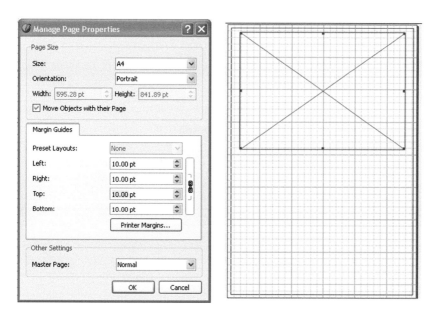

Figure 6-36. *Reducing the margins in Page Properties*

Color Sampling

Next, you need to import an image frame into the top half of the page, as illustrated in Figure 6-37.

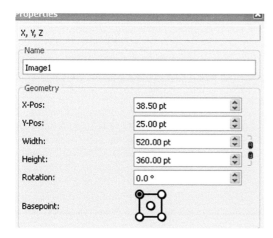

Figure 6-37. *Setting the frame size in the XYZ tab of the Properties Palette*

Using the XYZ tab in the Properties Palette, set the size of the frame to a width of 520 pts and a height of 360 pts, as shown in Figure 6-37.

You have now reached the stage where you need to insert a photo in the document. I have chosen a simple seaside scene, which is a TIFF image. It is copyright free and available to download from the book's page on the Apress website.

Right-click the image frame and select Get Image from the context menu. Insert the image into the top half of the page. You can also use a different photo or graphical image.

I had to adjust the image to the frame using the context menu, and as a result the width of the image is now 481.5 pts. If you feel the need, select the image, and move it around until it is located centrally within the top half of the page, as shown in Figure 6-38.

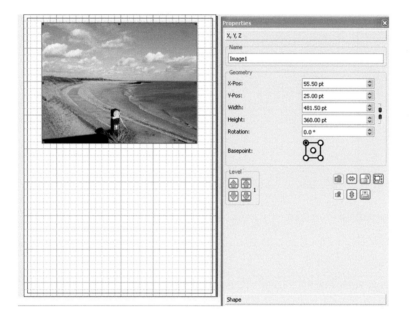

Figure 6-38. *The image is now inserted into the frame, and moved to a central position in the upper half of the paper*

Using the Toolbar, select and insert a rectangular shape ▢ ▾ so that it covers the top half of the page, and completely covers the photo up to the edge of the page, as in Figure 6-39.

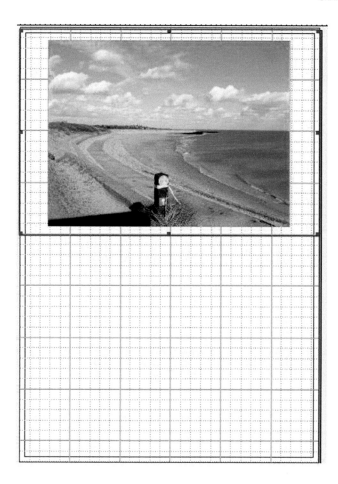

Figure 6-39. *The rectangular shape after it has been placed over the photo*

Now click the Eyedropper icon on the toolbar, select an area of color in the photo that you would like to reproduce, and (when the Save As dialog box appears) name your new color, as illustrated in Figure 6-40.

Color Not Found	?	X

The selected color does not exist in the document's color set. Please enter a name for this new color.

Frinton Sea

OK   Cancel

Figure 6-40. *Adding an on-screen RGB color from your photo to your palette*

To make this simple flyer, I captured the colors used for the sand, sea, and sky, and added them to my Scribus color palette. I then selected the background shape (which is now colored the same color as the sky in the photo), and I rolled it halfway up the photo, so that it is roughly level with the skyline, as in Figure 6-41.

Figure 6-41. *Moving the blue background up until it is level with the skyline*

Inserting a Linear Gradient

Now insert another rectangular shape that runs from the skyline to the halfway line just under the photo. Right-click your shape and select Properties. In the Color tab of the Properties Palette, select the Fill icon, then select the Horizontal Linear Gradient from the drop-down menu below the icon, click the left gradient stop, and select the first color in your color blend, as shown in Figure 6-42.

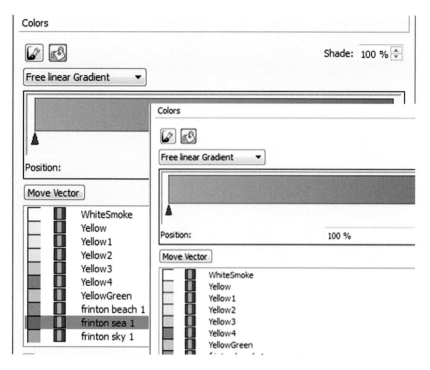

Figure 6-42. *Setting up your gradient using colors taken from the photo*

I chose the color of the Frinton sky for my first gradient color.

For the second color, clicking the right gradient stop, I chose the color of the Frinton sea in my photograph. You should now have a shape that changes slowly from your first color to your second color, and that matches the colors that appear in your photo, as shown in Figure 6-43.

Figure 6-43. *The two gradient colors that match the sea and sand*

If you have lost sight of your photo during the process of creating your color gradient, right-click the text frame, select Level, and then select Lower to Bottom. Your photo should now reappear.

You should, at this stage, have a photograph positioned over two shapes, and the lower shape should contain a linear gradient made up of colors that match the photo.

One final modification you should make to the top half of the flyer is to add a white margin to the photo so that it looks more like a three-dimensional holiday snap.

So select the image frame and increase the line width to 5 pts, as shown in Figure 6-44.

Figure 6-44. *Inserting white borders to achieve a postcard effect*

Right-click the border line of the rectangle with your mouse, and, with the Properties Palette open, select the Line tab, and increase the width of the line to about 5 points.

Now go to the Color tab, select the Stroke Color, and then select white as your stroke color.

Voila! You should now have a white border around the edges of your photo, making it look more like a holiday snap.

Text Frames and Margins

Finally, you need to position your shapes. I have added a rectangular shape to act as a colored background for the lower half of the flyer, and I have used the color of the Frinton sky as my background color, as shown in Figure 6-45.

Figure 6-45. *The completed background shapes with colors taken from the photo*

A background shape has also been added to the lower half of the flyer, which is also shown in Figure 6-45.

I then superimposed four rectangular shapes across the background frame, giving the top two a white background, and the lower two a Frinton Sea Blue background, as shown in Figure 6-46.

Figure 6-46. *The flyer with four text frames added to the lower half*

The text in the top two frames was set using Garamond bold at 25 points. The text was centered and I moved it away from the edges of the frame by adding margins in the Properties Palette.

How to Insert Margins in Your Text Frames

Inserting margins in your text frames is an important technique in Scribus that is often overlooked. To add margins to your text frame, use the Text tab in the Properties Palette.

Then select the Column and Text Distances expander, as shown in Figure 6-47.

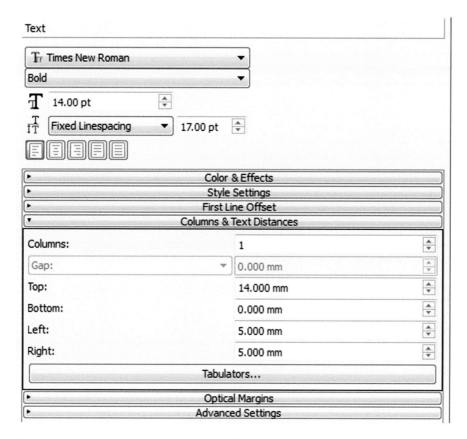

Figure 6-47. *Setting your frame margins in the Properties Palette*

You can now add your margins by increasing the measurements in the boxes for the top and left margins.

And there it is, your first flyer, created using Scribus in under 20 minutes!

Exporting Your Flyer as a PDF

When you are satisfied that you have got the flyer looking how you want it, preview it in the Print Preview window (File ➤ Print Preview).

If it looks okay, export it as a PDF file (File ➤ Save as PDF).

Ignore the errors in the Preflight Verifier for now, and go to the Save As PDF dialog.

In the General Tab, select the page you wish to export, select the image resolution, and name the file.

In the Fonts tab, check that you embedded all the fonts you have used.

In the Color tab, select Printer if you intend printing it, or Screen/Web if you intend to distribute it over the Internet.

Go back to the Color tab and click Save. Or consider exporting the flyer as a PNG or vector image in the File menu.

A Word on Layers

A layer in Scribus is a collection of objects on a page that can be moved as a group above or below other layers on the same page. The comparison that is often made is with sheets of transparent plastic, with graphical objects placed above or below each other on different sheets: some of them are hidden, some of them are opaque, and some of them are locked so that they cannot be moved.

Layers in Scribus are not to be confused with levels: a level refers to a single layer containing objects that can be stacked in a variety of stacking orders.

Layers can be used to compile multilingual documents, where different layers can be used to represent different languages. Layers also provide a useful design aid. If you are designing a four-fold brochure, layers can be used as a way of labeling each page during the design process. These labels can then be hidden prior to the process of printing or exporting to PDF.

You can also lock layers so that their objects cannot be moved or deleted accidentally, and you can use layers to produce semi-transparent images on the page background, or use them to overlap your text with graphics.

Many Scribus users find layers to be an indispensable part of their document design work. However, there will probably be many situations in which you do not need to use them. It's generally a matter of personal taste, but bear in mind that a Scribus document containing layers needs to be exported to PDF Version 1.5 or above if you wish to preserve the layer objects in the PDF file.

Exploring the Layers Window

To see the Layers window (shown in Figure 6-48), select Layers in the Windows menu (or press F6 if you are working in Windows).

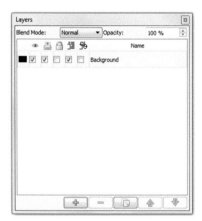

Figure 6-48. *The Layers Window*

To start with, each new document that is created in Scribus has just one layer, known as the Background Layer, and you need to click the + sign to add another layer. If you add a new layer, it will appear on top of the background layer, as shown in Figure 6-49, and it will appear highlighted as the active layer.

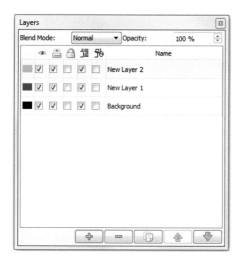

Figure 6-49. *Creating a new layer on top of the Background layer*

If you want to name the new layer, double-click NewLayer1.

You can use the Layers window to alter or toggle the visibility of a layer, using the toggle boxes to toggle it on and off.

The layer can also be locked in order to protect its contents from further editing.

If you have some layers on your page, you can lower and raise the active layer to another level by clicking the up and down arrows. You can also delete a layer.

Layer Properties in Scribus

Each layer that you add to the page will have properties that can be changed. Your layers can be locked, hidden, or moved within their standing order.

If a layer is locked, you will no longer be able to make changes to it, and if it is hidden, you will not be able to see its contents until it is made visible again. You can also change the order in which your layers are stacked. It is important to bear in mind, when stacking your layers, that the content that is placed on the layer that is at the top of a stack will hide the content that is placed on the lower layers.

Working with Layers

When working on your layers, it is important to ensure that you have the correct highlighted layer selected. Any new layer that you add will appear at the top of the stack and, once you have created it, it will become the active layer.

Moving Objects Between Layers

To move an object between layers, right-click it, and select Send to Layer from the context menu. Then select the layer to which you wish to move the object.

Changing Layer Opacity in the Layers Window

You can choose how much your active layer obscures the layers beneath it by lowering the opacity. You can change the opacity by using the drop-down box on the top right side of the Layer window. Remember that any layers you create will only be visible in a PDF if they are exported in PDF version 1.5 or higher.

Summary

This chapter showed you how to handle your preflight checks, how to export your documents as PDF files, and how to format a lightweight version of your PDFs for use with the Web or email. You also learned how to use your customized color palettes to create a simple flyer.

Scribus is quite good at handling graphical images, but it is still a page layout system rather than an image processor. If you really want to edit your images so that they look professional enough to use in a publication, you need to start using an image editor called GIMP.

In the next chapter, you will explore the GIMP workspace, and you will learn some editing tricks to apply to your images before you import them into Scribus.

CHAPTER 7

■■■

Working with GIMP

In the previous chapters, we showed you how to check your documents for errors before exporting them as PDF files. We also showed you how to customize your color palette, and how to use customized colors in the design of a simple flyer.

However, Scribus is a page layout system, rather than an image processor. If you need to lighten your photographs before importing them into Scribus, or you want to cut out a foreground object and delete the background, you need to use an image processor such as GIMP.

In this chapter, you shall be doing just that. You will learn about some of the effects that you can apply to your images, and you will learn how to use alpha channels to make your image backgrounds transparent.

In particular, you will learn the following:

- How to install GIMP 2.8

- How to find your way around the workspace

- How to crop an image

- How to apply transparencies to areas you wish to remove

- How to desaturate your images to black and white

- How to apply a soft-fade effect

GIMP stands for the GNU Image Manipulation system. It is a free, open source graphics editor that is used for creating, editing, cropping, and resizing digital images, as well as for creating photo montages and converting different image formats.

GIMP is considered by many to be a rival to Adobe Photoshop, and is considered to be suitable for professional artwork. If you need any proof, please download the latest version of *GIMP Magazine* (http://GIMPmagazine.org/), which contains some stunning artwork, all of it produced in GIMP and laid out using Scribus.

You are going to use this program to brighten your images and to cut out foreground objects so that you can import them into Scribus. The latest version of GIMP will work with Microsoft Windows, Mac OSX, and Linux.

First of all, though, you need to install the program.

Installing GIMP for Windows

Before you install GIMP, you need to check the recommended specifications. On a Windows PC, GIMP requires a minimum computer memory capacity of 128MB (256MB is better) and disk space of at least 100MB.

Then you need to go to http://www.GIMP.org/downloads/ and download the latest version of GIMP for your operating system.

When the file has finished downloading, double-click it to begin the installation process, and select your preferred language.

Installing GIMP on Linux Ubuntu

To download the latest stable version of GIMP on Ubuntu,

- Click the Ubuntu Icon, located in the upper left hand corner.
- Click More Apps.
- Search for GIMP.
- Click GIMP Image Editor.
- This will bring you into the software center on the install page for GIMP.
- Click Install.
- Enter your password.
- Wait for the application to finish installing.
- Click the Ubuntu icon again and search for GIMP.
- You should now see the application and be able to launch it.

To Install GIMP from the Terminal

Open the Terminal and type the following command:

sudo apt-get install GIMP

Enter your password. Wait for it to finish installing, and then launch the application to test it out.

Installing GIMP on Mac OSX

Since the 2.8.2 version GIMP runs on OSX natively, it now comes with a standard DMG installer. Open your web browser and visit the Downloads page at `www.GIMP.org/downloads/`. Then select GIMP for Mac OSX.

To install GIMP on your Mac, you just open the downloaded DMG file and, as you would do with other Mac apps, drag the `GIMP.app` to your `Applications` folder. The site contains a GIMP 2.8 DMG installer by developer Sven Claussner. It works on OS X 10.6 Snow Leopard and upwards. Just open the downloaded DMG and drag and drop GIMP into your `Applications` folder.

Opening GIMP for the First Time

When you open GIMP for the first time, the user interface can appear a little overwhelming, as shown in Figure 7-1.

Figure 7-1. *Welcome to the GIMP user interface*

Don't worry!

GIMP has been described as "Photoshop with its guts hanging out."[1] It might look complicated, but it is easier to use than you think. It will take some getting used to, though.

GIMP is available to use in two forms, single window mode and multiple window mode. GIMP 2.8 defaults to multiple window mode (if you happen to find yourself in single window mode, the toolbar and dialog windows can be opened from the Windows menu).

So instead of using a single window in which to load my images, I have separate windows for the images, toolbox, and layer controls. By default, my toolbox and tool options are on the left side, and my path, channel, and layer dialogs are on the right side, but they can all be moved around and resized at will, according to taste.

The Toolbox

Figure 7-2 shows the tools that are available in the GIMP toolbox. There are tools to help you draw and paint, tools to help you select image areas, and tools to help you convert and edit photos. (Note that it might look slightly different if the toolbox dialog is a different width).

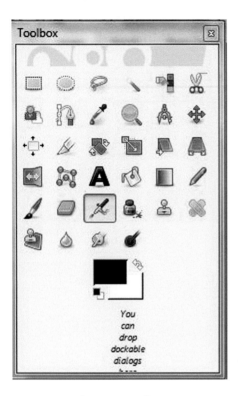

Figure 7-2. *The GIMP Toolbox*

Each tool has a tooltip to accompany it, and you can view it by hovering your mouse over the icon and keeping it there. The toolbox is really in two parts: the tools themselves, and the options for the tool that has been selected. The tools fall into approximately five categories. There are Selection tools, Paint tools (for changing colors), Transform tools (for altering the geometry of an image), Color tools (for altering the distribution of color across an image) and a group of Other tools (ones that do not fall into any of the above categories).

At the bottom of the toolbox is a black-and-white icon representing the current foreground and background colors. When selected, they open the GIMP Color Chooser, illustrated in Figure 7-3.

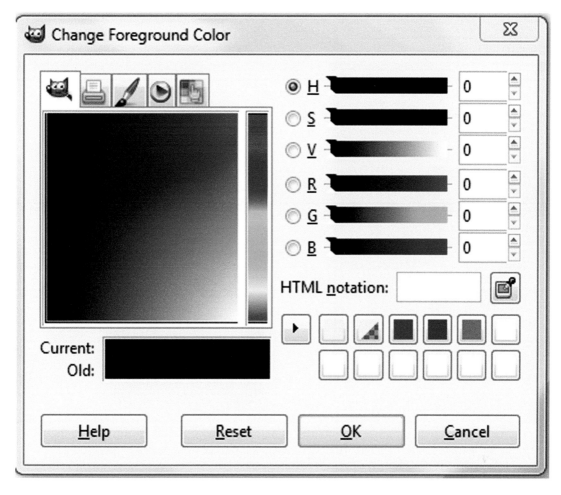

Figure 7-3. *The Color Chooser*

Below the Color Chooser is a dialog box called Tool Options, shown in Figure 7-4. In the default setup, Tool Options will appear each time a tool is activated. The set of options that it displays will change when a different tool is selected as the active tool.

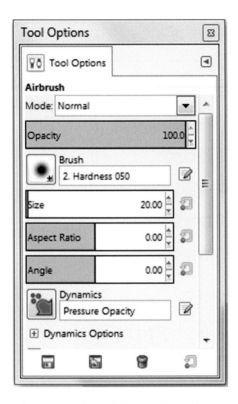

Figure 7-4. *The Tool Options box, as it appears when the Airbrush is selected*

On the other side of the image window, by default, you will find a lot of useful dialogs (such as the Layers dialog) that can also be opened via the Windows menu. You can see a list of the dockable dialog windows available in the Dockable Dialogs menu (Windows ➤ Dockable Dialogs). You can choose which dialog boxes to group together using a process known as docking. The Layers dialog is used to edit, manage, and modify layers.

Docking

Some GIMP tabs can be moved about at will in the GIMP workspace. Such tabs are known as dockable windows. The two most prominent examples are the Layers dialog and the Tool Options dialog. You can view a list of your dockable dialogs by choosing Windows ➤ Dockable Dialogs.

The Undo List

In GIMP, most actions that alter an image can be undone. If, like me, you occasionally get yourself into a terrible mix-up, your work can be undone. You can undo your most recent action by choosing Edit ➤ Undo from the Image menu. If you need to go backwards and forwards to undo and redo several steps at a time, you might find it easier to use the Undo History dialog. This is a dockable dialog box that enables you to see a small sketch of each step in your Undo History. You can access the Undo History dialog from the menu path Windows ➤ Dockable Dialogs ➤ Undo History.

Opening and Creating Files

You can open a file in GIMP by selecting the Open command in the File menu (Windows users can also perform this operating by dragging one of their images over the GIMP desktop icon).

GIMP uses the RGB color model as its default mode. A color model is a mathematical way of representing a color, and RGB, which is used to produce the colors on your computer, is one such example.

To create a new file, follow the menu path File ➤ New. The Create a New Image dialog will appear, as shown in Figure 7-5.

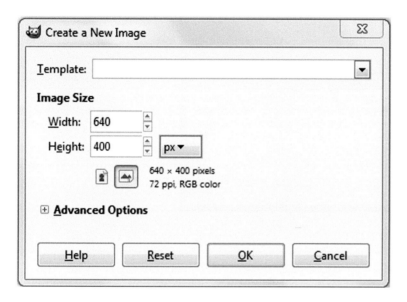

Figure 7-5. *The Create a New Image Dialog*

Here, you can select the size of template that you wish to work on (a template is a GIMP file with reusable contents that can be adapted, edited, or changed). You can then adjust the width and height, and select the units of measurement that you wish to work in. The pixel is the default unit of measurement, but you can also work in millimeters, centimeters, feet, inches, yards, and meters.

Scaling and Cropping

You can scale an image using the Scale Image dialog (Image ➤ Scale Image), as shown in Figure 7-6.

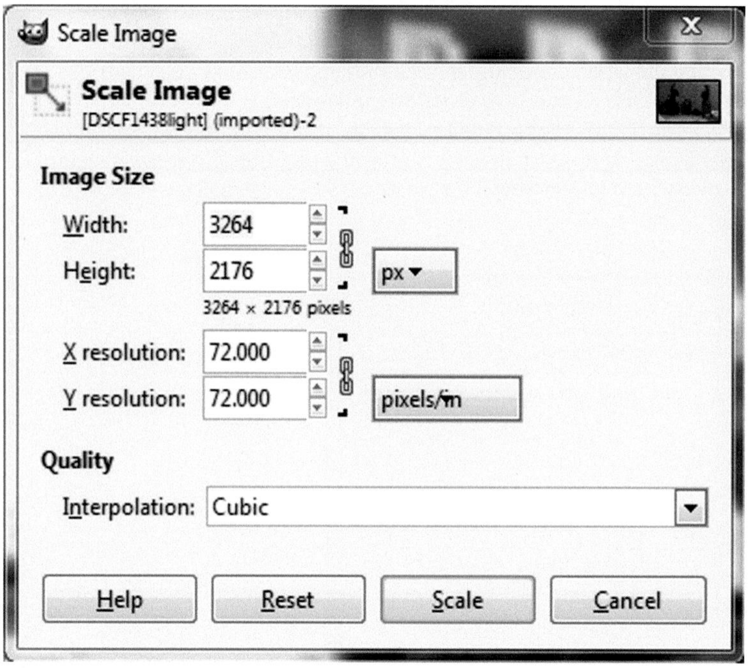

Figure 7-6. *The Scale Image Dialog*

The Resolution section of the dialog enables you to set the number of pixels (or other units) per inch in your image, although it does not change the size of the image. If you have a 300 ppi print image that you want to convert to 72 ppi, then this is the place to do it. You first need to change the width and height scale to something other than pixels, so select inches or centimeters. This is because you want the image to stay the same physical size, so that's what you need to look at. Make a note of the physical width of the image (you don't need to worry about the height because by default the two dimensions are locked together; change one and the other also changes). Now change the X resolution to 72 pixels/in. Click in the Y resolution box and you'll see that figure automatically change to 72. If you look up at the physical dimensions again, you'll notice that they've now changed to something much bigger. This is because by default GIMP is trying to keep the same number of pixels, so when you make the number of pixels per inch smaller, the physical size of the image gets bigger. That's not what you want to happen here, so click in the Width box and enter the width number that you made a note of earlier. If you click in the Height box, you'll see the number change proportionally. Now when you click Scale, the image will be adjusted to your requested resolution while keeping the same physical size. Note that some information in the image will be lost when you scale it this way, so it's best to always work on a copy rather than on an original file.

Another way to resize an image is to use the Scale Tool (Tools ➤ Transform Tools ➤ Scale). It is a bit more difficult to use, but it is also quite effective.

However, if what you want to do is reduce the dimensions of your image by cropping it, just click the Crop Tool icon in the Toolbox. ✎ The Crop tool enables you to select an area of the image and discard everything that lies outside it.

With your image open (and using your mouse), draw a rectangular shape of the area that you wish to keep. When you click inside the image, GIMP will then delete everything outside that area.

Light-Adjustment Tools

A common problem for Scribus users is that the images that they want to use in their documents are too dark to guarantee a good print quality. Luckily, GIMP has three light-adjustment tools that can help convert your images before you import them into Scribus. (Note that these effects are, at a basic level, also available within the Scribus image effects.) They can be accessed from the Colors menu or in Tools ➤ Color Tools.

Brightness-Contrast

The first tool is called Brightness–Contrast, as shown in Figure 7-7. It is simple to use, having one horizontal slider for brightness and another for contrast. It also has a Preview facility, which is available by checking the Preview checkbox. This enables you to view the effect of any changes that you make before they are applied to an image.

Figure 7-7. *The Brightness-Contrast Tool*

Levels

The second tool is called Levels, and it is displayed in Figure 7-8. The Levels tool might look rather confusing for a beginner, but there is no need to learn all of it at this stage. The Levels tool lets you adjust the brightness of the image by using three equidistant sliders (Shadow, Mid-tone, and Highlight) to control the input and output levels. Under the Input Levels slider, there are two eyedropper buttons, which you can use to select points in your image that should be all black or all white.

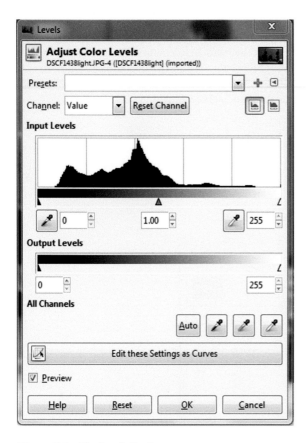

Figure 7-8. *The Levels Tool*

Curves

The third light-adjustment tool (and my favorite) is the Curves dialog (illustrated in Figure 7-9) which does the same thing as the Levels tool, but which I find more effective (one should note that Scribus itself has a similar, but much simpler, image effect).

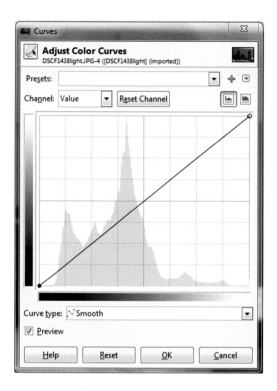

Figure 7-9. *The Curves Tool*

The Curves tool can be a daunting dialog for beginners, and it is not necessary to master it at this stage. However, if you want to use it on your image, click the straight line at its center and then drag it up with the mouse to make the image brighter, or pull it down to make it darker. You can pull the line in a second place further down to create a curve and alter the contrast. It's really rather fun to pull the line into a curve. I use it as a pre-press tool in my magazine in order to lighten some of my darker photos.

The really great thing about the Curves tool is the way that it lets you easily control which parts of your image get adjusted. You can use it to change the color, brightness, contrast, and transparency of an image.

The Threshold Tool

Another tool that I use (with some discretion) is the Threshold tool, shown in Figure 7-10. I can take some photographic images and convert them into black and white pictures akin to line art. (Mind you, it's not the only tool that can do this sort of thing). I sometimes use this tool to produce line drawings from photos, since I cannot draw.

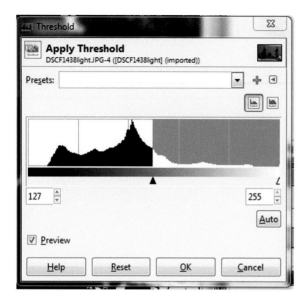

Figure 7-10. *The Threshold Tool*

You can access the Threshold tool in the Tools menu. Figure 7-11 shows a rather crude threshold conversion of a photo of a Kendo martial arts club.

Figure 7-11. *A photo of a Kendo Club converted to black and white*

Other Tools

The Posterize tool, shown in Figure 7-12 has a Posterize Levels slider that enables you to reduce the number of colors in your image, turning it into what looks like a minimalist print.

Figure 7-12. *The Posterize tool reduces the colors down to the level of a minimalist print*

The Desaturate Tool (Figure 7-13) replaces the colors with shades of grey. It lets you choose your shades of grey based on measurements such as Luminosity and Average, and it also gives you a preview of how your changes will look in the final image. This tool is a must if you need to convert color photos to black and white.

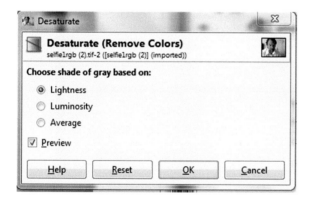

Figure 7-13. *The Desaturate Tool*

The Invert tool inverts the colors in your image, effectively turning it into a photographic negative. However, Scribus has an equally good Invert tool, and it is the one I tend to use.

The Map Objects tool (Filters ➤ Map ➤ Map Object, shown in Figure 7-14) enables you to take an image and wrap it around an object such as a cylinder, a box, or a sphere. You should be aware, however, that the Map Objects tool is a complex tool, and is not really aimed at beginners.

219

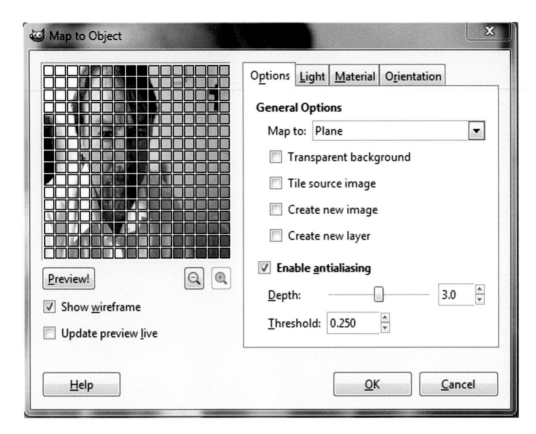

Figure 7-14. *Map Objects Tool*

The Text Tool

The Text Tool, shown in Figure 7-15 (Tools ➤ Text), acts a bit like a text editor, but it can be a little confusing for the unwary. It lets you add text to your image but it is easy to be put off your stride by the unwieldy shape of its text entry cursor. If you are a complete beginner it can take a bit of getting used to.

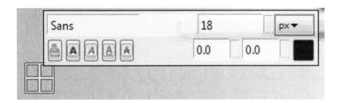

Figure 7-15. *The Text Tool*

Adding Text to an Image

To add text to your image, select the Text tool in your Toolbox, and click the area of the image where you want to add some text. After clicking the image window, the mouse/cursor adds a small and oddly shaped rectangle to the image. This is your text box where you enter your text.

However, if, like me, you are rather uncomfortable with this tool, you can revert to a more traditional form of text editor by checking Use Editor in Tool Options. This will open the more traditional-looking GIMP text editor, shown in Figure 7-16.

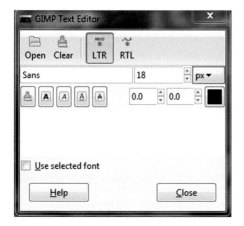

Figure 7-16. *The GIMP Text Editor*

The GIMP Color Chooser

You can access the Color Chooser (Figure 7-17) by clicking the Change Color icon at the bottom of the toolbox or the Color Button in the Text Tool Options.

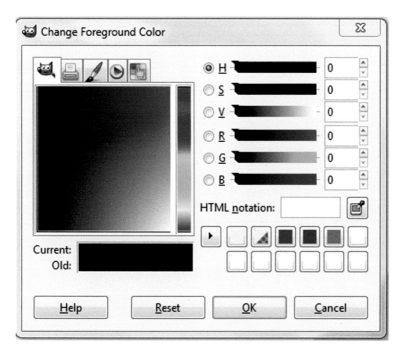

Figure 7-17. *The Color Chooser*

To choose a color, use the vertical color bar to pick a hue, and then use the square on the left to adjust the intensity and brightness of the color. You should be able to pick a place in the square that displays a color close to your needs.

There is an HTML notation box where you can select colors using the HTML codes. HTML codes represent the colors red, green, and blue in varying degrees using the format #RRGGBB.

To the right of the HTML Notation box is the eyedropper icon. You can also use this to select your color. Click the eyedropper, and then click anywhere within your image. This will change the active color to that which is located by the mouse.

The Blend Tool

The Blend Tool (Tools ➤ Paint Tools ➤ Blend) acts just like the Gradient feature in the Scribus Color tab, and creates a similar transition from one color to another.

GIMP's support for CMYK color is actually quite limited, but you can always use Scribus to convert from RGB color to CMYK color.

Removing Objects from Photographs

If you wish to cut out an object from a photo and remove its background, you need to make sure that your image has what is known as an alpha channel. An alpha channel is a special type of channel that can be added to an image to represent the transparency of the image. It will allow you apply transparencies to the areas of the picture that you wish to remove.

EXERCISE

To complete this exercise, you need to find an image containing an object that you wish to cut out. Let's cut out a standing cross from the photo shown in Figure 7-18; you can download it from the Apress website.

Figure 7-18. *Open the image that you wish to edit in GIMP*

Use the scaling control at the bottom of the image window to blow the image up to a scale of 100%. Then right-click the background layer in the layers window and select Add Alpha Channel. This will add a transparent background, even though you won't be able to notice any difference just yet.

Now, select the Paths Tool in the Toolbox. Starting anywhere you like on the outline of the cross,

left-click on its boundary to mark the outline that you wish to extract. You will be placing anchor marks around the entire outline, as illustrated in Figure 7-19.

Figure 7-19. *Anchors have been placed around the outline of the object you wish to extract*

When you get back to the anchor point where you started, click it to join the link together (make sure you are in Edit mode when you do this). Then right-click anywhere in the area that you wish to capture, and choose Select ➤ From Path in the context menu. This will select the cross by displaying a moving boundary of "marching ants" around it (make sure that View ➤ Show Selection is on in order to see them).

Finally, choose Select ➤ Invert to invert your selection, and press the Delete button on your keyboard to delete the background, as shown in Figure 7-20.

Figure 7-20. *The cross has been selected and the background has been deleted*

Et voila! The area around the cross has been selected and deleted. The background to your image should now look like a checkerboard. The checkered background tells you that it is transparent. To remove the selection in GIMP, choose Select ➤ None. To delete a path, choose, Windows ➤ Dockable

Dialogs ➤ Paths ➤ Delete Path. Export the file as a PNG file (File ➤ Export As ➤ cross.png).

Do not save this file as a JPEG file because this format does not support transparencies.

FURTHER EXERCISES

Graphics files are an important element in most successful publications; they can provide a powerful means of promoting your publication in the eyes of your potential advertisers, and they make great promotional material.

One particular graphic design element that has found its way into the quality broadsheets in recent years is the hedcut. A hedcut is a stipple or dot-ink portrait that accompanies a regular column in a newspaper. The creation of a hedcut involves the use of a stipple technique in which the subject's features are recreated using dots of varying sizes and weights. Hedcuts are designed to emulate the look of woodcuts from old-style engravings and newspapers, and are often associated with the Wall Street Journal.

Let's create one now. First of all, you need a photographic self-portrait, or selfie, like the one in Figure 7-21, which you can download from the Apress website.

Figure 7-21. *My photographic selfie, taken on an iMac*

Cropping the Image

You need to crop the image. So click the Crop Tool button in the Toolbox, or use Tools ➤ Transform Tools ➤ Crop in the image window. This changes the cursor and allows you to click and drag the rectangular shape you wish to preserve.

Click one corner of the desired crop area and drag your mouse to create your crop rectangle, as shown in Figure 7-22.

Figure 7-22. *Cropping the portrait*

After completing the click-and-drag motion, a selected rectangle is shown on the canvas. The darkened, rectangular area on the right shows the part of the image that will be discarded. This rectangle can be altered; you can then drag the rectangle's corners or edges to change the dimensions of the selected area. You can then click inside the darkened rectangular area to crop it. The portrait should now look like the image in Figure 7-23.

Figure 7-23. *A successfully cropped image*

At this point, you need to extract the figure from its background, by adding an alpha channel and inserting anchors around the figure.

So, using GIMP, zoom in so that it is big enough to edit the contours of the face and shoulders. Go to the Layers dialog, and to the image layer, where you select the background image using the mouse. Using the scaling control at the bottom, enlarge the image to a size that is workable; try 120%.

Next, right-click the image layer in the Layers window, and select Add Alpha Channel from the context menu. This will add a transparent background to the image.

Then, select the Paths tool in the Toolbox.   Starting in the left corner, click along the contours of

the shirt and shoulder to add anchors to the contours of the figure, as shown in Figure 7-24.

Figure 7-24. *The anchors being inserted along the boundary of the object to be extracted*

Left-click all the way along the boundary of the image you wish to extract. If you make a mistake, select File ➤ Undo Anchor and start again.

■ **Important** When you get to the last link in the chain (i.e. when you reach the anchor where you originally started), click it to connect the two remaining links, as shown in Figure 7-25.

Figure 7-25. *The connected chain of anchors. Note that there are two anchors in the bottom corners of this image*

Now, with the mouse, right-click within the area of the image you wish to cut out. When the context menu appears, choose Select ➤ From Path. This will select the background in your image. You will see a line of marching ants around the image, as was shown in the previous exercise.

Now choose Select ➤ Invert from the menu bar. This will invert the selection. You can now delete the background by pressing the Delete button on your keyboard. The background in the image should now look like a checkerboard, as shown in Figure 7-26.

Figure 7-26. *The image is retained and the checkerboard pattern lets you know that the background has been deleted*

The checkerboard background tells you that it is transparent.

Finally, export your file as a PNG file (do not use JPEG because that format does not support transparencies).

Try opening your image file outside GIMP. You now have a portrait minus the background, as shown in Figure 7-27.

Figure 7-27. *The portrait on a white background*

Converting the Portrait into a Line Drawing

Converting the picture into a line drawing can be quite a drawn-out process if you use tools such as Hue Saturation and Gaussian Blur, but you are just going to employ one of the effects available in the Colors menu.

So, from the Colors, menu, select the Desaturate tool and click OK. This will convert the photo into black and white, as shown in Figure 7-28.

Figure 7-28. *A desaturated version of the selfie*

With the desaturated version open, go to the Filters menu, and select Artistic ➤ Photocopy (Filters ➤ Artistic ➤ Photocopy). This will produce the window shown in Figure 7-29. The Photocopy window modifies the selected image so that it looks like a black and white photocopy.

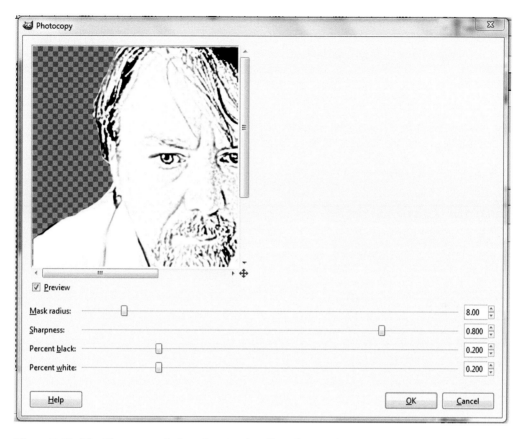

Figure 7-29. *The Photocopy window showing the effect when applied to the image*

In this window, you need to play around with the levels of the Mark Radius, Sharpness, Percentage Black, and Percentage White until you get an image that looks black enough for a line drawing while still retaining the important contours of the original image. I'm going to settle for the image shown in Figure 7-30, in which the portrait has been placed on a white background.

Figure 7-30. *The finished image, as it appears on a white background*

It's by no means perfect, but it's not bad. There are one or two scripts available for GIMP that enable the production of a proper stippled hedcut, but this will have to do for now. The next task is to open the image in Scribus and insert it into an editorial piece.

Uploading Your Line Drawing to Scribus

Start Scribus, and navigate to a document. Insert the line drawing in the top corner, where the hedcut would normally be placed. My version is shown in Figure 7-31.

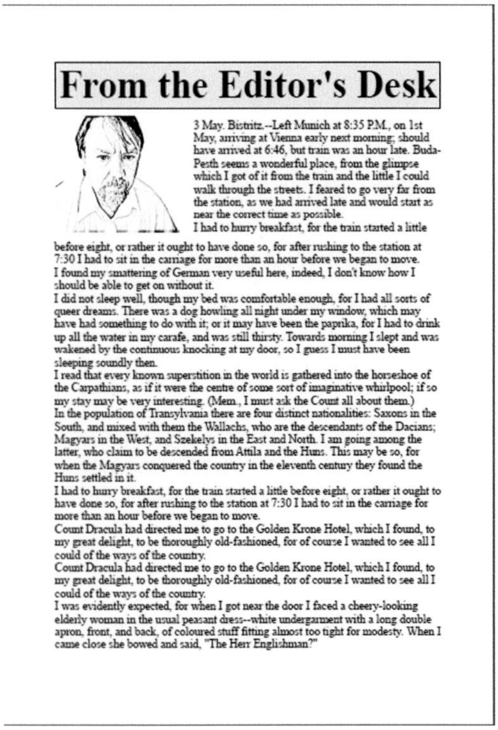

From the Editor's Desk

3 May. Bistritz.--Left Munich at 8:35 P.M., on 1st May, arriving at Vienna early next morning; should have arrived at 6:46, but train was an hour late. Buda-Pesth seems a wonderful place, from the glimpse which I got of it from the train and the little I could walk through the streets. I feared to go very far from the station, as we had arrived late and would start as near the correct time as possible.

I had to hurry breakfast, for the train started a little before eight, or rather it ought to have done so, for after rushing to the station at 7:30 I had to sit in the carriage for more than an hour before we began to move.

I found my smattering of German very useful here, indeed, I don't know how I should be able to get on without it.

I did not sleep well, though my bed was comfortable enough, for I had all sorts of queer dreams. There was a dog howling all night under my window, which may have had something to do with it; or it may have been the paprika, for I had to drink up all the water in my carafe, and was still thirsty. Towards morning I slept and was wakened by the continuous knocking at my door, so I guess I must have been sleeping soundly then.

I read that every known superstition in the world is gathered into the horseshoe of the Carpathians, as if it were the centre of some sort of imaginative whirlpool; if so my stay may be very interesting. (Mem., I must ask the Count all about them.)

In the population of Transylvania there are four distinct nationalities: Saxons in the South, and mixed with them the Wallachs, who are the descendants of the Dacians; Magyars in the West, and Szekelys in the East and North. I am going among the latter, who claim to be descended from Attila and the Huns. This may be so, for when the Magyars conquered the country in the eleventh century they found the Huns settled in it.

I had to hurry breakfast, for the train started a little before eight, or rather it ought to have done so, for after rushing to the station at 7:30 I had to sit in the carriage for more than an hour before we began to move.

Count Dracula had directed me to go to the Golden Krone Hotel, which I found, to my great delight, to be thoroughly old-fashioned, for of course I wanted to see all I could of the ways of the country.

Count Dracula had directed me to go to the Golden Krone Hotel, which I found, to my great delight, to be thoroughly old-fashioned, for of course I wanted to see all I could of the ways of the country.

I was evidently expected, for when I got near the door I faced a cheery-looking elderly woman in the usual peasant dress--white undergarment with a long double apron, front, and back, of coloured stuff fitting almost too tight for modesty. When I came close she bowed and said, "The Herr Englishman?"

***Figure 7-31.** The line drawing as it appears in my regular monthly column*

Turning Your Selfie into a Photographic Portrait

Of course, you might prefer to insert a photographic self-portrait rather than a computer-generated line drawing.

No problem!

GIMP can provide your portrait with a beautiful fade effect that is really quite pleasing to use.

With GIMP still open, close the current view and open up the original self-portrait, like the one shown in Figure 7-32.

Figure 7-32. *Self-Portrait*

If you are starting from the original print and have not done so already, crop the image using the Crop tool, as demonstrated above.

Creating the Soft-Fade Effect

In the toolbox, select the Rectangle tool.

In the Tool Options dialog, select Round Corners and choose a radius for the corners, as shown in Figure 7-33. For this image, I used a radius of 25 pixels.

Figure 7-33. *Rectangle Tool Options Dialog Box*

When you have done that, select the portion of the image you want to keep by dragging a rectangle onto the image, selecting the area that you wish to protect, as in Figure 7-34.

Figure 7-34. *Dragging a rectangle to mark the area that you wish to keep*

At this point you can, if you wish, adjust the radius of the corners.

Now go to the menu and choose Select ➤ Invert. Then go to the menu again and choose Select ➤ Feather. A pop-up window will appear, prompting you to choose the amount of feathering that you wish to apply to the selection, as shown in Figure 7-35.

Figure 7-35. *The Feathering window*

The process of feathering creates a smooth transition between a selection and its surroundings. The Feather Selection window controls how much of the image will be faded out. For this exercise, use 50 pixels. Click the OK button.

Now create the soft fade by hitting the Delete key on your keyboard.

Et Voila! The soft-fade effect should envelope the frame of your portrait, just as in Figure 7-36.

Figure 7-36. *The soft fade effect as applied to the photo*

Your fade effect is now complete. All you need to do now is export the file under a new name and import it into Scribus.

CAPTURING A SCREENSHOT IN GIMP

Using GIMP, you can also grab a screenshot of an entire webpage. Go to File ➤ Create ➤ From Webpage.

To grab a snapshot from a webpage, you are first prompted to enter the URL of the webpage, as shown in Figure 7-37.

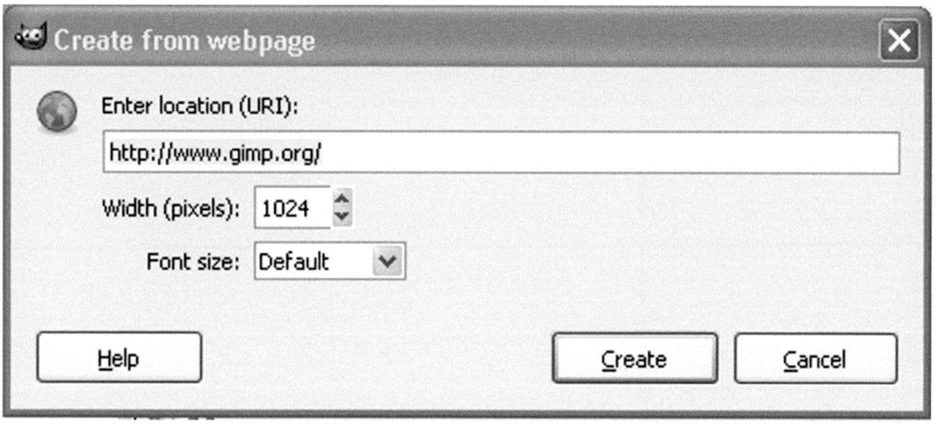

Figure 7-37. *The Create from Webpage Dialog Box*

The default width in pixels is given as 1024. GIMP will then attempt to capture the entire web page, which will produce a very long page if the web page that you happen to capture takes the form of a blog.

There are two other ways of taking a screenshot using GIMP. You can grab a screenshot of the whole screen, or you can grab a screenshot of a single window.

To grab a screenshot, follow the path File ➤ Create ➤ Screenshot, which will produce the WinSnap window, as shown in Figure 7-38.

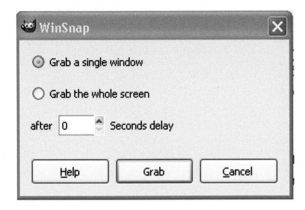

Figure 7-38. *The WinSnap Window*

The WinSnap window gives you the option of grabbing a single window or the whole screen. It also allows you to set a time delay before grabbing the window in case you want to grab something that would otherwise disappear from the screen when you clicked the grab button.

If you select the option to Grab a Single Window, and then click the Grab button, you will be presented with the Select Window, which contains a set of crosshairs, as shown in Figure 7-39.

Figure 7-39. *The Select Window with Crosshairs*

Dragging the crosshairs over to another window produces an XCF file of the window. A dark border will then appear around this window. The image can now be exported as a PDF file (see Figure 7-40).

Figure 7-40. *A screen capture of the Layers dialog. Notice the dark blue border around its perimeter*

If you want to introduce a time delay after grabbing the window, you can specify a delay.

If you opt to grab the whole screen, you will be presented with an image of the whole screen, as shown in Figure 7-41, which you are prompted to save as an XCF file.

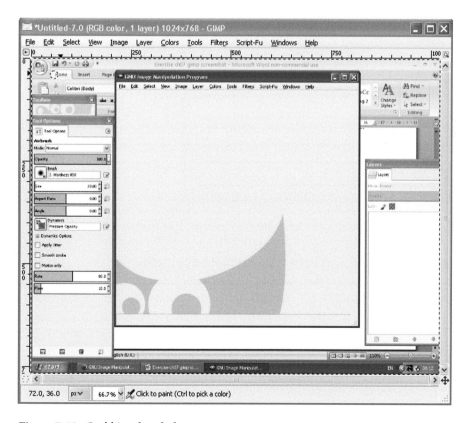

Figure 7-41. *Grabbing the whole screen*

The screen capture tools in GIMP are quite handy, but you might also want to consider using a free and dedicated screen capture program such as SnagIt or Greenshot. Most of the screen shots in this book were produced using Greenshot, which is available to download at `http://getgreenshot.org/`.

ADDING DROP SHADOWS TO YOUR SCREEN CAPTURES

Drop shadows can be used in order to add emphasis to images on the page, such as screen shots.

To add a drop shadow to an image, use the command Filter ➤ Light & Shadow ➤ Drop Shadow.

This will produce the Script-Fu: Drop Shadow window, shown in Figure 7-42.

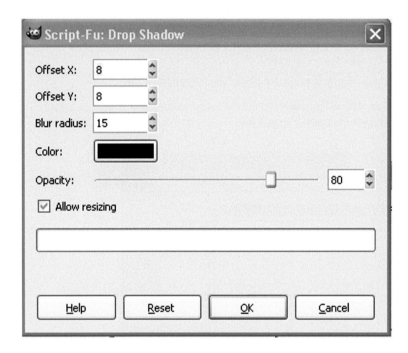

Figure 7-42. The Script-Fu: Drop Shadow window. Make sure the Allow resizing box is checked

Figure 7-43 shows the before and after illustrations of the effects of a drop shadow.

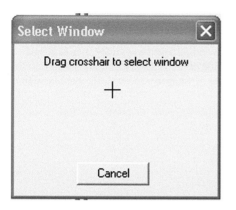

Figure 7-43. *The image before and after the drop shadow has been applied*

HOW TO REMOVE A BACKGROUND COLOR

Sometimes, if you are inserting an image or a logo, the image will contain a background color that is incompatible with your layout. It is possible to remove this color by following these steps.

Load your image or logo, as in Figure 7-44.

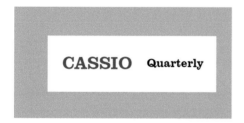

Figure 7-44. *A TIFF image with a background color that needs to be removed*

Select the Select By Color tool in the Toolbox.

Click the color that you wish to delete. Then add an alpha channel. Right-click the image and select Layer ➤ Transparency ➤ Add Alpha Channel.

Finally, select Clear from the Edit menu (Edit ➤ Clear) to clear the background color. The background color should now be clear.

Summary

In this chapter, you learned how to download the open source image editor known as GIMP. You explored GIMP's tools and workspace, and you learned how to go about scaling and cropping your images, and adding some effects. You also learned how to add a transparent layer to your images that will enable you to select a foreground object while deleting its background.

In the next chapter, you will see how to speed up your productivity by using styles, scripts, and templates to do all the donkeywork.

References

1. Graham Harwood, quoted by latsami in "Open Source Publishing: design tools for designers," `https://github.com/latsami/PleaseMakeMeDesign/blob/ master/texts/design%20tools%20for%20designers.mkd`.

CHAPTER 8

■ ■ ■

Automating Scribus

In this chapter, you will learn the following:

- How to use the Style Manager to save time when formatting a document
- How to apply a paragraph style
- How to create a drop cap style
- How to insert a template
- How to create master pages
- How to add page numbers using master pages
- How to run a Python script
- How to add a Python script using a plain text editor
- How to design a threefold brochure

In the previous chapter, you learned how to edit your images by opening them up in GIMP. If you work with images regularly in Scribus, GIMP could become a valuable part of your publishing workflow. The ability to select the areas of your image that you wish to edit (using the Paths tool) and the ability to make colored pixels transparent (using Color to Alpha) could save you lots of time when you lay out your images in Scribus.

However, Scribus can help you optimize your workflow still further by automating some of the more boring and repetitive tasks. You can, for example, use character and paragraph styles to automate the typesetting in your longer documents. You can also use templates to cut down on the amount of repetitive layout work.

Scribus has a large collection of built-in templates that accompany its distribution download. If you decide to use one of these templates, you will find that much of the layout work has already been done for you. All you need to do is modify the template to suit your own personal preferences. Furthermore, you can use master pages to save, store, and apply any fixed elements that appear in your documents.

Some of the more tedious and repetitive layout tasks in Scribus can be automated using Python scripts. Scribus has some built-in Python scripts that can help you design a calendar or preview your fonts, and there are many more scripts available on the Scribus Wiki.

Finally, after you have learned about styles, layers, and templates, you will apply this new knowledge to the design of a threefold brochure.

The Need for Consistency in Your Documents

One word that you will hear time and again in the field of document design is "consistency." Consistency is considered to be a mark of good design, but maintaining a high level of consistency throughout your documents can be a real problem.

It is especially important that you maintain a high level of consistency when applying fonts to your documents, particularly when selecting font families, font sizes, weights, and colors. It's a common nostrum in desktop publishing that the choice of font size and font type really needs to be the same for all your headings and the same for all your body text. But perhaps it is more accurate to say that your choice of typeface depends on what is needed for the design.

In Scribus, the best way to achieve a consistent look in your documents is to use the feature known as a style. A style is a set of properties that have been saved collectively under one name, so that they can be reused within the document. So when a style is applied to part of a document, all these attributes are applied with it. Thus, with a single click of the mouse, you can apply a complete set of font styles to parts of your document in one go. You can use them to format a character, a line of text, a paragraph, or a line.

In the first part of this chapter, you will learn how to apply styles to your documents. You will see how to create styles, how to edit them, and how to reuse them.

Styles

Styles are incredibly important in document layout, especially at a professional level. I use them to format my Word tables because they offer an easy way to manage the text within my longer and more complex documents.

Advantages of Styles

The use of styles will save you a great deal of time once you have mastered them and established an efficient workflow. Instead of entering the font type, the font size, and linespacing for every paragraph in a long document, you can save your preferred settings as a style and apply all your formatting in one go.

Eventually, you will find that you cannot do without them. In fact, some people regard them as the killer feature of Scribus.

In Scribus, there are three types of styles that can be defined: character styles, paragraph styles, and line styles.

What Is a Paragraph Style?

A paragraph style is a collection of paragraph attributes that you name so that they can be applied to other paragraphs in one go, thus obviating the need to apply text formats to each paragraph individually.

A paragraph style can be used to set the margins, indents, and linespacing. You can also include drop caps and justified text.

How to Set a Paragraph Style

To set a paragraph style, follow the Edit ➤ Styles menu to open the Styles Manager, as shown in Figure 8-1.

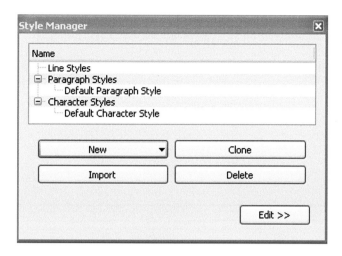

Figure 8-1. *The Styles Manager*

Click the New button, and, from the drop-down list, select Paragraph Style. Then enter a name for your style, as shown in Figure 8-2.

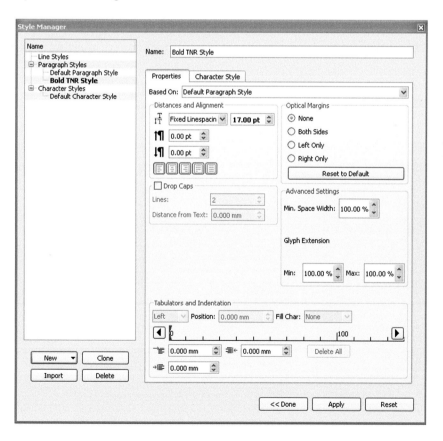

Figure 8-2. *Setting a new style in the Style Manager*

Now you can enter the paragraph attributes (font type, size, color, etc.) to suit your requirements. When you have everything to your liking, click the Apply button. Your new style should now appear in the top left dialog box, as shown in Figure 8-3.

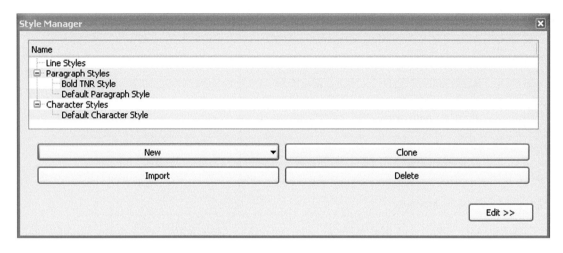

Figure 8-3. *Selecting a style in the Style Manager*

How to Apply a Paragraph Style

To apply a paragraph style, select the text frame that you wish to format. In the Text tab of the Properties Palette, open the Style Settings expander and replace New Style with the name of the style you just created (which should now be listed, just like the new TNR Bold Style in Figure 8-4).

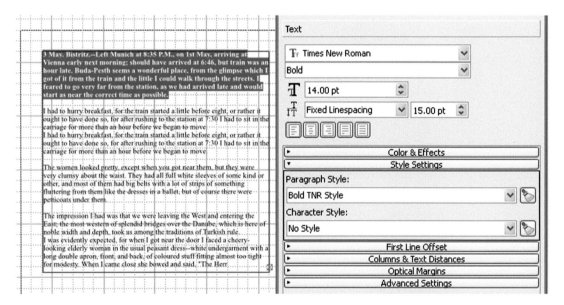

Figure 8-4. *A new style is available in the Style Settings expander of the Properties Palette*

If you have done everything correctly, the text in your text frame should now change to conform to your new format.

Create a Drop Cap Style

A drop cap is the first letter of a paragraph that has been enlarged in size so that it is able to "drop" down by a few lines into the surrounding body of text, as shown in Figure 8-5.

Having had some time at my disposal when in London, I had visited the British Museum, and made search among the books and maps in the library regarding Transylvania; it had struck me that some foreknowledge of the country could hardly fail to have some importance in dealing with a nobleman of that country.

Figure 8-5. *A drop cap that drops three lines below the text*

To create a style that creates a drop cap at the start of your paragraph, open the Style Manager (by using the Edit ➤ Styles menu), select New, and then select Paragraph Style. Enter a name for your style, such as Drop Cap Style, as shown in Figure 8-6.

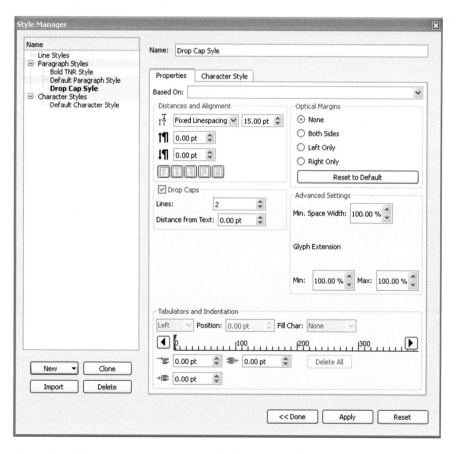

Figure 8-6. *The settings for a drop cap in the Properties tab*

243

Check the box for Drop Caps and enter the number of lines you wish the capital to drop and the distance from the rest of the text. Then click Apply.

Now go to the Properties tab, and check the entry for Drop Cap Style (as shown in Figure 8-6) so that it is turned on. Then choose a line height for your drop cap. Let's try two lines.

Finally, in the Character Style tab, select the required font type and size. Click to apply and then close the Style Manager dialog.

Applying the Drop Cap Style

Select the text frame and highlight the paragraph where you wish to apply a drop cap. You can now apply your drop cap style. To do this, go to the Text tab in the Properties Palette, select the Style Settings expander, and, in place of No Style, select the Drop Caps Style.

As you can see in Figure 8-7, I got rather carried away with applying my "one-click" drop caps.

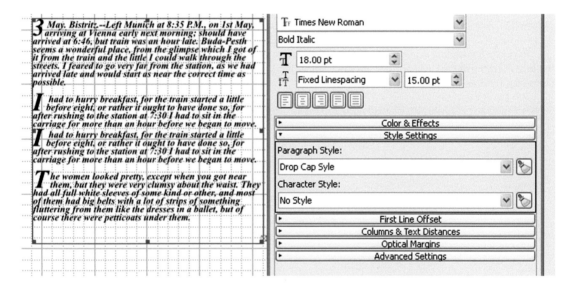

Figure 8-7. *Drop caps after they have been inserted using the Style Expander*

Styles really are rather fun!

Character Styles

In the same way that you have just set the style for a paragraph, it is possible to set the style for individual characters or words.

To do this, highlight the word or character that you wish to format in your text frame and open the Style Manager (using Edit ➤ Styles). Select New, then Character Style, and enter a name for your style. In the Character Style tab, select the required font. Finally, click Apply.

To apply your character style, select your text frame, highlight the word or character that you wish to format, select New, and then Character Style. In the Properties Palette Text tab, under Style Settings, select your new character style.

Line Styles

Use a line style if you want to format the use of lines consistently throughout your documents.

To set a line style, open the Style Manager (Edit ➤ Styles), select New, and then choose Line Styles. After you have named the new style, click the Apply button and close the Style Manager.

To apply your new line style, select the line (or anything with an outline) that you wish to format, and then select the Properties Palette Line tab.

In the Line tab, select your new style. The line should now change to reflect the settings in your new line style.

Templates

Instead of saving a particular style as part of your document, you might prefer to work with some ready-made layouts.

If you follow the path for File ➤ New from Template, you will be presented with the selection of built-in Scribus templates that accompanied your original installation, as shown in Figure 8-8. These templates provide the Scribus user with ready-made layouts under categories such as brochures, business cards, newsletters, PDF presentations, and posters.

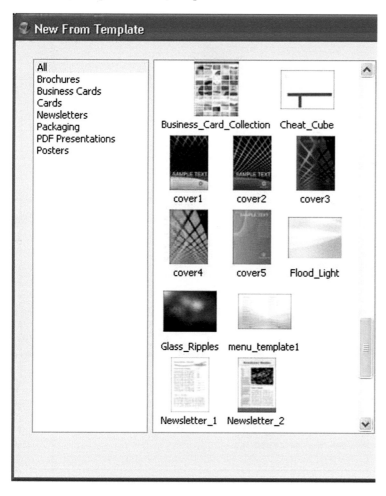

Figure 8-8. *The range of built-in Scribus templates*

In Scribus 1.4.4, there is a rather good template for a newsletter in the lower right corner (see Figure 8-9). This template contains default columns of text boxes for your newsletter title, table of contents, and body text, and some image frames for inserting your own images.

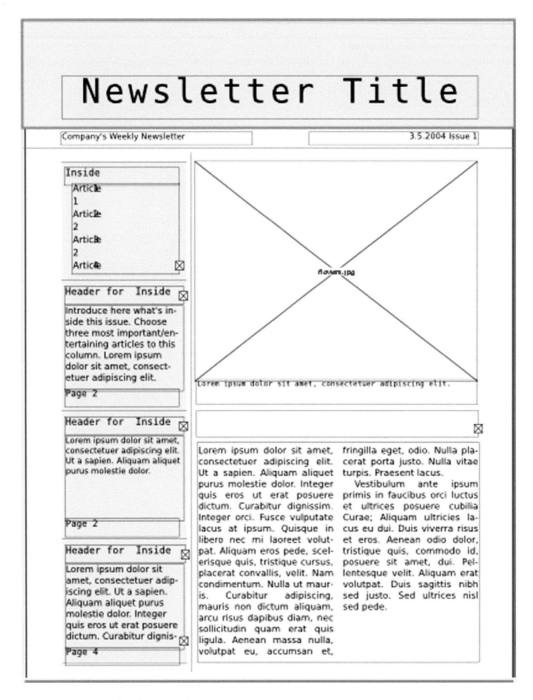

Figure 8-9. *A template for a newsletter*

The selection of brochure templates also includes some rather impressive cover designs, and there is an interesting newsletter template as well as some fairly basic templates for business cards. These templates can all be customized to suit your own requirements.

Saving a Document as a Template

If you have created a document that you wish to save as a template, select File ➤ Save as Template and enter a name for it. Windows users can store their templates in the Scribus templates folder at `C:\Program Files\ Scribus 1.4.5\share\templates`.

You will find some useful templates on the Scribus Stuff website (`http://scribusstuff.org/?xconten tmode=642`).

Master Pages

So far, you have seen how to reproduce complex formatting using styles, and you have seen how to reproduce editable layouts using templates. However, there will be occasions when you will want to reproduce the same objects throughout your documents. I am thinking here in particular of headers, footers, logos, page numbers, and (if you design magazines) a magazine folio. In magazine publishing, a folio contains the magazine's name and issue date alongside the page number. You can see an example of one in Figure 8-10.

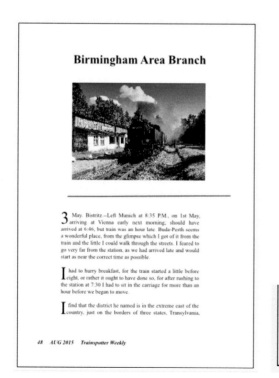

Figure 8-10. *A typical magazine folio, as seen in many A3-sized local magazines*

If you need to reproduce such items on a regular basis, but only want to edit them occasionally, you should use master pages.

To begin with, when you open a new document, Scribus automatically creates a default master page. A metaphor that is often used to describe master pages is that of the "transparent sheet" or "underlay." The objects that you include on your master page will appear in the background of every page to which your master page is applied, and they cannot be changed unless you do it via the Edit ➤ Master Pages tool. Furthermore, the link between your objects and your master page will be preserved, so that if the master page is changed in any way, the other pages that are based on it will also change.

You can create a master page from scratch or from an existing page.

Creating a Master Page from Scratch

To create a master page from scratch, follow the Edit ➤ Master Pages menu, and click the menu bar icon to Edit Master Pages, as shown in Figure 8-11.

Figure 8-11. *The Edit Master Pages dialog*

The New Master Page dialog will appear, prompting you for a name, as shown in Figure 8-12.

Figure 8-12. *The New Master Page dialog*

Name the new master page, and then click OK to save it.

Creating a Master Page from an Existing Page

It is possible to turn a normal Scribus page into a master page, although reports vary as to the reliability of this method. If you want to turn a page into a master page, go to the Page menu and select Convert to Master Page, as shown in Figure 8-13.

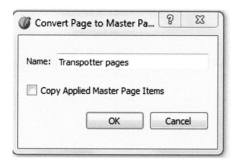

Figure 8-13. *The Convert Master Page dialog box*

I find it works okay, and I sometimes use this method for my headers and footers.

You can also duplicate a master page. To do this, you need to select Master Pages from the Edit menu (see Figure 8-14). When the Edit Master Pages window appears, click the Duplicate icon.

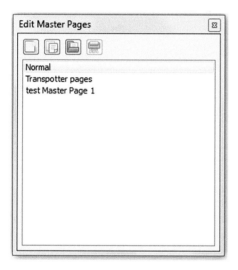

Figure 8-14. *The Edit Master pages window*

Using Master Pages to Add Page Numbers

If you wish to add page numbers to the pages in your document, so that they have page numbers on the bottom right of the front page (recto) and the bottom left of the reverse page (verso), this is how you do it.

Create a new document with double-sided pages, as shown in Figure 8-15. Go to the first left page.

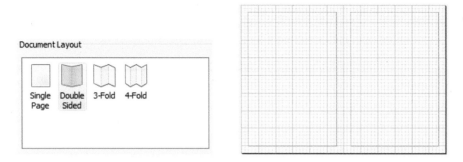

Figure 8-15. *Creating a double-sided document*

Open the Edit Master Pages window (Edit ➤ Master Pages). Click the icon to Add a New Master Page and call it First Left page, as shown in Figure 8-16.

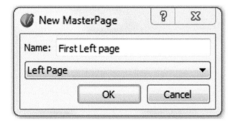

Figure 8-16. *Nominating a left-hand page*

With the Edit Master Page window open, highlight "First Left page," and then add a text frame for the page number. After you have done this, you can enter a page number. You do this by opening the Story Editor, and selecting Insert ➤ Character ➤ Page Number, or you can insert special characters as inline characters.

Selecting this menu item inserts a hash symbol (#) in the text frame. Make the symbol 14 points and Times New Roman Regular and ensure that it is left-aligned. Then click the green arrow to close. You should now see the hash symbol in your text frame. This represents your page number for your left hand page.

Now format a page number for the right-hand page. Click to Add a New Master Page. Name it First Right page. With the Edit Master Pages box still open, click the menu bar icon to Add a Text Frame and position it on the lower right side of the page.

Then open the Story Editor. Select Insert ➤ Character ➤ Page Number. Set the hash symbol to 14 points, Times New Roman Regular, and right-aligned, and click OK.

A hash symbol now appears on the right side of the page. And there you have your page number.

To apply the master pages to your document, make sure that you have closed the Master Page Edit window, go to a page, and select Apply Master Page from the Page menu (or right-click the page background and select Apply Master Page from the context menu). The Apply Master Page dialog box will appear, as in Figure 8-17.

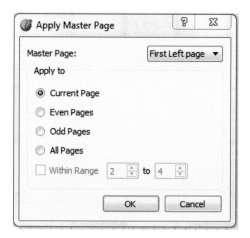

Figure 8-17. *A master page being applied to a normal page*

Go to the first left page. Select First Left Page as your current page at the top of the dialog box, and click OK. A page number will then appear under the main editable layer.

The page numbers can be applied individually or automatically throughout your document.

Applying a Master Page

To apply a master page to a normal page, select Apply Master Page from the Page menu. This will bring up the Apply Master Page window.

You can then assign (or reassign) your master pages to various document pages by using the Windows ➤ Arrange Pages dialog. The Arrange Pages dialog provides a list of your document pages and master pages, as shown in Figure 8-18.

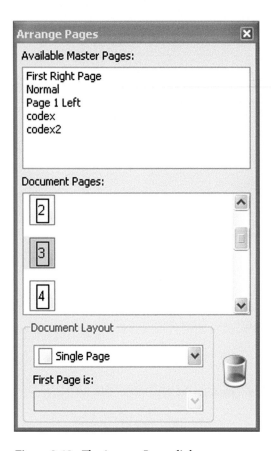

Figure 8-18. *The Arrange Pages dialog*

Navigating Your Master Pages

You can navigate your master pages by using the Windows ➤ Arrange Pages dialog.

The top part of the dialog shows the available master pages. The middle section shows the pages in your document, with the numbers representing their relative positions. At the bottom you can select document layouts or move individual pages to the trash bin.

You can also do this from Windows ➤ Outline window, as shown in Figure 8-19.

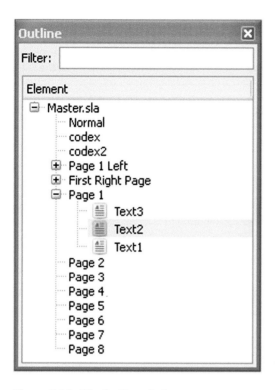

Figure 8-19. *The Outline window*

Clicking a master page will display it for editing, and bring up the Edit Master Page dialog.

Scripting with Python

Styles, templates, and master pages offer time-saving ways of formatting your documents. However, if you are looking to automate a really ambitious task, you might need to rely on a Python script. Scripts can do the formatting for complex page-layout tasks, such as calendar layouts, but they can do more than that; they can enable you to add your own functionality to Scribus. This is quite an exciting prospect if you plan on taking your Scribus usage to a more advanced level.

You should consider using scripts whenever you have a lot of complex, repetitive tasks that you wish to implement in Scribus, particularly if you wish to apply those tasks to more than one document. There are two types of scripts, normal (or basic) scripts and extension scripts. A basic script will execute the task for which it has been written, and then finish. So you need to run the script again if you want to use it again.

What exactly are scripts? Scripts are plain text files with a .py extension written in the Python programming language. Python is a powerful, yet versatile, language that is easy to learn, making it an ideal language for all Scribus newbies.

More importantly, if you happen to write a Python script and it fails to work, you will not damage Scribus when you run it (although you might make a mess of your document, so it's best to save first). You will need to learn some of the Python syntax and vocabulary in order to write such scripts.

There are lots of scripts available for the Scribus user, and you will find many of them in the Scribus Wiki at http://wiki.scribus.net/canvas/Category:Scripts.

Starting a Script

Scribus has a selection of built-in scripts that come with the installation download. You can use them to extend the functionality of Scribus, but you can also use them as a way of familiarizing yourself with the Python programming language. Once you have become familiar with these scripts, you can start adapting and improving them for your own personal use.

When you find a script that you like, and it does the things that you want, you can set about trying to modify and improve it. This is perhaps the easiest way to learn a programming language. So you're going to use a script as an example and then start trying to customize it. This way, you will get to understand the Python language.

The best way to do this is to make a copy of the script and then edit or customize it. Windows users will find scripts at `C:\Program files\Scribus 1.4\share\scripts`.

The following scripts are included in your Scribus installation:

- **Calendar Wizard**, which helps you create a calendar layout.

- **Font Sample**, written by Steve Calcott, which creates a Scribus document containing samples of all the fonts available on your computer. See Figure 8-20.

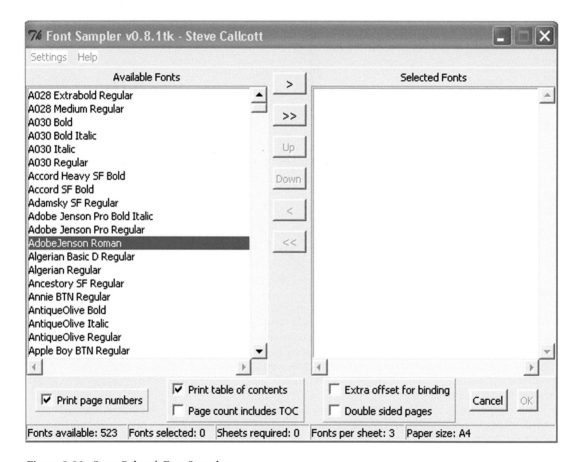

Figure 8-20. *Steve Calcott's Font Sampler*

- **Infobox**, which produces an information box containing the settings used in a selected text frame.

- **Importcsvtable**, which imports CSV data from a spreadsheet into a Scribus document and then creates a table.

Running a Script

There are three different ways to run a script in Scribus, and all of them are accessible from the Script menu.

To start a Python script, go to the Script menu, and select Extension Script, or Scribus Scripts, or Script ➤ Recent Scripts. You will find even more scripts on the Scribus Wiki.

Beginner's Scripts

The following scripts, which are listed on the Scribus Wiki, are said to be suitable for beginners:

- **Drawing Circles with Radii**, which creates a circle with 30 spokes radiating from the center.

- **Making a Dot Gradient**, which uses some Python programming loops to create a customizable dot-gradient image.

- **Adding DRAFT to a Document**, which places a light-grey DRAFT watermark on a new layer.

- **Automatically Creating a Graph**, which is an interactive script in two parts that generates a graph.

- **Discovering an Item's Properties**, which selects an item and runs this script to see the properties that are available to the script. It's useful for programming.

- **Bullets**, which selects a paragraph and the script inserts bullets.

- **Bullets and Numbered Lists**, which is an improved version of the previously mentioned script and inserts bullets and numbered lists.

- **Split Image Across Gutter**, which selects an image, runs the script, and extends the image across the binding between two pages.

- **Calendar Wizard**, which inserts a calendar layout.

■ **Calendar Wizard** is a simple but effective script with which to start. The script allows the user to set up a calendar with a choice of one week or one month per page. You also get the option of adding an image, as shown in Figure 8-21.

Figure 8-21. *A month-per-page calendar generated from the script, with an image of my choice*

Adding a Script

If you like the idea of using some more scripts in your page layout work, the best thing to do is to browse the collection of scripts at `http://wiki.scribus.net/canvas/category:scripts`.

Under the Scripts category, you will find a large selection of scripts, together with some instructions on how to use them. Read the instructions before you run your scripts: sometimes you need to have a document open and an item selected before you can run them.

If you wish to install one of these scripts in your Scribus installation, highlight and copy the script, and paste it into a plain text editor, such as Notepad++ or Gedit. Make sure to save the file name using the extension `.py`, and (if you are a Windows user) save it to `C:\Program Files\Scribus 1.4\share\scripts`.

Read the accompanying instructions, if any, and then run your script by selecting Scripts ➤ Execute Script.

Extension Scripts

As mentioned, there are two types of Python scripts that are used in Scribus: normal (or regular) scripts and extension scripts. Regular scripts use the normal Scribus feature set, whereas extension scripts can run outside Scribus and can make changes to the Scribus environment. Extension scripts can create Scribus objects, such as dockable windows, dialog boxes, and floating palettes that continue to run after the script has finished. Scripts that involve programming a graphical environment usually require access to a GUI toolkit known as PyQt.

A good example of an extension script requiring the installation of PyQt is the Pantone script created by Olivier Berten. This Pantone script allows the user to import Pantone colors into Scribus.

Designing a Threefold Brochure

Now that you're halfway through this chapter, it seems like a good time to reinforce some of the things you have learned by doing some practical work. Let's design a threefold brochure using a couple of old holiday snaps. In order to complete the design, you will need to use layers, some image editing, and some styles for the text.

The threefold brochure is a popular format that is used to promote everything from small businesses to the cultural and arts events on offer in your local library. The design consists of two pages: one side representing the three inner panels, and one side representing the three outer panels. When you open the brochure, the three inner panels possess the potential to provide a full-page spread, which you can use to promote your message.

However, designing the three outer panels requires a lot of preparation. The front panel needs to look attractive enough to make the reader want to see what's inside, while the back panel often displays a bullet list of important points. The middle panel (at the rear of the brochure) usually lists the contact details, such as a phone number, a website, and an email address.

You could use one of the built-in templates that comes with Scribus. A template for a training guide that I rather like is shown in Figure 8-22.

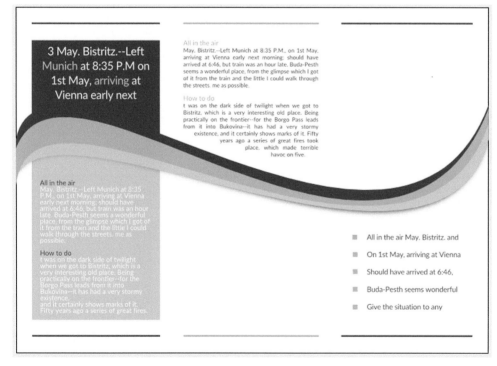

Figure 8-22. *The Training Guide template*

There is also a rather good one that includes some vector drawings of fruit, which is shown in Figure 8-23.

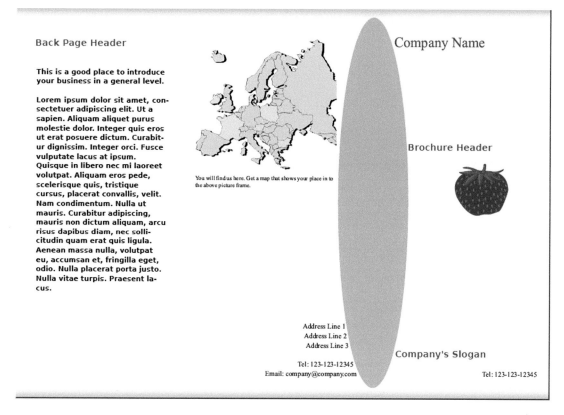

Figure 8-23. *The outer three panels of a threefold brochure template*

As you can see from Figure 8-23, the design is a basic one. There is an oval vector shape linking two of the panels, and the use of a white-to-light green gradient underlines the fact that this template has been designed with bleeds and full page color printing in mind.

The inner panels are shown in Figure 8-24.

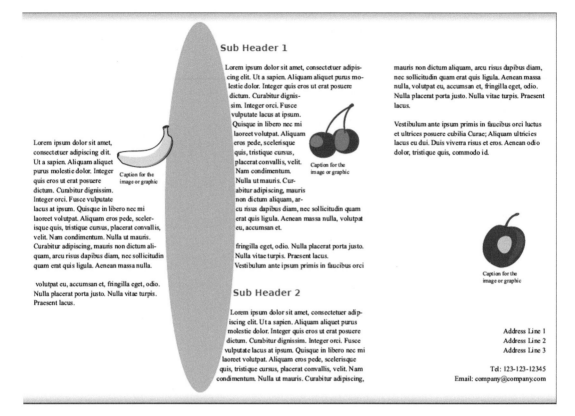

Figure 8-24. *The inner panels of the brochure*

The image frames and text frames are there to be manipulated and edited, and you might be able to create a heritage or travel brochure using such a layout. However, let's now turn to laying out a threefold brochure from scratch.

CREATING A THREEFOLD BROCHURE FROM SCRATCH

For this brochure, you'll use some of the images that are available on the website Pixabay.com. The images that were downloaded are shown in Figure 8-25.

Figure 8-25. *A selection of images available on Pixabay for free download*

They are royalty-free and freely available for commercial use. So download them now and save them into a folder that you have created for this purpose. You can locate them by searching for color wheels, color gradients, rgb, cmyk, and chromatic circle.

Then open a new document in Scribus (File ➤ New). In the New Document window, set the default unit to millimeters, set an 8 mm margin guide, and select an A4 Single Page layout with landscape orientation, as shown in Figure 8-26.

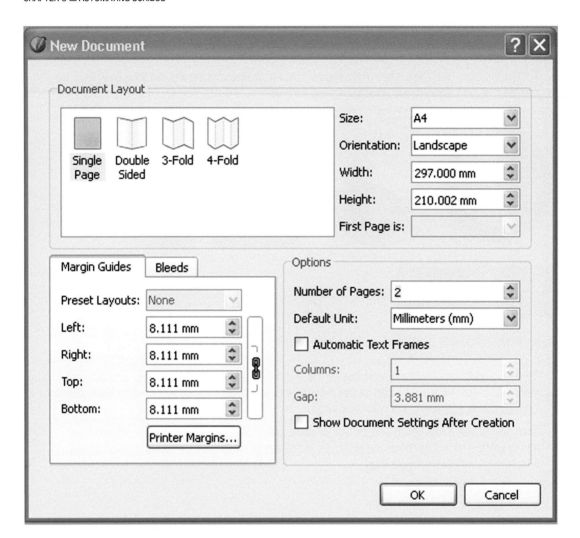

Figure 8-26. *The New Document window with settings adjusted for the brochure*

Click OK and name the document.

At this point you may wish to zoom out of your page a bit so that you can see the entire document.

Next, you need to set some guides in order to divide the page into panels. So open the Manage Guides dialog (Page ➤ Manage Guides). Since you want to divide the page into three panels, you will need two vertical guides. So go to the Column/Row tab, shown in Figure 8-27.

Figure 8-27. Setting the guides and gap in the Guide Manager

In the Verticals section, add two vertical guides, check the Use Gap box, and enter 16mm for the column gap. Next, select Margins because we want the columns to be based on the margins rather than the full page, and click Apply to All Pages.

Then close the Guide Manager.

If you want to make it easier to follow along, you could add some names to the bottom of each panel, in order to make them easier to identify, as shown in Figure 8-28.

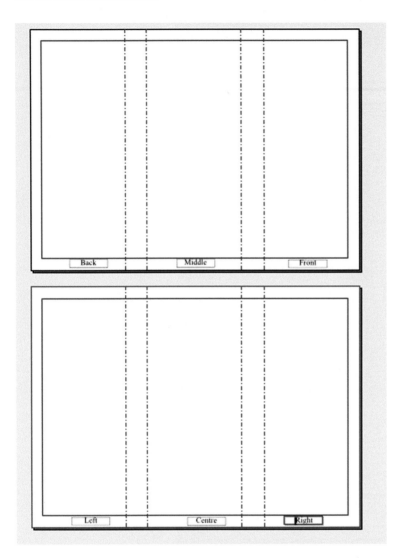

Figure 8-28. *Adding labels to the bottom of each text panel*

So insert a text frame at the bottom of the top right panel.

Double-click in the frame, and enter the word "Cover." Then, making sure the text is selected in the Properties Text tab, increase the size of the text to 30 points. Copy the text frame, and paste it into a similar location at the bottom of the five remaining panels by positioning the cursor at the bottom of each panel and clicking Edit ➤ Paste. You should now have six panels, all containing the label called Cover at the bottom, as in Figure 8-29.

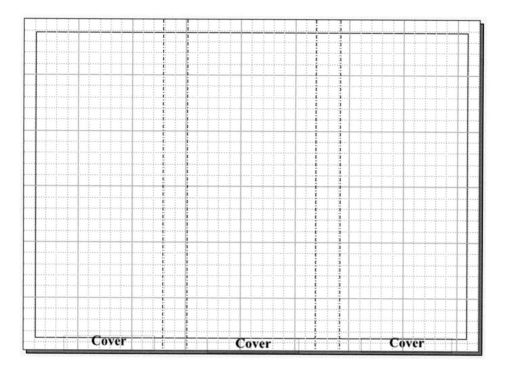

Figure 8-29. *A text frame has now been copied to the bottom of every panel*

You now need to alter the names of the five other panels, so double-click each text frame, and change the names so that they resemble the names in Figure 8-30, with the top page containing panels for Flap, Back, and Cover, and the lower page containing the panels for Left, Center, and Right.

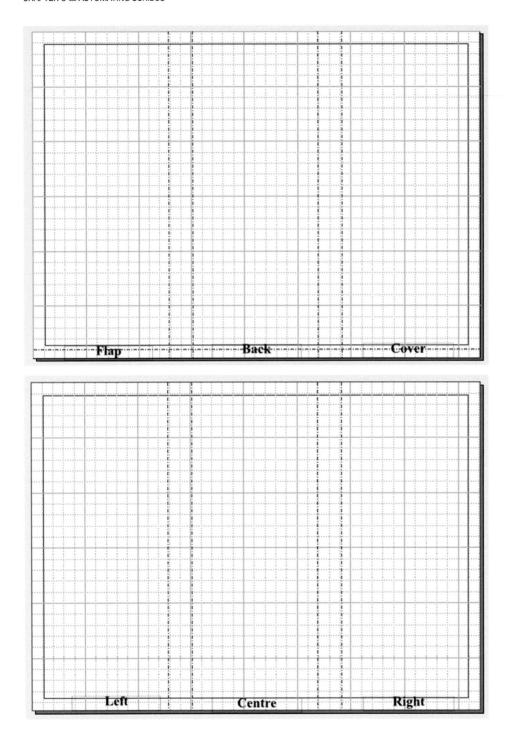

Figure 8-30. *The labels for the upper and lower panels*

Using Layers To Hide Your Labels

These labels are intended as a design aid, so they will not be part of the final brochure. They are meant to help you identify each panel. When you have finished laying out your design and you want to hide the labels, you can turn off the visibility of this layer.

So open the Layers dialog (Windows ➤ Layers) and select Add a New Layer. Select the new layer (which will have the name New Layer) and change its name to Top Layer, as shown in Figure 8-31.

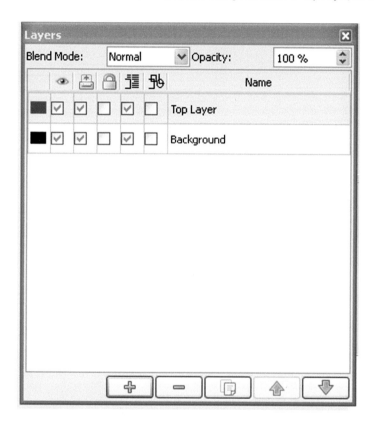

Figure 8-31. *Adding a new layer and changing the layer name to Top layer*

If you now uncheck the second checkbox down on the left side (which is the Make Layer Visible checkbox for the Background layer), you will notice that your panel names disappear, as shown in Figure 8-32.

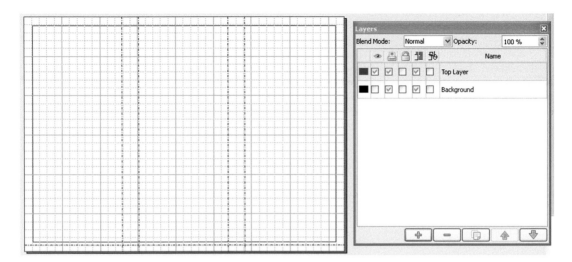

Figure 8-32. *Unchecking the visibility of the Background layer*

Check the Visibility box for the Background again and turn the labels back on.

On the top layer, add some text frames to create a layout for your panels. Insert text frames into all three panels (Flap, Back, and Cover) and insert some sample text into the first two frames (Insert ➤ Sample Text). You need to link the first two frames by selecting the Flap text frame, clicking the Text Link icon on the Toolbar, [icon] and clicking the text frame on the Back panel. So click the frame on the panel

labeled Flap, click the Link icon on the toolbar [icon] , and then click the text frame in the Back panel.

Your frames should now be linked and you can begin filling them with sample text (Insert ➤ Sample Text). So select the text frame in the fold panel, and select File ➤ Sample Text. Select whichever language you wish the sample text to be in. Now format the text in the Flap and Back panels using Times New Roman Bold at 14 points.

For the text frame in the Cover panel, enter the words "Introduction to Color Theory," center them, and set the text as 34 points Times New Roman Bold with a fixed linespacing of 46 points. The completed text boxes should look like the ones in Figure 8-33.

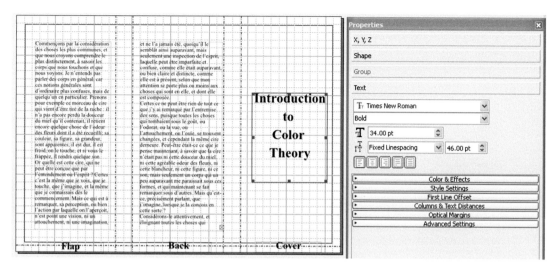

Figure 8-33. *The top three panels with their formatted text frames*

Adding Margins to Text Frames

Okay. The text frames are good, but if you decide to place them on a dark or colored background, the text would either be difficult to see or it would look cramped because it flows to the edge of the border. So let's add some margins to the text frames, just in case.

Select the Cover panel, then select the Properties Text tab, and then select the Columns & Text distances expander. Add 5mm to each side of the text frame, so that it looks like the frame in Figure 8-34.

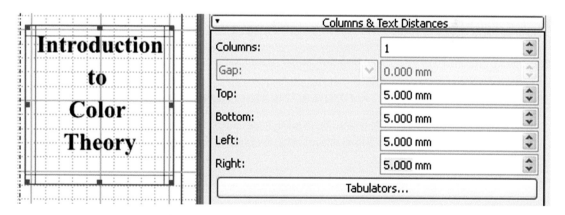

Figure 8-34. *A 5mm margin has been added to the frame*

Now repeat the process for the other panels. All three panels should now look like the ones in Figure 8-35. As a finishing touch, add a chromatic color circle that you downloaded from Pixabay to the top of the title frame.

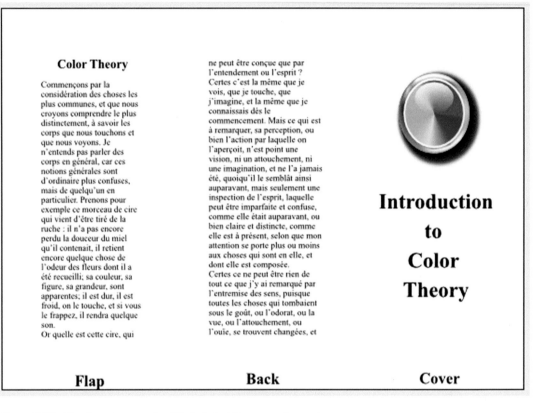

Figure 8-35. *The three top panels with their text frames and margins*

Formatting the Back Page

Now you need to format the inside pages. You're going to design the brochure's inner panels so that each panel has both a text frame and an image frame, as shown in Figure 8-36.

CMYK

RGB

The Color Wheel

Commençons par la considération
des choses les plus communes, et
que nous croyons comprendre le
plus distinctement, à savoir les
corps que nous touchons et que
nous voyons. Je n'entends pas
parler des corps en général, car
ces notions générales sont
d'ordinaire plus confuses, mais de
quelqu'un en particulier. Prenons
pour exemple ce morceau de cire
qui vient d'être tiré de la ruche : il
n'a pas encore perdu la douceur
du miel qu'il contenait, il retient
encore quelque chose de l'odeur
des fleurs dont il a été recueilli; sa
couleur, sa figure, sa grandeur,
sont apparentes; il est dur, il est
froid, on le touche, et si vous le

Commençons par la considération
des choses les plus communes, et
que nous croyons comprendre le
plus distinctement, à savoir les
corps que nous touchons et que
nous voyons. Je n'entends pas
parler des corps en général, car
ces notions générales sont
d'ordinaire plus confuses, mais de
quelqu'un en particulier. Prenons
pour exemple ce morceau de cire
qui vient d'être tiré de la ruche : il
n'a pas encore perdu la douceur
du miel qu'il contenait, il retient
encore quelque chose de l'odeur
des fleurs dont il a été recueilli; sa
couleur, sa figure, sa grandeur,
sont apparentes; il est dur, il est
froid, on le touche, et si vous le
frappez, il rendra quelque son.

Commençons par la considération
des choses les plus communes, et
que nous croyons comprendre le
plus distinctement, à savoir les
corps que nous touchons et que
nous voyons. Je n'entends pas
parler des corps en général, car
ces notions générales sont
d'ordinaire plus confuses, mais de
quelqu'un en particulier. Prenons
pour exemple ce morceau de cire
qui vient d'être tiré de la ruche : il
n'a pas encore perdu la douceur
du miel qu'il contenait, il retient
encore quelque chose de l'odeur
des fleurs dont il a été recueilli; sa
couleur, sa figure, sa grandeur,
sont apparentes; il est dur, il est
froid, on le touche, et si vous le
frappez, il rendra quelque son.
Or quelle est cette cire, qui ne

Left   **Centre**   **Right**

Figure 8-36. *The three inner panels with text and images*

So go ahead and insert some images in the top third of each panel.

■ **Note**   The Pixabay website (from which these images have been taken) allows you to download these images as bitmap images. You can also download them as vector images, but you will need to register with the website before you can do so.

The first image is a color wheel, and the second one is known as "CMYK eye." The third image is that of an RGB color intersection. Position and scale your images. Right-click each image after it has been loaded into the image frame, and select Scale to Image Frame in the Context menu. After you have positioned and scaled your images, insert a text frame under each image, and fill it with sample text. Format the text to 14 points Times New Roman, and add three headings (at 20 points Times New Roman bold for the text frames on the Left, Center, and Right panels, respectively). Finally, add some 5mm margins to the text frames using the Columns & Text Distances expander.

You should now have a set of panels like the ones you saw in Figure 8-35 and Figure 8-36.

Removing the Labels

Before you export these pages as PDF files for printing, you need to remove the labels at the bottom of each panel. You can do this using the Layers dialog. Select Windows ➤ Layers and uncheck the Background layer's visibility, as shown in Figure 8-37. The checkbox to uncheck is the second one down on the left, next to the black square.

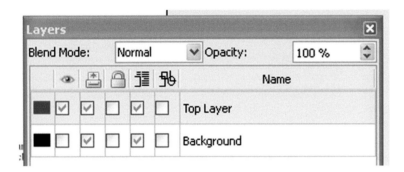

Figure 8-37. *Unchecking the background layer's visibility in the Layers dialog*

Save your file.

You should now have six basic panels for your threefold brochure, as shown in Figure 8-38.

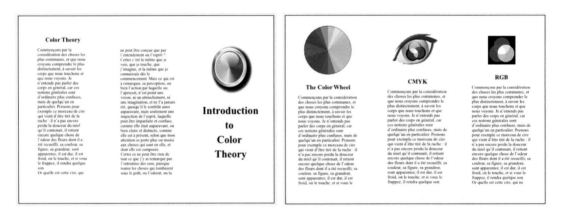

Figure 8-38. *The finished panels of the threefold brochure*

Modifying Your Brochure

One modification that you might want to make to your lower panels is to move the headings above the images. This can easily be done without creating any new text boxes by simply flowing the text around the images.

If you want to do this, move the panel images onto the text frames beneath them, and press the Use Bounding Box button in the Shape tab, as shown in Figure 8-39.

Figure 8-39. *Select the button to Use Bounding Box and fit your image into the text*

The end result, shown in Figure 8-40, looks much better.

The Color Wheel

Commençons par la considération des choses les plus communes, et que nous croyons comprendre le plus distinctement, à savoir les corps que nous touchons et que nous voyons. Je n'entends pas parler des corps en général, car ces notions générales sont d'ordinaire plus confuses, mais de quelqu'un en particulier. Prenons pour exemple ce morceau de cire qui vient d'être tiré de la ruche : il n'a pas encore perdu la douceur du miel qu'il contenait, il retient encore quelque chose de l'odeur des fleurs dont il a été recueilli; sa

CMYK

Commençons par la considération des choses les plus communes, et que nous croyons comprendre le plus distinctement, à savoir les corps que nous touchons et que nous voyons. Je n'entends pas parler des corps en général, car ces notions générales sont d'ordinaire plus confuses, mais de quelqu'un en particulier. Prenons pour exemple ce morceau de cire qui vient d'être tiré de la ruche : il n'a pas encore perdu la douceur du miel qu'il contenait, il retient encore quelque chose de l'odeur des fleurs dont il a été recueilli; sa couleur, sa figure, sa grandeur, sont apparentes; il est dur, il est froid, on le touche, et si vous le frappez, il rendra quelque son. Or quelle est cette cire, qui ne

RGB

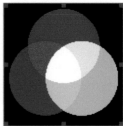

Commençons par la considération des choses les plus communes, et que nous croyons comprendre le plus distinctement, à savoir les corps que nous touchons et que nous voyons. Je n'entends pas parler des corps en général, car ces notions générales sont d'ordinaire plus confuses, mais de quelqu'un en particulier. Prenons pour exemple ce morceau de cire qui vient d'être tiré de la ruche : il n'a pas encore perdu la douceur du miel qu'il contenait, il retient encore quelque chose de l'odeur des fleurs dont il a été recueilli; sa

Figure 8-40. *The modified lower panels with text flowing around the images*

Adding Colors to Your Panels

Let's add some background images or colors to both pages, then color them in the Properties Palette, and send them to a lower level. It will make the brochure look more eye-catching and professional. So insert an image frame and add a blue and white vertical gradient using the Color tab. Then, send the colored frame into the background by right-clicking it and using the path Levels ➤ Send to Bottom Level. The result should look like Figure 8-41.

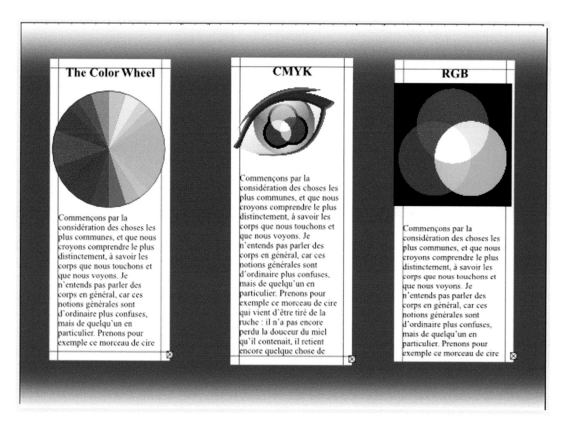

Figure 8-41. *The lower panels with image frame in background, colored to a blue and white vertical gradient*

POSTSCRIPT: CREATING BULLETED LISTS

Many professionally designed business brochures display bullet points listing their events or the advantages of using their business or product. Unfortunately, at the present time, there is no automatic method for formatting bulleted or numbered lists in Scribus. At the time of writing, you have the choice of formatting the bullet points manually or using a Python Script to do the job for you.

Formatting a Bulleted List Manually

To format a bulleted list manually, insert your text frame, enter your list in the Story Editor, and then enter a bullet point by using the menu Insert ➤ Character ➤ Bullet.

This method will insert individual bullet points at the start of each list, which you can then tabulate so that there is a gap between the bullets and the text. The finished list should look similar to the one in Figure 8-42.

- Monday Tea dance
- Tuesday Bingo
- Wednesday Whist Drive
- Thursday Early Night
- Friday Bowls Club
- Saturday
- Sunday

Figure 8-42. *A bulleted list constructed manually in the Story Editor*

Formatting a Bulleted List Automatically

However, there is a Python script that will format the bulleted list for you. Visit the Scribus Wiki website and locate the script called "Bullets and Numbered Lists," which can be located at http://wiki.scribus.net/canvas/Bullets_and_numbered_lists.

Highlight the Python code, copy it, and paste it into a text file (I use Notepad++). Save the file as a .py file with a name like Bullets.py, and save it to the scripts folder in your Scribus program files (for Windows users, these can be found using the path Scribus ➤ share.scripts).

To execute your Python code, select the text frame containing the list you wish to format, and then select Execute Scripts from the Scripts menu. Your Bullets script should appear in the list of Python scripts. Select the script and it will ask you to select the bullet or number format of your choice. The result will look like the list in Figure 8-43. I think that the Python-generated list looks more professional, but you may feel otherwise.

❏　Monday Tea Dance
❏　Tuesday Bingo
❏　Wednesday Bridge
❏　Thursday Whist drive
❏　Friday Bowls Club
❏　Saturday
❏　Sunday

Figure 8-43. *A bulleted list formatted using a Python script*

Formatting a Bulleted List Using Styles

In Scribus, there is no default bulleted list or number list method. If you pasted the text in, you must format each line manually, but you can use styles in order to help create the list. And create a new style.

Insert a new text frame on the panel labeled Back, and using the Story editor, paste in your text.

Select Edit ➤ Styles to open the Style Manager. Click the New button to create a new style. Name it Bullet List.

Then choose your requirements: a font size of 25 points in Times New Roman Bold and a fixed linespacing of 25 points.

You could choose to indent your text at this stage by going to the section headed Tabulation & Indentation and slightly indent the first row of text by dragging the right-hand triangle away from the brackets, as shown in Figure 8-44. But let's leave them as they are and add some spaces in the Story Editor at a later point in the exercise.

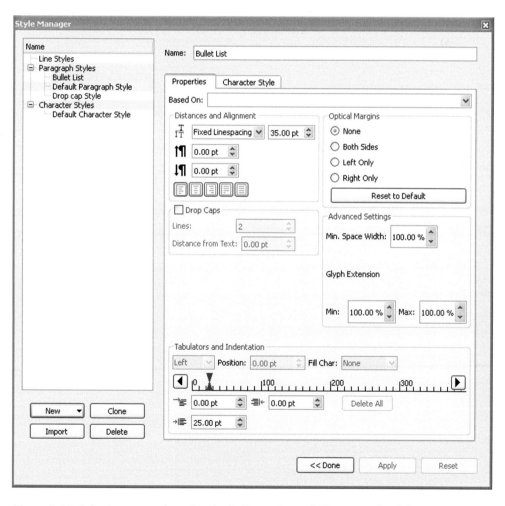

Figure 8-44. *Selecting your style settings in the Properties and Character tabs of the Style Manager*

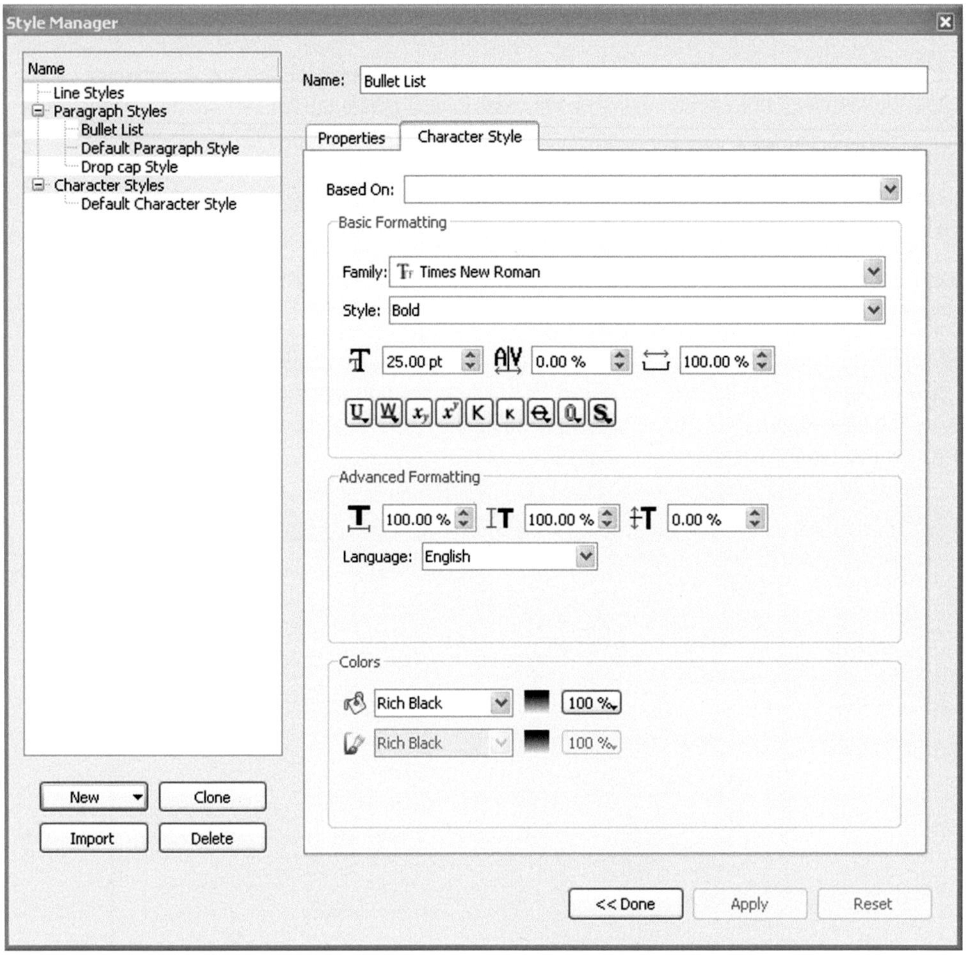

Figure 8-44. (*continued*)

Click Save.

In the Properties ➤ Style Settings expander, chose the style setting in the left corner. Click the arrow beside No Style and select Bullet List, as shown in Figure 8-45.

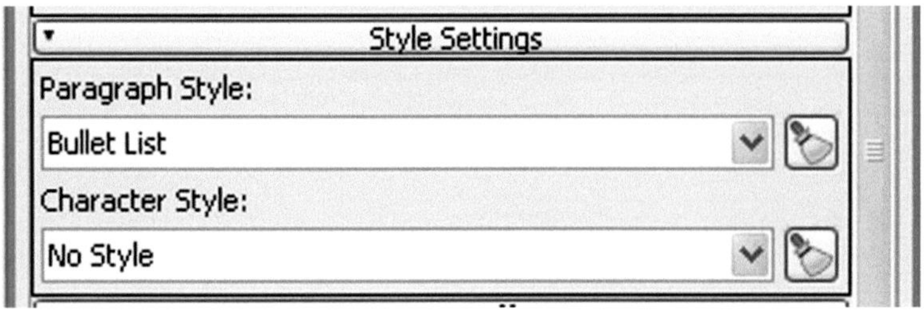

Figure 8-45. *Selecting the Bullet List style in Style Settings*

Now everything that you paste will take on this style.

Click Update.

You now need to insert some bullets.

Move the cursor to the first line and in the Story Editor, select Insert ➤ Character ➤ Bullet.

Then add a couple of spaces and click Update (see Figure 8-46).

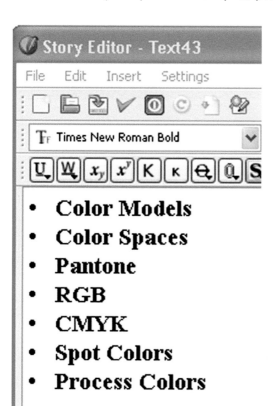

Figure 8-46. *The bulleted list as it appears in the Story Editor*

You'll find you might have to add or remove some spaces in order to align the text.

Now, in the Story Editor, copy the bullet and the spaces, and paste them into the beginning of each other entry in the list.

Click Update and close the Story Editor.

Check the list in preview mode (see Figure 8-47).

Color Theory

Commençons par la
considération des choses les
plus communes, et que nous
croyons comprendre le plus
distinctement, à savoir les
corps que nous touchons et
que nous voyons. Je
n'entends pas parler des
corps en général, car ces
notions générales sont
d'ordinaire plus confuses,
mais de quelqu'un en
particulier. Prenons pour
exemple ce morceau de cire
qui vient d'être tiré de la
ruche : il n'a pas encore
perdu la douceur du miel
qu'il contenait, il retient
encore quelque chose de
l'odeur des fleurs dont il a
été recueilli; sa couleur, sa
figure, sa grandeur, sont
apparentes; il est dur, il est
froid, on le touche, et si vous
le frappez, il rendra quelque
son.
Or quelle est cette cire, qui

Color Theory

- **Color Models**
- **Color Spaces**
- **Pantone**
- **RGB**
- **CMYK**
- **Spot Colors**
- **Process**

Introduction to Color Theory

Figure 8-47. *The bulleted list as viewed in preview mode*

Using Glyphs

Instead of using bullets, you could insert some glyphs into your list by choosing Insert ➤ Glyph.

There is a large range of glyph characters that you can choose from that are dependent on the font that you have chosen, as shown in Figure 8-48.

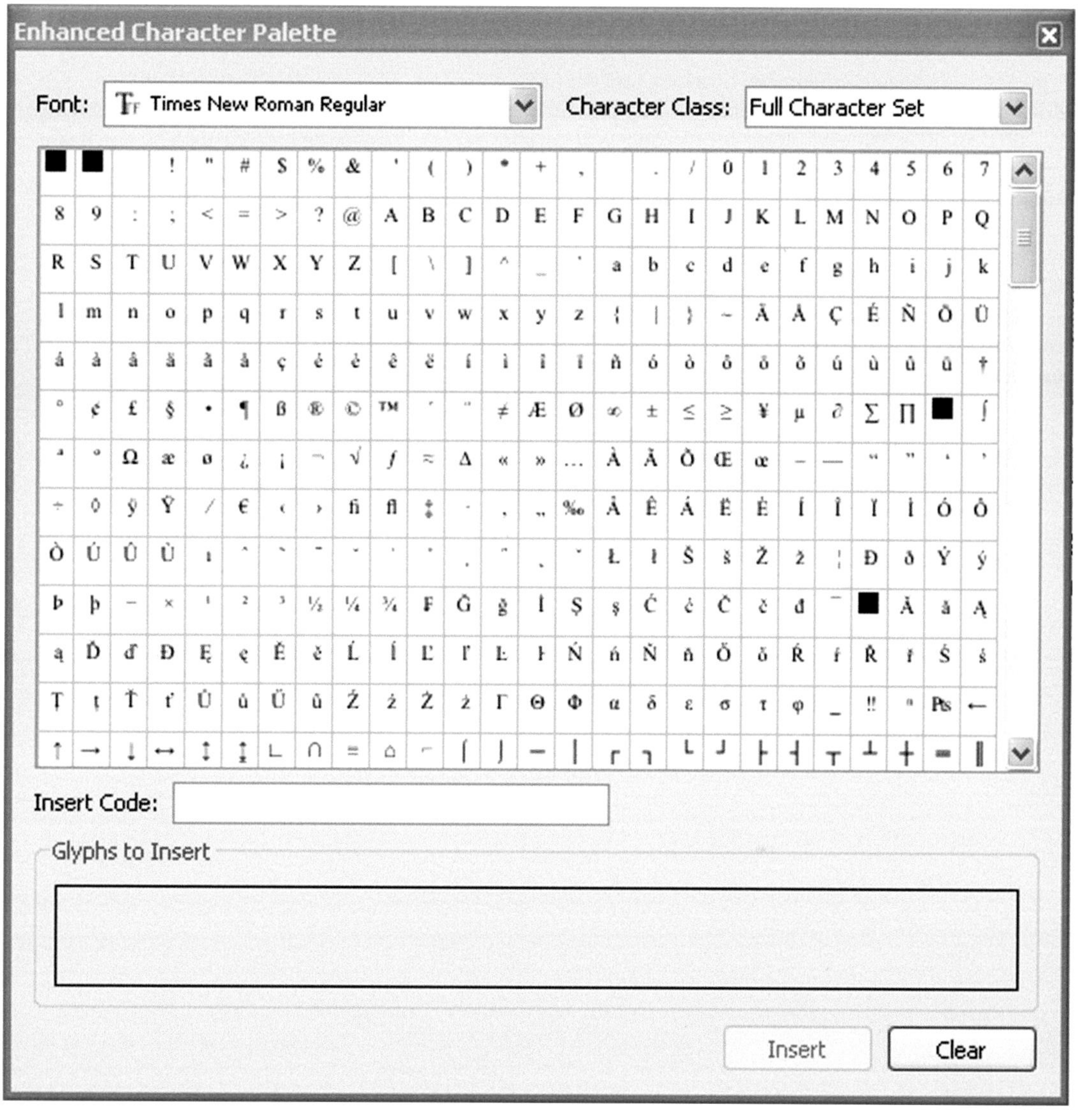

Figure 8-48. *The Glyph selection for Times New Roman*

Summary

Typesetting a large document can be a long and drawn-out process. After you finish setting the fonts individually for over 30 pages of text, you may conclude that there has to be an easier way of doing this.

Well, there is! The Style Manager can help you format your headers, footers, and body text, and if you need a ready-made newsletter or brochure layout in a hurry, you can open a template and customize it to suit your own requirements.

Page numbers, which can be very fiddly when installed manually, can be inserted very quickly using master pages. And complex page layouts, such as the ones used to create grids and calendars, can be inserted in less than a minute by running a Python script.

We will be returning to the subject of scripts in a later chapter. However, in the next chapter, you will learn a few graphic design principles, and then you will apply what you learned so far to the design of a magazine.

■ ■ ■

CHAPTER 9

Designing Magazines

In the previous chapter, you looked at the ways in which you can automate your page layout tasks in Scribus via styles, scripts, and master pages. In this chapter, you're going to examine the design process and then apply all of your new knowledge to some design exercises.

Because page layout programs are used in the main to produce magazines and newsletters, you are going to be looking at the design of a glossy magazine, one that contains full page color bleeds, and that can be sent to a professional high street printer for processing.

In this chapter, you will do the following:

- Look at the use of space in document design

- Design a magazine front cover

- Insert a barcode

- Design a masthead and editorial letter

- Design an advertorial

- Learn how to export PDF files to the Web

Efficient Magazine Design

The goal of this book is to show you how to get the most out of a desktop publishing program, but, when designing documents, learning the program is only half the battle. You also need plenty of practice.

Scribus is capable of producing some amazing page layouts, but learning to use it will not turn you into a graphic designer overnight. The sobering truth is that the documents you produce using Scribus will be no better than the design concepts that lie behind them.

Scribus can help you with the layout of your pages, but you are ultimately responsible for the success of the concepts that lie behind them. A full account of the design process, from the first flash of inspiration to the finished product (and including the principles of graphic design), is beyond the scope of this book. Although a brief study of its principles will not necessarily provide you with an easy answer to your design problems, it could provide you with a rich set of design possibilities.

Choosing Your Format

Firstly, you need to be clear about the intended audience for your document. Knowing your intended audience will help you choose the right format for the message that you want to communicate. For example, if you wish to communicate a message to a large group of people in a public space, you probably need to produce a large format piece such as a poster, something that uses large images and fonts that can be viewed at a distance. If you intend to communicate your message on a one-to-one basis, you would be better off producing a small set of flyers. To a certain extent, the format that you choose will determine the size and shape of the page that you have to work with, and the amount of information that can be included within it. These are all factors that will influence how you go about placing your elements on the page.

Using Grids

The use of grids can help you to place these elements on the page with more precision. Grids provide a hidden framework for your design and help define your proportions. This is important because a carefully proportioned set of contents on a page will help the reader to access and assimilate the contents more easily.

The grids and guides that are available in Scribus are hidden by default, but you can reveal the grids by using the View ➤ Show Grids menu. And you can use guides by dragging them off the rulers at the side and top of the page. To reveal them initially, however, you need to use the menu View ➤ Show Guides. After you have done that, you will be able to magnetically attach objects to your guides by selecting Page ➤ Snap to Guides.

It is possible to create a visually appealing sense of proportion on your page by dividing it up into thirds, using one third of the page for the graphics or whitespace, and two thirds of the page for the text. Another way to make your page layouts look attractive and inviting is to use guides and to include a generous proportion of linespacing. Linespacing is the distance between the text baselines, the baseline being the line upon which most letters sit. In Scribus, the baseline grid is used to ensure that the lines of text in parallel columns or text frames are precisely aligned.

Achieving a Sense of Flow

The careful placement of visual elements on the page will aid the viewer in scanning through its contents; in a sense, your layouts help you control the way that the reader navigates through the material. One element in your page design that can help you lead the reader from one element of the page to another is what is known as active whitespace.

Whitespace

You should think of whitespace as an important element in your overall design. Whitespace is the area of blank space that lies between the elements in your composition. The word refers not only to the spaces that contain no images or text (major whitespace) but also to the smaller spaces between words/letters and images/captions (micro whitespace). It can also refer to the spaces that can be created through the use of increased linespacing, kerning, the addition of margins, and a change of fonts (passive whitespace). The addition of a little passive whitespacing can make a big difference to the readability of a document, as shown in Figure 9-1.

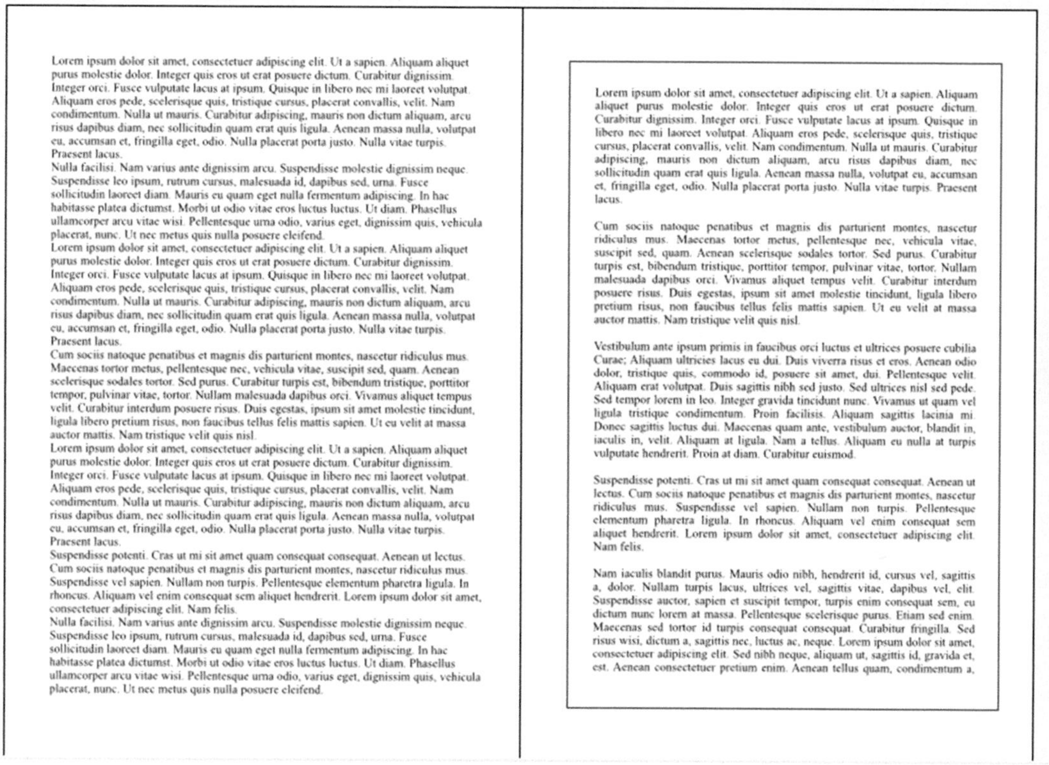

Lorem ipsum dolor sit amet, consectetuer adipiscing elit. Ut a sapien. Aliquam aliquet purus molestie dolor. Integer quis eros ut erat posuere dictum. Curabitur dignissim. Integer orci. Fusce vulputate lacus at ipsum. Quisque in libero nec mi laoreet volutpat. Aliquam eros pede, scelerisque quis, tristique cursus, placerat convallis, velit. Nam condimentum. Nulla ut mauris. Curabitur adipiscing, mauris non dictum aliquam, arcu risus dapibus diam, nec sollicitudin quam erat quis ligula. Aenean massa nulla, volutpat eu, accumsan et, fringilla eget, odio. Nulla placerat porta justo. Nulla vitae turpis. Praesent lacus.

Nulla facilisi. Nam varius ante dignissim arcu. Suspendisse molestie dignissim neque. Suspendisse leo ipsum, rutrum cursus, malesuada id, dapibus sed, urna. Fusce sollicitudin laoreet diam. Mauris eu quam eget nulla fermentum adipiscing. In hac habitasse platea dictumst. Morbi ut odio vitae eros luctus luctus. Ut diam. Phasellus ullamcorper arcu vitae wisi. Pellentesque urna odio, varius eget, dignissim quis, vehicula placerat, nunc. Ut nec metus quis nulla posuere eleifend.

Lorem ipsum dolor sit amet, consectetuer adipiscing elit. Ut a sapien. Aliquam aliquet purus molestie dolor. Integer quis eros ut erat posuere dictum. Curabitur dignissim. Integer orci. Fusce vulputate lacus at ipsum. Quisque in libero nec mi laoreet volutpat. Aliquam eros pede, scelerisque quis, tristique cursus, placerat convallis, velit. Nam condimentum. Nulla ut mauris. Curabitur adipiscing, mauris non dictum aliquam, arcu risus dapibus diam, nec sollicitudin quam erat quis ligula. Aenean massa nulla, volutpat eu, accumsan et, fringilla eget, odio. Nulla placerat porta justo. Nulla vitae turpis. Praesent lacus.

Cum sociis natoque penatibus et magnis dis parturient montes, nascetur ridiculus mus. Maecenas tortor metus, pellentesque nec, vehicula vitae, suscipit sed, quam. Aenean scelerisque sodales tortor. Sed purus. Curabitur turpis est, bibendum tristique, porttitor tempor, pulvinar vitae, tortor. Nullam malesuada dapibus orci. Vivamus aliquet tempus velit. Curabitur interdum posuere risus. Duis egestas, ipsum sit amet molestie tincidunt, ligula libero pretium risus, non faucibus tellus felis mattis sapien. Ut eu velit at massa auctor mattis. Nam tristique velit quis nisl.

Lorem ipsum dolor sit amet, consectetuer adipiscing elit. Ut a sapien. Aliquam aliquet purus molestie dolor. Integer quis eros ut erat posuere dictum. Curabitur dignissim. Integer orci. Fusce vulputate lacus at ipsum. Quisque in libero nec mi laoreet volutpat. Aliquam eros pede, scelerisque quis, tristique cursus, placerat convallis, velit. Nam condimentum. Nulla ut mauris. Curabitur adipiscing, mauris non dictum aliquam, arcu risus dapibus diam, nec sollicitudin quam erat quis ligula. Aenean massa nulla, volutpat eu, accumsan et, fringilla eget, odio. Nulla placerat porta justo. Nulla vitae turpis. Praesent lacus.

Suspendisse potenti. Cras ut mi sit amet quam consequat consequat. Aenean ut lectus. Cum sociis natoque penatibus et magnis dis parturient montes, nascetur ridiculus mus. Suspendisse vel sapien. Nullam non turpis. Pellentesque elementum pharetra ligula. In rhoncus. Aliquam vel enim consequat sem aliquet hendrerit. Lorem ipsum dolor sit amet, consectetuer adipiscing elit. Nam felis.

Nulla facilisi. Nam varius ante dignissim arcu. Suspendisse molestie dignissim neque. Suspendisse leo ipsum, rutrum cursus, malesuada id, dapibus sed, urna. Fusce sollicitudin laoreet diam. Mauris eu quam eget nulla fermentum adipiscing. In hac habitasse platea dictumst. Morbi ut odio vitae eros luctus luctus. Ut diam. Phasellus ullamcorper arcu vitae wisi. Pellentesque urna odio, varius eget, dignissim quis, vehicula placerat, nunc. Ut nec metus quis nulla posuere eleifend.

Lorem ipsum dolor sit amet, consectetuer adipiscing elit. Ut a sapien. Aliquam aliquet purus molestie dolor. Integer quis eros ut erat posuere dictum. Curabitur dignissim. Integer orci. Fusce vulputate lacus at ipsum. Quisque in libero nec mi laoreet volutpat. Aliquam eros pede, scelerisque quis, tristique cursus, placerat convallis, velit. Nam condimentum. Nulla ut mauris. Curabitur adipiscing, mauris non dictum aliquam, arcu risus dapibus diam, nec sollicitudin quam erat quis ligula. Aenean massa nulla, volutpat eu, accumsan et, fringilla eget, odio. Nulla placerat porta justo. Nulla vitae turpis. Praesent lacus.

Cum sociis natoque penatibus et magnis dis parturient montes, nascetur ridiculus mus. Maecenas tortor metus, pellentesque nec, vehicula vitae, suscipit sed, quam. Aenean scelerisque sodales tortor. Sed purus. Curabitur turpis est, bibendum tristique, porttitor tempor, pulvinar vitae, tortor. Nullam malesuada dapibus orci. Vivamus aliquet tempus velit. Curabitur interdum posuere risus. Duis egestas, ipsum sit amet molestie tincidunt, ligula libero pretium risus, non faucibus tellus felis mattis sapien. Ut eu velit at massa auctor mattis. Nam tristique velit quis nisl.

Vestibulum ante ipsum primis in faucibus orci luctus et ultrices posuere cubilia Curae; Aliquam ultricies lacus eu dui. Duis viverra risus et eros. Aenean odio dolor, tristique quis, commodo id, posuere sit amet, dui. Pellentesque velit. Aliquam erat volutpat. Duis sagittis nibh sed justo. Sed ultrices nisl sed pede. Sed tempor lorem in leo. Integer gravida tincidunt nunc. Vivamus ut quam vel ligula tristique condimentum. Proin facilisis. Aliquam sagittis lacinia mi. Donec sagittis luctus dui. Maecenas quam ante, vestibulum auctor, blandit in, iaculis in, velit. Aliquam at ligula. Nam a tellus. Aliquam eu nulla at turpis vulputate hendrerit. Proin at diam. Curabitur euismod.

Suspendisse potenti. Cras ut mi sit amet quam consequat consequat. Aenean ut lectus. Cum sociis natoque penatibus et magnis dis parturient montes, nascetur ridiculus mus. Suspendisse vel sapien. Nullam non turpis. Pellentesque elementum pharetra ligula. In rhoncus. Aliquam vel enim consequat sem aliquet hendrerit. Lorem ipsum dolor sit amet, consectetuer adipiscing elit. Nam felis.

Nam iaculis blandit purus. Mauris odio nibh, hendrerit id, cursus vel, sagittis a, dolor. Nullam turpis lacus, ultrices vel, sagittis vitae, dapibus vel, elit. Suspendisse auctor, sapien et suscipit tempor, turpis enim consequat sem, eu dictum nunc lorem at massa. Pellentesque scelerisque purus. Etiam sed enim. Maecenas sed tortor id turpis consequat consequat. Curabitur fringilla. Sed risus wisi, dictum a, sagittis nec, luctus ac, neque. Lorem ipsum dolor sit amet, consectetuer adipiscing elit. Sed nibh neque, aliquam ut, sagittis id, gravida et, est. Aenean consectetuer pretium enim. Aenean tellus quam, condimentum a,

Figure 9-1. *The text frame on the right has more passive whitespace. The result is easier on the eye and more readable*

285

DESIGNING A MAGAZINE

At this point, let's run through the process of designing an eight-page double-sided magazine in Scribus, using bleeds in order to facilitate full page color reproduction with a photo-lithographic printer.

But before you open Scribus, let's look at the anatomy of a traditional magazine so that you can find your way around it. Figure 9-2 shows a magazine page.

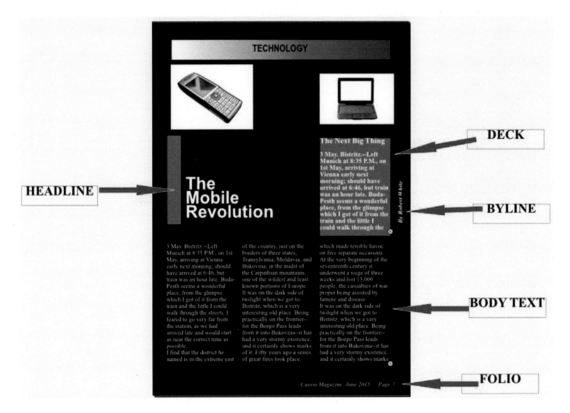

Figure 9-2. The anatomy of a magazine page

The project for this chapter is the design of a mock-up of a magazine called **ALANA**. The design process for Alana should be straightforward enough; you start by opening a new document and establishing your document settings. These will include settings for the bleed area and crop marks, and will utilize a double-sided page format. Then you will design a cover page. After that, you will design an editorial and a masthead (or imprint).

So open Scribus, and when the New Document window appears, enter the settings shown in Figure 9-3.

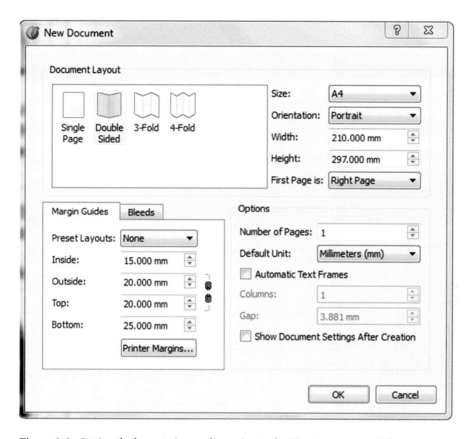

Figure 9-3. *Setting the layout, size, and margins in the New Document window*

Then click OK to create the document. Once the document is opened on the first page, click View ➤ Fit to Height and then turn the grid on (View ➤ Show Grid). Now you can start adding the features that will appear throughout the document, such as the page number, or folio.

For our next exercise, we are going to create a mock-up of the fashion magazine Alana.

CREATING A FRONT PAGE IN SCRIBUS

The aim of this exercise is to create a magazine front page and a logo (or nameplate), then add a photo of a model to act as the center of visual interest (CVI), and finally add headlines and a barcode along the side of the page. To cut out the figure of the model, you will use the GIMP photo editor.

The magazine is called Alana, as mentioned, and it's a fashion magazine for the woman of today. It carries regular monthly features on fashion, cooking, gossip, DIY, and shopping. The finished design should look like the one in Figure 9-4.

Figure 9-4. *The finished mock-up for the Alana front cover*

Fonts

In order to complete this exercise, you will need to have the following fonts (or a Scribus substitute) installed on your computer:

Garamond Bold

Century Gothic Bold

Images

You will also need an image of a fashion model so that you can position it down the center of the page. I downloaded an image from the Pixabay website. I chose it because it looked like it would provide a good CVI and it would also enable me to fit plenty of text frames for the headlines around the sides of the page. So if you need an image, go to www.pixabay.com and search for images of fashion models (although there are many other websites that will let you download stock free images). Using the Pixabay search filter, you can search for pictures with a **vertical orientation**, which are more suited to fitting on a cover page. You want to download the highest quality image that is available. When you locate an image you like, download it and save it to your magazine folder.

So create a folder for your magazine now, and save it to your desktop, and then download your chosen image.

Deleting the Image Background in Gimp

There is a tradition in fashion magazine design of positioning the front page model so that she partially obscures the center of the logo. In order to do this, you need to delete the background in the image of the model; that way you will be able to push the image over the Alana logo at a later stage in the design.

So open the image in Gimp 2.8 (by selecting Edit ➤ Edit Image ➤ Gimp 2.8), and open the image of the fashion model that you downloaded, as in Figure 9-5.

Figure 9-5. *The image of the fashion model at it appears in Gimp 2.8*

Introducing Intelligent Scissors

Normally, you would use the Paths tool to select the image that you want to save, but this time, you will be using Intelligent Scissors, which are useful for selecting a region that is defined by strong color changes.

Click the Scissors icon in the Gimp toolbox.

Choose a point where you want to start cutting out the figure, and click the edge of the shape where the model meets the background. Then click all around the contours of the model, dropping anchors as you go, until you reach the point where you started. Click your original anchor to complete the selection, as shown in Figure 9-6.

Figure 9-6. *The background has been selected by dropping anchors around the outline of the model*

At this point, while the Intelligent Scissors tool is still selected, go to its associated Tool Options box, and check the entry for feathered edges, as shown in Figure 9-7.

Figure 9-7. *Check the box to add feathering. This will create a smooth selection*

Press the Enter key to turn the area into a selection, and then add an alpha channel. To add an alpha channel, select Layer ➤ Transparency ➤ Add Alpha Channel.

Finally, choose Select ➤ Invert to invert the image so the background gets deleted.

You can now click the Delete button on your keyboard, and the image should look like the one in Figure 9-8.

Figure 9-8. *The figure of the fashion model has been saved and the background has been deleted*

Export the finished image as a PNG file (File ➤ Export ➤ model.png).

Now it's time to set up your document.Document Setup

Switch over to Scribus and click File ➤ New Document to set your document up. You want to set up a four-page document. If you were actually designing a real magazine with bleeds, you would be using a double-sided page layout. However, for the purpose of this exercise, use a single page layout. Set the document size to A4, and the number of pages to 4. Then set the default units to millimeters, and the margins to 15 mm (left), 20mm (right), 20mm (top), and 25mm (bottom), as shown in Figure 9-9.

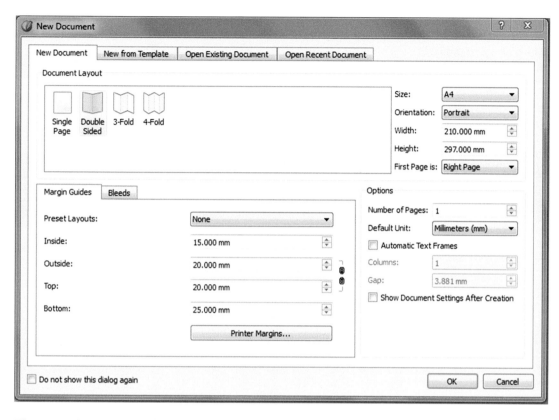

Figure 9-9. *Starting a new document for the magazine*

Setting the Bleed

Most magazine covers that are printed today bleed off the edge of the paper, so you will also add a bleed in Scribus. In the Bleeds tab of the New Document dialog, set the bleeds to 3mm for top, right, and bottom, as shown in Figure 9-10. Note that 3mm is a standard measurement for bleeds in the UK and the rest of Europe; in the US, the standard is 1/8 of an inch.

Margin Guides	Bleeds	
Inside:	0.000 mm	
Outside:	3.000 mm	
Top:	3.000 mm	
Bottom:	3.000 mm	

Figure 9-10. *The bleeds as set in the Bleeds tab of the New Document dialog*

As a rule of thumb, bleeds are usually set between 3mm and 5mm past the edge of the page (known as the trim). If you were getting this page printed professionally, you would need to check the required bleed setting with your printer.

Click OK to create the document, and select View ➤ Fit to Height so that you can view the entire first page on your screen.

You will want to align some of the headlines that run down the sides of the cover page, so you need to set some guides that so that you can snap to them. Make sure that Page ➤ Snap to Guides is checked. In addition, follow the menu File ➤ Document Setup ➤ Guides and select In the Foreground.

INSERTING A BACKGROUND

Insert a rectangular shape (Insert ➤ Shape ➤ Rectangle) and drag it out so that it covers the entire area

of the page. ☐ With the shape still selected, go to the Properties Color tab, and select Horizontal

Gradient. In the Gradient Fill box, set the red color pointer on the left to khaki, and set the color pointer on the right to white. Then click in the middle of the gradient fill box to add a third color, and set that to ivory. The finished gradient and the background shape should look like the one in Figure 9-11, with the gradient running from khaki on the left, through to ivory in the middle, and white at the end.

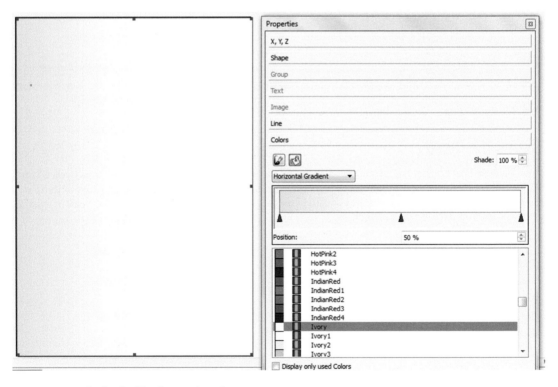

Figure 9-11. *The finished background gradient*

Creating a Logo

Now let's create a magazine logo, or nameplate, as shown in Figure 9-12. You are going to be using Garamond Bold for the font, which is widely available.

Figure 9-12. *The logo*

Open the Layers window (Windows ➤ Layers) and click the + button to add a new layer. Double-click the name New Layer 1 and change it to Logo, as shown in Figure 9-13.

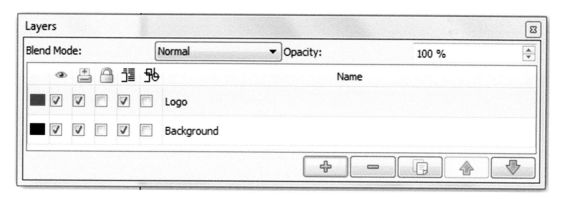

Figure 9-13. *The Layers dialog with a newly created layer*

To create the magazine logo, select the Insert Text Frame icon on the Toolbar, ▤ (Insert ➤ Insert Text Frame) and drag out a text frame until it covers the top fifth of the page up to the margins at the side. With the text frame still selected, double-click and type the word ALANA into the frame.

In the Properties Text tab (shown in Figure 9-14), select Garamond Bold as the font, and select a font size of 170 points, and then center the text. Next, open the Story Editor, and select the Outline icon (which you can also access from the Color & Effects expander in the Properties Text tab). ▣

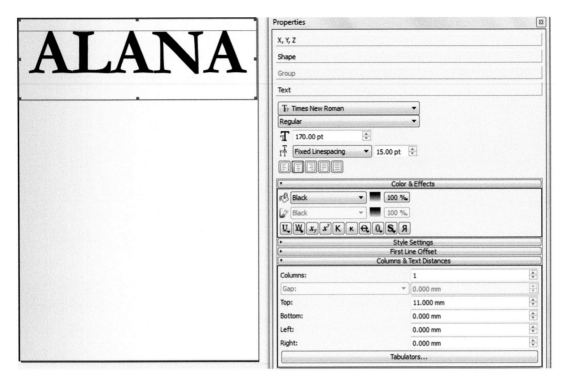

Figure 9-14. Formatting the logo using the Text tab

This will enable you to edit the outline stroke width of the text. In the Properties ➤ Text tab, select the Outline icon to turn the text into an outline. Increase the stroke width from 1 point to 4 points. Then choose your logo colors. For the stroke color, select black, and for the fill color, select gold. Finally, click the Shadowed Text icon to add some drop-shadow to the text. Then click to save the document. Your results should match Figure 9-15.

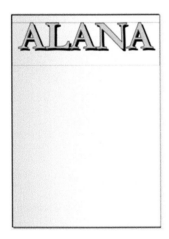

Figure 9-15. The text now has an outline and drop-shadow applied to it

Toggling the Background Layer

Throughout this exercise, there will be times where you will want to see the grid and then go back to seeing the background gradient. To toggle the background layer on and off, simply turn to the Layers dialog (Windows ➤ Layers) and uncheck the Visibility Checkbox for the Background layer, as shown in Figure 9-16.

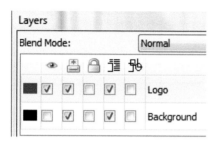

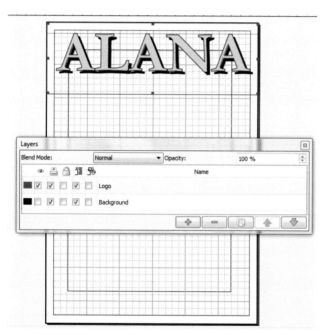

Figure 9-16. *Uncheck the Background layer visibility to see the grid*

Adjusting the Manual Tracking of the Logo

Now that you have selected your colors, you will probably want to adjust the tracking between the letters that make up the logo. After the initial placement of text on the page, it is likely that the characters will either look too squashed or too far apart. See Figure 9-17.

Figure 9-17. *The initial placement of characters with varied amounts of white space between them*

In all likelihood, you will want to kern the text of your logo so that the individual letters are on the point of touching. To do this, you will need to alter the manual tracking and the scaling width of your letters. You will also want to adjust the scaling height of the letters to 130.00%, as shown in Figure 9-18.

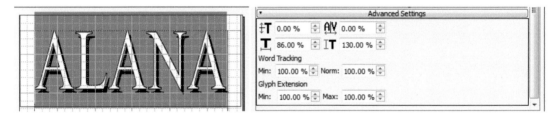

Figure 9-18. *The tracking and scaling settings for the magazine logo*

So open the Advanced Settings expander in the Text tab. With your cursor, highlight any pairs of characters that you wish to move closer together or further part, and use the Manual Tracking control to effect the desired change. A|V 0.00 %

Next, using the Scaling Height control, increase the scaling of the logo characters to around 130% using the upwards arrow. IT 130.00 %

Laying Out the Cover Page

Add a new layer to the document (by clicking the + button in the Layers dialog), and rename the layer as Image.

Now you can start laying out your cover page in Scribus, by adding your new PNG file. The PNG file is going to act as your CVI; it will help anchor the page and provide visual impact. Insert an image frame from a position just under the logo, and drag it all the way to the bottom of the page, so that it takes up roughly a third of the page, but leaves plenty of space by the side margins, as shown in Figure 9-19. Then insert the PNG image you created earlier in the chapter using GIMP.

Figure 9-19. *Position the newly edited image so that it inhabits the central column of the page and obscures some of the center of the logo*

You will probably have to scale the image to frame size (by right-clicking the image and selecting Scale to Frame Size).

Laying Out Your Text

Add a new layer using the Layer's dialog and name this layer Headlines.

Now the fun begins. You can start placing text frames around the side of the image. You can use the guides to do this simply by clicking the vertical rule that runs along the side of the page, and dragging one onto the page along the left margin, and then start adding your text frames.

Insert a text frame to the left of the model's head, and insert the text "Foodbanks To Die For" inside the frame. Then format the text so that it is left-aligned at 30 points Century Gothic Bold. In the Text tab, select the Outlines button and then select black as the stroke color and brown as the fill color (you can, if you wish, also use red as a fill color to emphasize certain words, as I have done).

Now copy the text frame a further five times and add the following text: "60 Fun Cake Mixes" "The Wombles: 40 Years On," "Connectionism: Where's The Harm?," "Travis T on that break-up" and "Sun, Sand & Ikea."

Place the text frames so that they run down both sides of the page, as shown in Figure 9-20. The completed page is shown on the right.

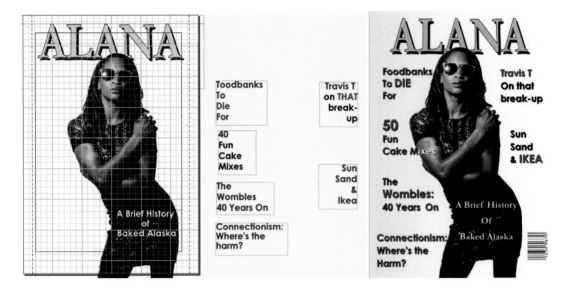

Figure 9-20. *The formatted text frames, before and after they have been moved into position on the page*

<ins>Inserting a Barcode</ins>

If you want the cover to look more realistic, you could add a bar code in the lower right corner of the page.

The details of how to obtain a code (such as an International Standard Serial Number) are beyond the scope of this book; however, you insert a barcode on your front cover by simply following the Insert ➤ Barcode menu. This will produce the Insert Barcode dialog shown in Figure 9-21.

Figure 9-21. *The Insert Barcode dialog*

There are barcodes for the U.S. Postal Service, the UK Royal Mail, QR codes, various retail codes, and codes used in the shipping and packing industry. However, the codes that interest me are the codes named EAN 2 and 3 (which are used for marking periodicals at retail point-of-sale terminals) and the ISBN (or International Standard Book Number), which is used for book labelling by publishers.

So select a barcode type, check the entries for Include Text in Barcode, and (if available) Include Checksum Digit, enter your code, and click OK. Next, click a point on the page with your cursor in the place where you want to paste it.

■ **Note** The barcode generator will sometimes refuse to work if your installation of Ghostscript is not up-to-date. (Ghostscript helps interpret your Postscript and PDF files.)

When I finished adjusting the positioning of the barcode, I had a front page that looked like the one in Figure 9-22.

Figure 9-22. *A magazine front cover with barcode*

ADDING A FOLIO

A folio is an identifying label that often accompanies the page number, and you are going to add one to the foot of the page. This feature could be saved as a style and applied to the document as a master page.

So, begin by going to Page 2, and creating a text frame along the bottom left corner of the page on the left (known as the verso page). Create another text frame for the bottom right corner of the page on the right (known as the recto page).

Fill your text frames with the title of the publication (which is Alana Magazine), the month of publication (which in this case is May), and the page number. The frames should appear just like the ones illustrated in Figure 9-23.

Alana Magazine   *May 2015*   *Page 3*

Figure 9-23. *The folio and page numbers*

If the magazine were larger, I might have used master pages for the folios, but for this exercise, I have only used folios on pages 3, 6, and 7. The name of the publication and the issue date are also included as part of the footer.

CREATING A MASTHEAD

The *masthead* is a single-page informational overview that you will often find on Pages 2 or 3 of many high street magazines. It lists the editorial staff, the publishers, the publication details, and contact information relating to the production of the magazine.

In the UK, the masthead is sometimes referred to as the *impressum*, or imprint, and the word masthead itself is often used to refer to a magazine's logo or nameplate, as it appears at the top of the front page.

In this section, you will learn about how to design a masthead from scratch in Scribus. For the sake of clarity, I have used the American interpretation of the word masthead, meaning a page given over to the staff listing and publication details.

Go to Page 2 of your magazine document.

Add a background frame to the page by choosing the Rectangle shape on the toolbar  and then extend it across the entire page, as shown in Figure 9-24.

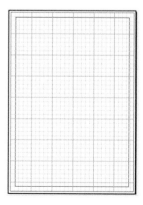

Figure 9-24. *Extend the shape across the whole page*

Insert a long text frame down the right side and color it black in the Text tab. Copy and paste some small image frames along the right side. I pasted in about 10 frames, as you can see in Figure 9-25.

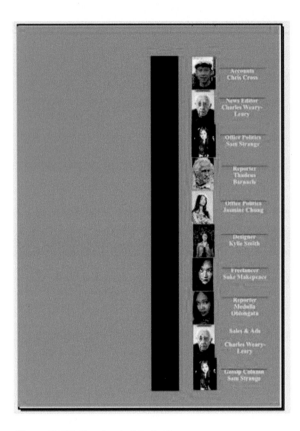

Figure 9-25. *Pasting in 10 photos*

Visit Pixabay.com and search for 10 faces that you can link to the 10 image frames, and use as portraits in the staff listing (see Figure 9-26).

Figure 9-26. *Portraits taken from Pixaby.com for use in the staff listing*

You should end up with a layout like the one in Figure 9-27.

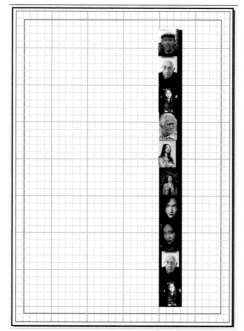
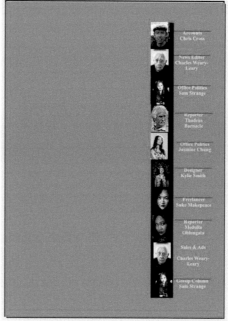

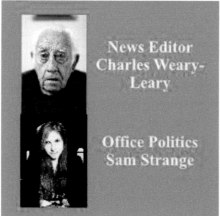

Figure 9-27. *The layout of the staff profiles*

Select the background frame, and in the Properties Color tab, turn the fill color to cyan.

Create a text frame to act as the first entry for the staff list, copy it, and paste it all the way down the right side.

Edit the text frames for the staff list by adding an imaginary name and job title to each frame. Then, using the Color tab, set the background (Fill) color to cyan and the color of the font (in the Text tab) to white. Center the text and use 14 points Times New Roman Bold for the font. See Figure 9-28 for a visual guide.

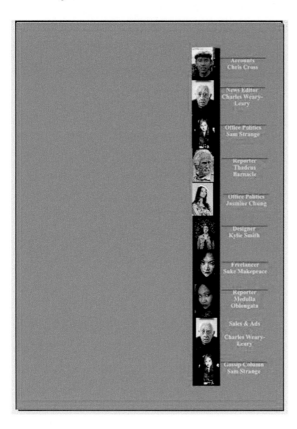

Figure 9-28. *The staff listing with photos*

Add a vertical guide to run along the left side of the vertical line of image frames, as shown in Figure 9-29.

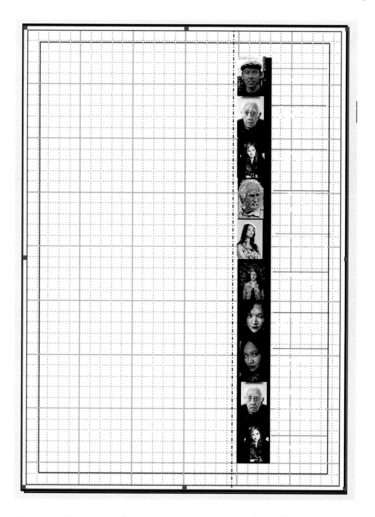

Figure 9-29. *A guide (which has been moved to the left) was used to align the photos*

Figure 9-30 shows the final result.

Figure 9-30. *The staff portraits*

These portraits can be selected and snapped to the guide (Page ➤ Snap to Guide).

Add the portrait of the Editor, as shown in Figure 9-31. To do so, insert an image frame in the top left corner of the page, and insert another photographic portrait in it. You can download a copy of my photo from the Apress website at www.apress.com.

Figure 9-31. *Portrait of the Editor*

Alongside the Editor's portrait, insert a text frame to represent the editorial heading. Underneath it, run a narrow horizontal text frame to act as an advertising banner. Using the Properties Color tab, give the frame a red background fill, and add some yellow text for the stroke in the Text tab. See Figure 9-32 for reference.

Figure 9-32. *The hedcut and title for the Editor's letter*

Select each of the image frames down the right side, and then select Snap to Grid from the Page menu. This has the effect of straightening them so that they run in a straight vertical line.

The photos that I used in the staff list are all different sizes. In order to straighten the appearance of the image frames on their right side, insert a long rectangular shape as a column that inhabits the area taken up by the staff portraits. In the Properties Color tab, select a fill color of black. It will now obscure the view of the photos, so select it and then select Item ➤ Level ➤ Lower. Your portraits should reappear, with a uniform straight line running down both sides.

Add a text frame to represent the Editorial letter. Add some sample text in Latin to represent the body of the letter (File ➤ Sample Text), and add an introductory line at the top, and a signature at the bottom, using the font Handscript SF Regular at 20 points. Add a white background in the Properties Color tab. See Figure 9-33 for reference.

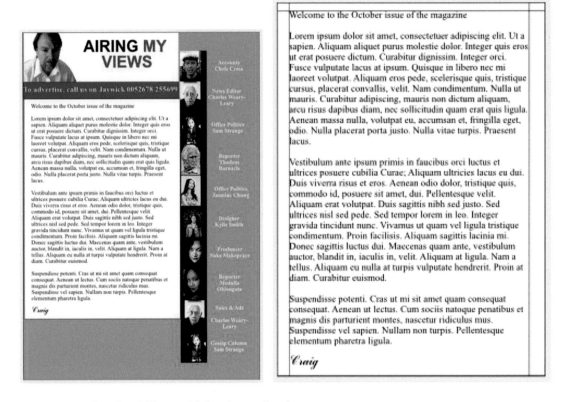

Figure 9-33. *The Editorial letter added to the masthead*

Add a rectangular text at the bottom of the page for the publication date, and then add some text, center it, and give it a cyan background (see Figure 9-34).

Figure 9-34. *The text frame for the publication date*

Finally, select the rectangular shape that covers the entire page, and give it a blue fill color in the Color tab.

And there you have it: a masthead that looks almost as good as the ones displayed inside many local magazines. See Figure 9-35.

Figure 9-35. *The finished masthead*

HOW TO DESIGN A PRINTED ADVERT

In this section, you will learn how to design a printed advert in Scribus.

An effective printed advert requires a headline or banner, a visual image that helps to reflect your message, and a call to action that encourages you to contact the seller.

The advertisement you are going to design contains all three elements (see Figure 9-36). It contains a headline banner, a photo obtained from Pixabay.com, a call to action, and some contact details.

Figure 9-36. *The elements of your printed advertisement*

The advert is made up of six elements.

First, there is the headline text frame containing the name of the business, the nature of the business, and the website address, shown in Figure 9-37. The name is centered and set at 65 points Script MT Bold Regular. The supporting text is 18 points Arial Regular.

Figure 9-37. *Featuring the name and website address of the business*

The photo shown in Figure 9-38 is the result of a search for interior designs at Pixabay.com. It is more than adequate in terms of PPI for a decent print image (759 x 759), given that actual PPI is the resolution of the image at 100% size.

Figure 9-38. *This photo can be downloaded from pixabay.com*

The advert also contains a list of unique selling points, consisting of a text frame with internal left margins and a 20 point fixed linespacing, as shown in Figure 9-39.

Local Office & Easy Parking	Good Customer Service
Local Knowledge	Online Database
Accurate Valuations	Guided Viewings

Figure 9-39. *The universal selling points*

I have also added a Contact frame with the address and telephone number, formatted in 30 points Times New Roman with the phone number in Bold, as shown in Figure 9-40.

01255 539053902
3 The Parade
Jaywick Sands

Figure 9-40. *The contact details*

And finally, I added two transparent shapes that were flipped horizontally, and then vertically, and then horizontally again in the XYZ tab, so that they fit together to form a rectangle. You'll explore the flipping process in more detail in a moment. The font was set at 20 points Times New Roman Regular. See Figure 9-41.

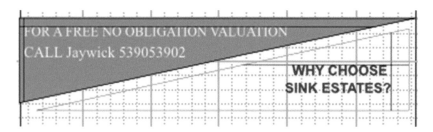

Figure 9-41. *The two triangles, with the lower one still awaiting its formatting*

Working with Shapes

Format the text and image frames with the formatting instructions described above. When you have finished, you should have six objects that are ready to be moved into position on the page, as shown in Figure 9-42.

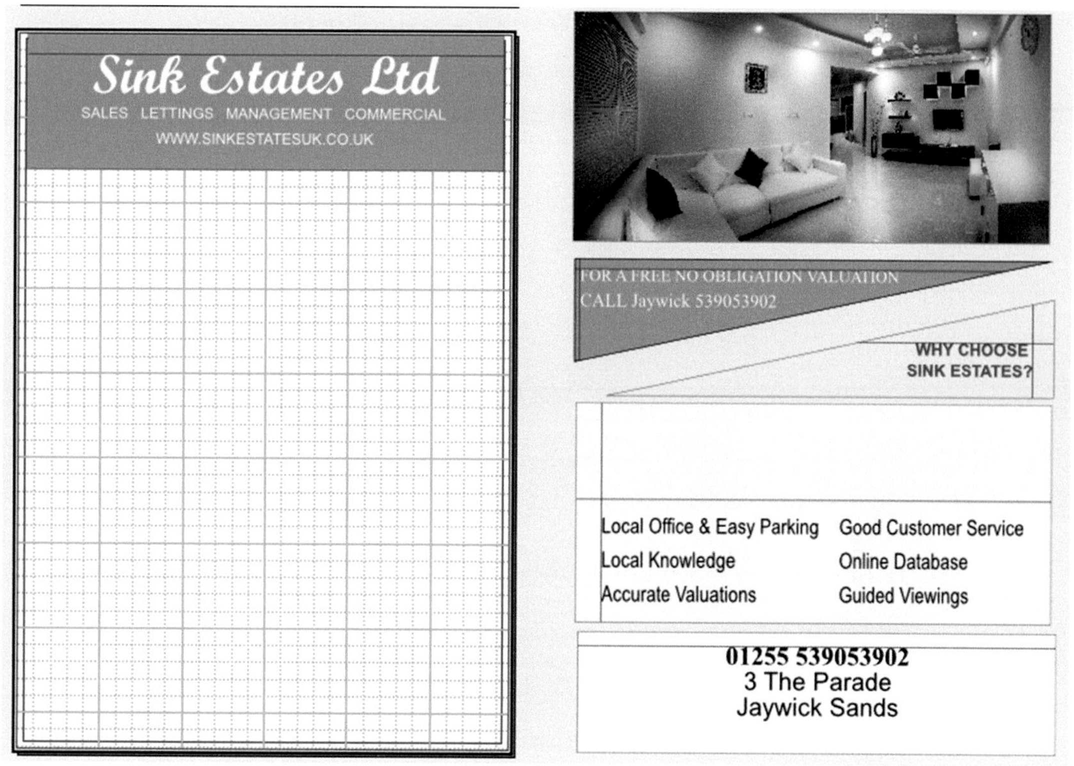

Figure 9-42. *The individual elements of the advert*

Move the logo or banner to the top of the page. Then move the photo so that it fits underneath it. Move the contact details to the bottom, and then fit the unique selling points above that.

That just leaves the formatting of the call to action frame, which consists of a set of two triangles. As a way of emphasizing the call to action in the advert, I inserted and flipped two triangular shapes so that they fit together to form a rectangle.

Insert this triangular shape from the list of shapes on the toolbar, shown in Figure 9-43.

Figure 9-43. *The triangle shape*

Select it, copy it (Edit ➤ Copy), and then paste it below the original (Edit ➤ Paste).

This gives you two individual triangles, as shown in Figure 9-44.

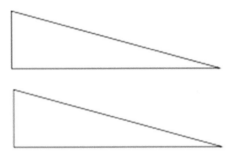

Figure 9-44. *The two triangles, ready for flipping*

Now flip them around using the Flip Horizontal button.

Take the second triangle and flip it using the Flip Vertical button.

Then flip it horizontally again, using the Flip Horizontal button again.

This will leave you with two compatible triangular shapes that can join up to form a rectangle, as shown in Figure 9-45.

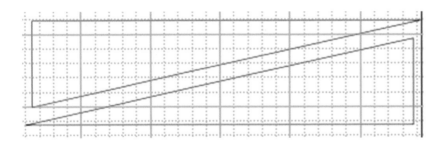

Figure 9-45. *The two triangular shapes after their final flipping*

Select each one in turn and select Item ➤ Convert to ➤ Text Frame. Open the top one in the Story Editor, type in the call to action text, right-align it, and format it at 20 points.

Your finished ad should look like the one in Figure 9-46.

Figure 9-46. *The finished advert*

Creating an Advertorial

An advertorial is an extended advertisement found in magazines that resembles an editorial in style but promotes the advertiser's product or services. They are very common in both the local press and in free-to-reader magazines, so this magazine ought to have one.

Figure 9-47 shows an advertorial layout for the magazine. It uses a gradient for the header, two image frames, and three columns of text, and it took about ten minutes to paste it all up. The image of the mobile phone and laptop were obtained from www.freeimages.com.

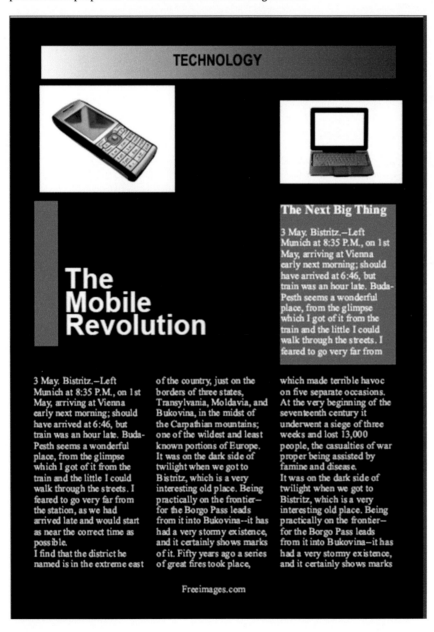

Figure 9-47. *The advertorial*

318

Note that you need to add a line of text indicating that the advertorial is an advert (and not a feature).

EXPORTING TO PDF

It's probably down to a question of individual taste, but I find it easier to export and view these pages in Adobe Reader PDF format, using the two-page view, before creating the final PDF file. The reason for this is that it is easy to check the symmetry of the pages using the PDF two-page view. One can then return to Scribus and quickly make the necessary adjustments.

So exporting your Scribus file to PDF is something that you might want to do more than once before you produce the finished article.

When exporting this magazine file to PDF, you will need to think about the version of PDF that you wish to use. The Preflight Verifier will produce its diagnostic check, but it will also ask you for a PDF profile. PDF 1.4 is fine if you have not used any layers, but as some of my pages contain layers, they work better in 1.5.

So select File ➤ Export ➤ As PDF, and when prompted, choose PDF version 1.5, choosing (for the sake of this exercise) to "Ignore Errors." This will produce the Save As PDF dialog box, shown in Figure 9-48.

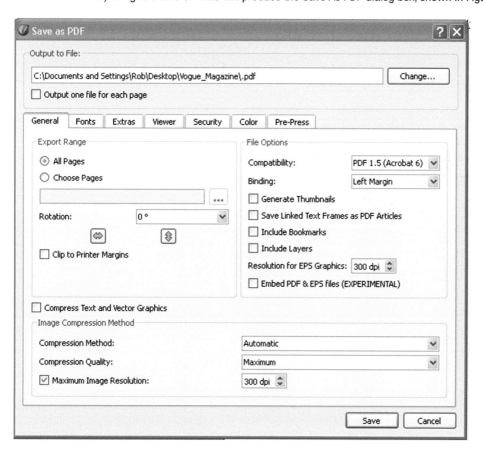

Figure 9-48. *The Save As PDF dialog box*

Select the page range that you wish to produce in PDF and the resolution of your images. Most print shops require a minimum of 300 dpi.

Look at the Fonts tab to check that the file includes all the fonts you have used. Ideally, you will want to embed all your fonts so that the font is saved along with the PDF file. However, some fonts cannot be embedded in Scribus, and when this happens, Scribus will automatically move the fonts to the Outline box so that they will be outlined instead. With outlining, the text is converted into paths and fills in order to keep the appearance of the type.

In the Color tab, select Printer as the Output Intended For option, as shown in Figure 9-49.

Figure 9-49. *The Color tab set to Printer*

Finally, in the Pre-Press tab, check the boxes for crop marks and bleed settings. Also, check the Use Document Bleeds box, as shown in Figure 9-50.

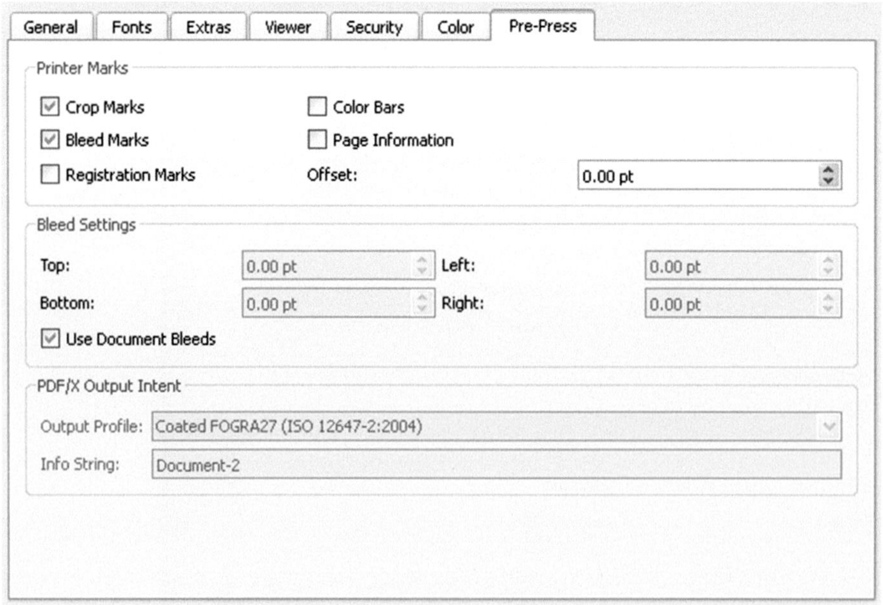

Figure 9-50. *The Pre-Press tab*

Crop marks are the lines in the corner of your document that show the printer where to trim the paper. Check the setting to Use Document Bleeds so that your document margins and bleed settings are the same as when you first set up the file.

Finally, when you are satisfied with the selections that you have made, click the Save button.

EXPORTING YOUR PDF FILES TO THE WEB

It is possible to configure the PDF Export dialog to produce a lightweight version of your PDF that is small enough to post onto the Web or send as an attachment via email.

To export your PDF file for the Web or as an email attachment, select the Screen or Web option in the Color tab of the PDF Export dialog, as shown in Figure 9-51.

Figure 9-51. *Saving your PDF in a web-friendly format*

You might also consider reducing the image resolution by entering an image resolution of 72 dpi in the File Options section of the General tab. See Figure 9-52.

Figure 9-52. *Using an image resolution of 72 dpi in the General tab*

If your PDF file is still too large and you need to reduce its size still further, you can check the box to Compress Text and Vector Graphics, as shown in Figure 9-53.

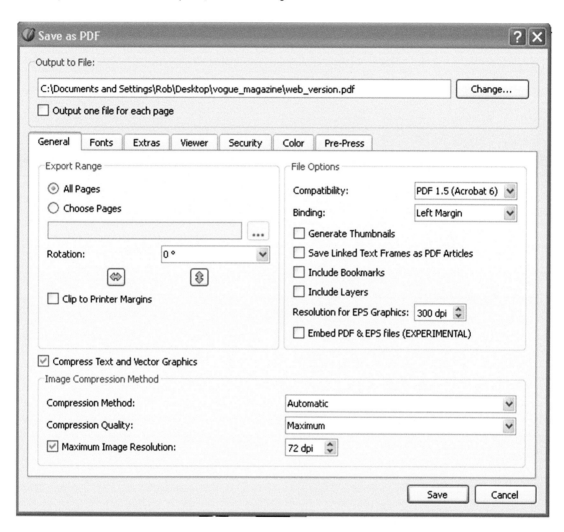

Figure 9-53. *Reducing the resolution to 72 dpi and checking the box for Text Compression*

Summary

This chapter consisted of several practical design exercises. You examined the use of whitespace in document design, You designed a front cover for a women's magazine, and you designed a logo using a drop shadow effect. You also designed a magazine masthead, an advertorial, and an editorial letter, and you looked at how to add bleeds to your page layouts, ready for export to the high street printer.

In the next and final chapter, you will be looking at the ways in which Scribus can make your experience of PDFs more interactive.

CHAPTER 10

■ ■ ■

Interactive PDFs

In Chapter 9, you designed some pages for a local magazine and exported them in two different PDF formats, one for the printer, and one for publishing on the Web.

In this tenth and final chapter, you will be looking at the ways in which you can customize how your web-based PDF is viewed, so as to make it easier to navigate between the pages and add notes in the sidebar.

You will also learn how to turn your PDF file into a slide show presentation, and how you can use Scribus to create interactive forms in the PDF format.

In this chapter, you will modify your Portable Document Format files by doing the following:

- Learning how to add bookmarks

- Learning how to add hyperlinks

- Learning how to add page transition effects

- Learning how to create a PDF form

- Learning how to modify that form using JavaScript

Adding Page Transition Effects to Your PDF Files

As a document designer, Scribus has the ability to let you determine how your PDF file will appear when it is opened in a PDF viewer (although these visual customizations tend to work best when they are viewed in Adobe Acrobat Reader). You should think carefully before customizing your PDF files, however, because some of the non-Adobe PDF readers do not support customization.

The options for customizing the visual appearance of the PDF can be found within two tabs in the Save as PDF dialog box: the Viewer tab and the Extras tab. Let's look first at the Extras tab.

If you have a PDF file that you would like to use as a slide presentation, it is possible to modify the appearance of that file in the Save as PDF dialog box, before it is exported as a PDF file (see Figure 10-1).

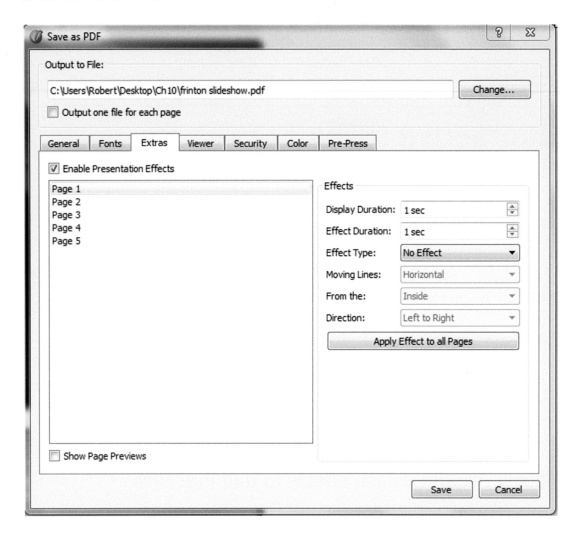

Figure 10-1. The Extra tab in the Save As PDF dialog box

The Extras tab contains a list of the settings that will enable you to create page transition effects for your PDF presentation. Page transitions are special effects that appear in between the pages of your presentation, and they are best viewed in a reliable PDF viewer, such as Adobe Acrobat Reader.

There is a choice of special effects to choose from, and it is possible (although not advisable) to use a different transition effect for each page. If you do decide to add a transition effect to your presentation, I recommend using only one effect per presentation; too many effects can spoil the show.

EXERCISE: ADD A PAGE TRANSITION TO YOUR PRESENTATION

You can introduce page transition effects into your PDF file at the same stage that you export your Scribus document as a PDF file: in the Save as PDF dialog box.

So open the Scribus file to which your wish to apply your transition effects, and select Export ➤ As PDF from the File menu. Ignore any warnings that you see in the Preflight Verifier and go to the Save as PDF dialog box.

Now, select the Extras tab that you looked at in Figure 10-1. You will see a list of settings for managing page transitions, as shown in Figure 10-2.

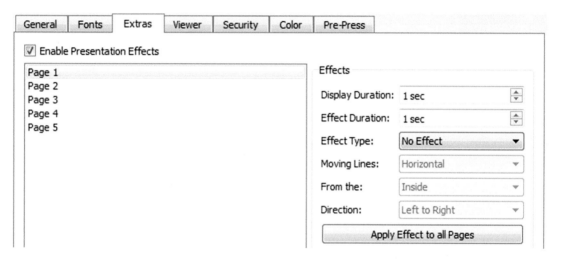

Figure 10-2. *The controls for managing page transitions*

You will need to ensure that the checkbox labeled Enable Presentation Effects is checked, as this will enable you to choose an effect type. Then all you need to do is choose your settings for the page duration and effect duration, and then choose your page transition effect.

There are ten transition effects to choose from: Blinds, Box, Dissolve, Glitter, Split, Wipe, Push, Cover, Uncover, and Fade (although Push, Cover, Uncover, and Fade are not available in MAC OSX).

Also in the Effects panel are the settings for controlling the starting point and direction of movement of some of the transition effects.

Checking the checkbox to Show Page Previews will enable you to obtain some thumbnails of the images in the Preview pane, as shown in Figure 10-3, although these page previews do not actively preview the transition effects themselves; instead, they provide thumbnails of the pages.

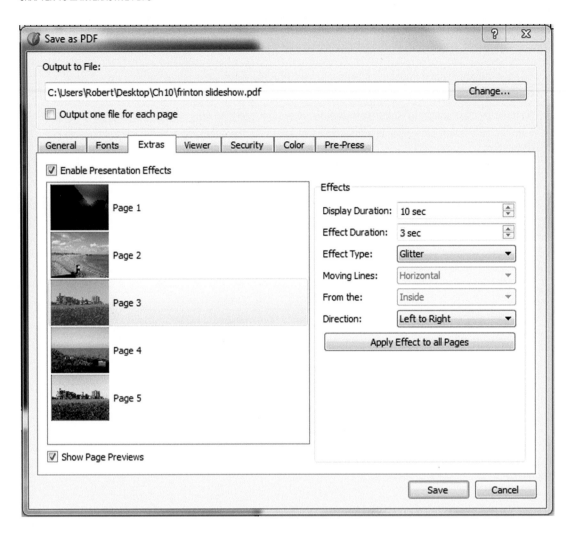

Figure 10-3. *The Extras tab, with Show Page Previews enabled*

In Figure 10-3, the Glitter effect is chosen to run from left to right. The Display Duration has been set to 10 seconds, and the Effect Duration is set to 3 seconds.

When you have finished setting the parameters for your page transition effect, select the page to which you want to apply the effect, and select your effect. When that is done, you can go ahead and export the PDF by clicking Save in the General tab. Make sure that the Color tab output is set for Screen/Web or Greyscale.

Testing Your PDF

Open up the PDF in your Acrobat Reader and observe the effect as the pixelated glitter sweeps across the slides from left to right.

The Viewer Tab

The Viewer tab, which is shown in Figure 10-4, enables you to choose how your PDF file will appear when it is displayed in the PDF reader. The Document Layout panel on the left lets you choose between different layout styles, such as Single Page, Double Page Right, Double Page Left, or Continuous.

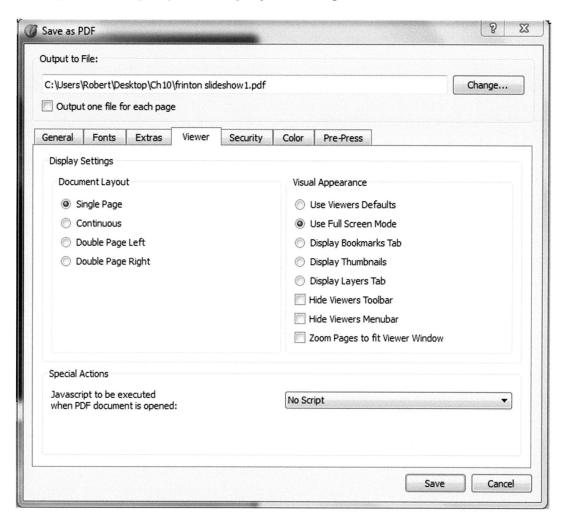

Figure 10-4. *The Viewer tab in the Save As PDF dialog box*

If you select the layout for Double Page Right, the PDF file will open in a traditional book format, with the front page on the right side, followed by a sequence of double pages placed side-by-side. However, the default setting is for a Single Page layout. This is generally thought to be easier to navigate, and (depending on how the reader is viewing it) it could be said to offer a more comfortable viewing experience for the reader.

You can also modify the visual appearance of your PDF file so that it displays bookmarks, thumbnails, or alters the page so as to fit the viewer's window.

Adding Thumbnails

It's actually rather fun to add thumbnails to your document. Thumbnails provide a fancy alternative to a table of contents, and they make it easy for the reader to navigate through your documents.

As illustrated in Figure 10-6, you can display thumbnail images down the left side of your PDF file by ensuring that you have checked the box for thumbnail display in the Viewer tab of the Save as PDF dialog box, which is shown in Figure 10-5.

Thumbnails form a part of the next exercise.

EXERCISE: CUSTOMISING THE APPEARANCE OF YOUR PDF

Let's create a PDF using a double-page format.

Open one of the documents that you created in the last chapter (I used the magazine center spread), open the Save As PDF dialog box, and then select the Viewer tab. In the Document Layout section on the left side, select Double Page Right, as shown in Figure 10-5.

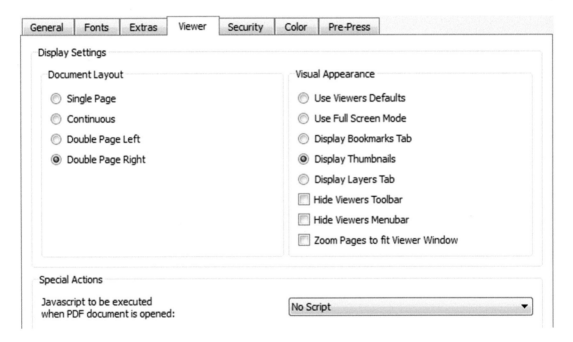

Figure 10-5. *Selecting Double Page Right in the Viewer tab's Document Layout panel*

In the Visual Appearance column on the right side, select Display Thumbnails.

Now generate the PDF. When you open up your PDF in Adobe Reader, you should see your thumbnails, as shown in Figure 10-6.

Figure 10-6. *The PDF for the magazine layout with added thumbnails on the left side*

Thumbnails are useful as they aid the reader's navigation if there is no table of contents.

Inserting Bookmarks

Bookmarks provide another way of enhancing the navigation within a PDF file. They are often used to navigate between a table of contents and the destination content. Note, however, that some frames (such as image frames that do not contain text) cannot be used as PDF bookmarks.

EXERCISE: CREATE A BOOKMARK

To create a bookmark, right-click the frame that you wish to bookmark and, from the context menu, select PDF Options ➤ Is PDF Bookmark. Or, if you prefer, use the same path in the Item menu.

Now, go into the General tab of the Save As PDF dialog box, as shown in Figure 10-7.

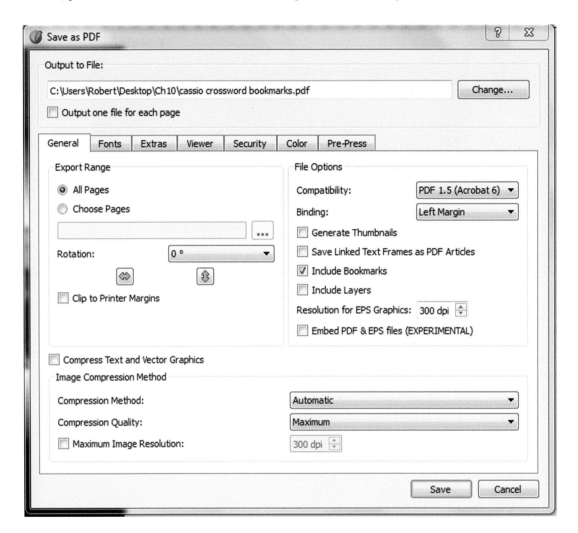

Figure 10-7. The General tab, with a check in the checkbox to include bookmarks

Check the box to include bookmarks and make sure that the button for displaying bookmarks is also selected in the Viewer tab. When you come to generate your PDF, you will notice that your bookmarks have been added along the left column, as shown in Figure 10-8.

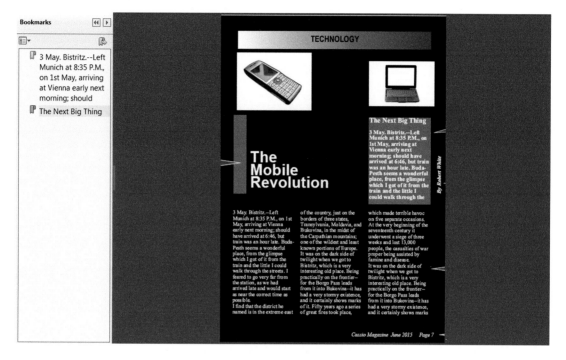

Figure 10-8. *A column with two bookmarks is displayed down the left side*

Adding Hyperlinks

Once you have got the hang of preparing your PDFs in Scribus, you will probably want to add links into your documents so that you can navigate to other chapters within them and to their associated websites.

The good news is that you can add hyperlinks to your PDF files in Scribus, and they work just like the hyperlinks used to link web pages.

PDF links in Scribus help the reader to navigate between one part of a document and another, but they can also be used to navigate to other documents, web pages, and email addresses.

There are three levels of hyperlink in Scribus: internal links, external links, and external web links.

INTERNAL LINKS

To establish a link between two parts of the same document, first select the Insert Link tool on the PDF Tools Toolbar.

With the Link tool selected, draw a rectangle around the source text. (Alternatively, to make a link on an existing frame, right-click and choose PDF Options ➤ Is PDF Annotation, then right-click and choose PDF Options ➤ Annotation Properties.

Introduction

If you now double-click the source text frame, this should produce the appearance of the Annotation Properties box, as shown in Figure 10-9.

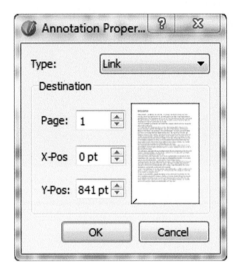

Figure 10-9. *The Annotation Properties box appears when you double-click your source text frame*

Select Link from the drop-down list, and under Destination, select the page number that you wish to nominate as your destination page. If you fancy being a bit more adventurous, you can try using the X and Y coordinates to place your link with more precision, although these coordinates may not be suitable for all purposes. There is a cross-hair cursor that will move up the page as you decrease the numbers for Y-Pos, and it will move across the page as you increase the numbers for the X-Pos setting. But you are better off clicking on the page preview to set the coordinates.

Generate your PDF in Scribus in the usual way and open up the PDF file in the Adobe Reader. When you reach your link, click it with the mouse pointer. The link will now take you to your destination text.

EXTERNAL WEB LINKS

The easiest way to demonstrate how to create an external web link is to set one up in your current document. Let's add a link to the official Scribus website (www.scribus.net) within the text.

Start by clicking the Insert Link Annotation tool.

Next, draw a rectangle around the source text, which in this case ought to refer to Scribus.

Designed using **Scribus 1.45**

After you've done that, double-click the box. This will bring up the Annotations Properties dialog box again, only this time you choose an external web link, as shown in Figure 10-10.

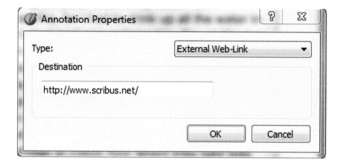

Figure 10-10. *The Annotations Properties dialog with settings for the web link and destination web address*

Enter the web address as the destination page for your link, and then click OK.

Most of the time, you will want to enter a web address, but it is also possible to enter an email address as long as you enter it in the usual format, which consists of a user name, followed by an @ symbol, followed by the domain name, as in somebody@somewhere.net.

Generate you PDF as usual, and then test your hypertext link in the PDF. I tend to work in Adobe Acrobat, but most PDF readers will automatically open a web browser when needed. My Firefox web browser opened up at the correct site with no prompting. Your link should now take you to the Scribus website. (Note that most PDF readers automatically parse URLs that are in the document text and provide links automatically for them. However, the URL will have to be displayed in full rather than as a nice-to-read alternative).

TEXT ANNOTATIONS

If you find yourself in a situation where you need to add notes to your documents, it is possible to add them in Scribus before the document is exported as a PDF file. Annotations enable you to provide notes to accompany the main body of text in a Scribus document.

To create a text annotation, select the Insert Link Annotation tool again, and draw a frame around the text that you wish to annotate. Then double-click the frame and, instead of selecting a link, select Text in the Annotation Properties dialog, as shown in Figure 10-11.

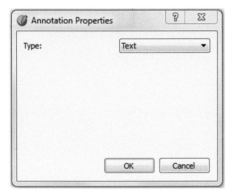

Figure 10-11. *The Annotation Properties dialog set to receive textual input in the PDF file*

And that is all there is to it. Generate your PDF file in the usual way, and when you open it up in your Adobe Reader, you will notice a small notepad icon by your selected text. Double-click this icon, and you will open up a text frame in the right column that is ready to receive your notes, as shown in Figure 10-12.

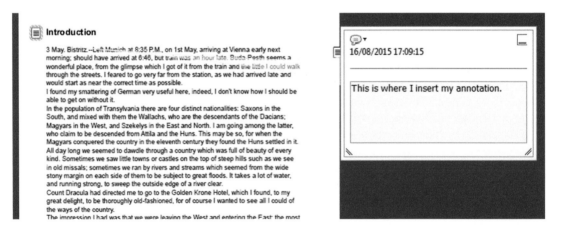

Figure 10-12. *Double-clicking the notepad icon in the main text opens up a text box on the right side of your PDF*

You can annotate your text here, and when you have finished adding your comments, you can access more settings by clicking the quotation bubble (if you are using Adobe Reader) in the top left corner of the annotation box. 💬▾

Or you can minimize the annotation by clicking the minimize symbol in the top right corner. ▭

Interactive Forms

In addition to creating slide presentations, Scribus can also create PDF forms that contain interactive elements. These forms can contain text fields (where you can add your own information), checkboxes (which allow you to enter a check mark that represents a yes or no answer), and list boxes and combo boxes, which provide you with a list of options.

In this section, you will learn how to add interactive elements to a PDF form so that the recipient can enter some data. While it is possible to print out the data on these forms, it is not so easy to save that data; you will probably need Adobe Acrobat X Pro in order to do so.

Using an interactive form, a recipient is able to add their own data to the form, which can then be printed, or saved and emailed back to the original sender.

If you are going to start designing PDF forms, you need to make yourself familiar with the PDF Toolbar, shown in Figure 10-13.

Figure 10-13. *The PDF Toolbar, which you will be using a lot when you create PDF forms*

Most of what you will do when making PDF forms involves the use of the PDF Toolbar. The toolbar can be found on the right of the main Scribus toolbar, although some of its options can also be found in the Item ➤ PDF menu, and any item context menu. It contains tools for creating buttons, text fields, checkboxes, combo boxes, and list boxes, as well as the tools you have been using to create annotations and hyperlinks.

So let's create a simple PDF form. Select the Insert PDF Text Field tool that is located in the right corner of the Scribus Toolbar. ▤

Next, select the Insert PDF Text Field tool that is located in the right corner of the Scribus Toolbar.

Move your mouse to the right of the Name field.

When you lick your pointer, the Enter Object Size box will appear, as shown in Figure 10-14.

DESIGN A SIMPLE PDF FORM

The first thing to do is to design a form in Scribus using ordinary text frames. Generally speaking, you create your forms as you would a normal document intended for printing. Any features that can be found in Scribus can be added to your form: tables, text frames, images, and shapes. Then you use the PDF Toolbar to activate those areas in your form that you wish to use for interactive feedback.

Let's make this a very simple form suitable for ordering seats in a multiplex cinema, based on the structure shown in Figure 10-14.

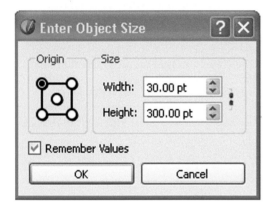

Figure 10-14. *The Enter Object Size box*

Enter a height of 30 points and a width of 300 points. You should end up with a rectangular shape that is exactly the right size for your name box.

Adding a Text Field

Now you are going to repeat the process with the fields for the address, town, and ZIP code. Select the Insert Text Field tool and drag out fields next to the labels for the address, town, and ZIP code, as shown in Figure 10-15.

Figure 10-15. *A basic form (left) that you will be turning into an interactive PDF form (right)*

The form as it has been designed so far contains eight text frames. However, using the PDF Toolbar, you can insert some PDF elements, including five text fields, one checkbox, and a combo box.

Now that you have a basic design structure for the form, the next stage is to add some interactive elements. You'll start with the text field.

Adding a Checkbox

You add the checkbox in the same way as you did with the text field. Select the Input PDF Checkbox tool on the Toolbar.

Move your pointer down to the right side of the entry for Non-Smoking, and drag the pointer over the checkbox area to create a small square that's about 30 x 30 points.

Adding a Combo Box

Finally, you need to add a combo box for the list of seats that are available. Select the Input PDF Combo Box tool on the Toolbar.

The Edit Object Size box should appear. Enter the required size of the combo box, which in this case is about 360 pts wide and 30 pts high. Click OK. With the Combo Box selected, right-click it and open the Story Editor.

With the Story Editor open, type in each seating area to be included in the list, but use a separate line for each entry, as shown in Figure 10-16.

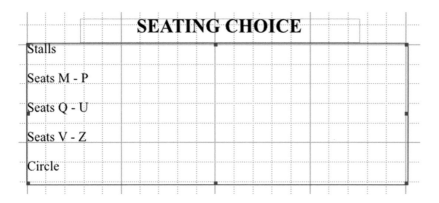

SEATING CHOICE

Stalls

Seats M - P

Seats Q - U

Seats V - Z

Circle

Figure 10-16. *The entries for the combo box, which were made using the Story Editor*

Finally, save and exit the Story Editor by clicking the green checkbox.

Now when you try saving the form as a PDF file, and then open it in the Adobe Reader, you should find that the combo box works perfectly.

When you open the PDF form, you will find that the interactive elements work perfectly, and that you can enter and save the text that you enter in the text fields, as displayed in Figure 10-17.

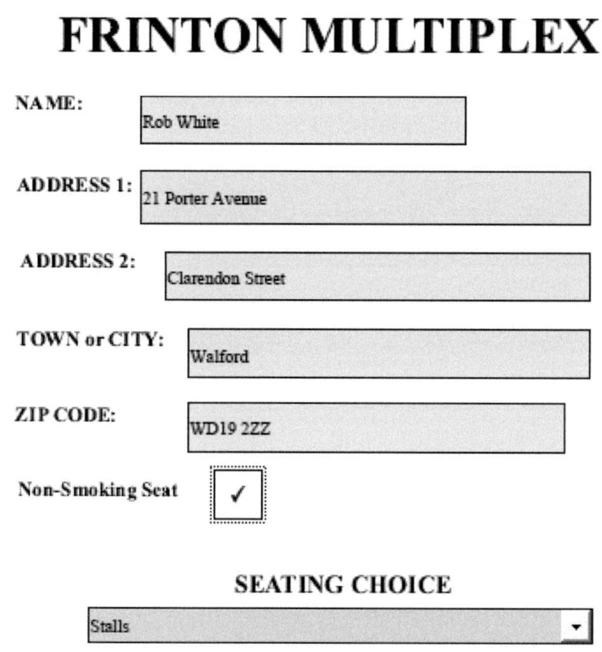

FRINTON MULTIPLEX

NAME: Rob White

ADDRESS 1: 21 Porter Avenue

ADDRESS 2: Clarendon Street

TOWN or CITY: Walford

ZIP CODE: WD19 2ZZ

Non-Smoking Seat ✓

SEATING CHOICE

Stalls ▼

Figure 10-17. *The completed booking form for the multiplex cinema*

Editing PDF Forms with JavaScript

So far, so good! Now that you have learned how to create and edit a PDF form, you are probably wondering if you can customize the elements and actions of the form still further. The answer is yes, but you can only do so by attaching some JavaScript code to the elements on the form.

Unfortunately, a comprehensive introduction to JavaScript programming is outside the scope of this book, but there are plenty of examples that are available on the Scribus Wiki. You are going to finish by adding two new features to your booking form. One is a text field that inserts the current date when the PDF is opened, and the other is a Print button for sending the form to the printer. Both of these projects are taken from the Scribus Wiki, which is a really valuable source of information for Scribus users.

You can find the code snippet for this JavaScript project at

http://wiki.scribus.net/canvas/How_to_enhance_your_PDF_forms_with_JavaScript.

EXERCISE: INSERTING THE CURRENT DATE INTO THE PDF

Go back to your version of the cinema booking form, and add a text frame label for the date of booking, as shown in Figure 10-18.

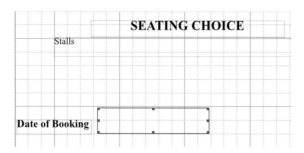

Figure 10-18. *Adding a text frame label and a text entry field to the booking form*

Then, using the PDF Toolbar, add a text field to run alongside the Date of Booking entry, by dragging out a rectangle alongside it.

Now you need to edit the text field for the Date of Booking entry. So double-click the text field to open the Field Properties Box. To the right of the entry for Name, enter the name DateField, as shown in Figure 10-19.

Figure 10-19. *The Field Properties box with the name DateField entered at the top*

Click OK. Now you need to add a function to the text field. So go to the Edit menu and select JavaScripts. When the Edit JavaScripts box opens, click the Add button, as shown in Figure 10-20.

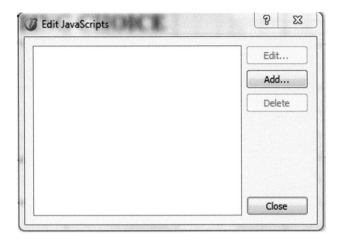

Figure 10-20. *The Edit JavaScripts box*

When you click on the Add button, the New Script window will open. Accept the default name that is offered and enter the following script:

```
function date() {
   var fld = this.getField("DateField");
   fld.value = util.printd("dd mmmm yyyy",new Date());
   }
   date(); // call my function
```

Don't worry if it does not make a lot of sense. I simply copied and pasted it from the Scribus Wiki web page mentioned:

http://wiki.scribus.net/canvas/How_to_enhance_your_PDF_forms_with_JavaScript

Now all you need to do is OK the editor, close the Edit JavaScripts dialog, and generate a new PDF file.

When you come to saving the file in the Save As PDF dialog, be careful to add the JavaScript that you have just created. In particular, you should go to the bottom of the Viewer tab, and select New_Script in the panel marked Special Actions (as illustrated in Figure 10-21). If you don't, your JavaScript will not work.

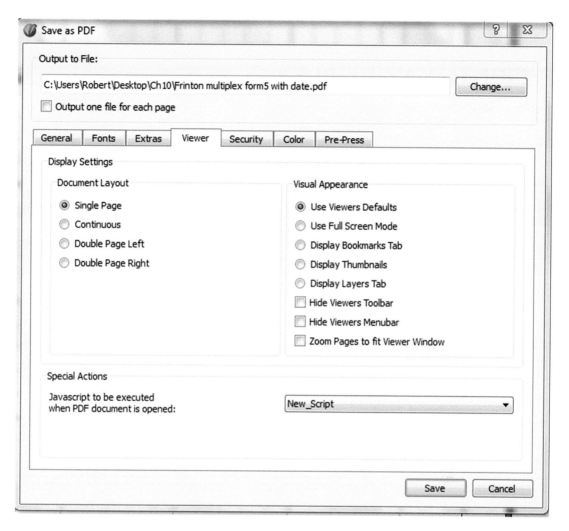

Figure 10-21. *Selecting the New_Script JavaScript in the Viewer tab*

When you generate a new PDF, you should find that the current date is included in the form, as shown in Figure 10-22.

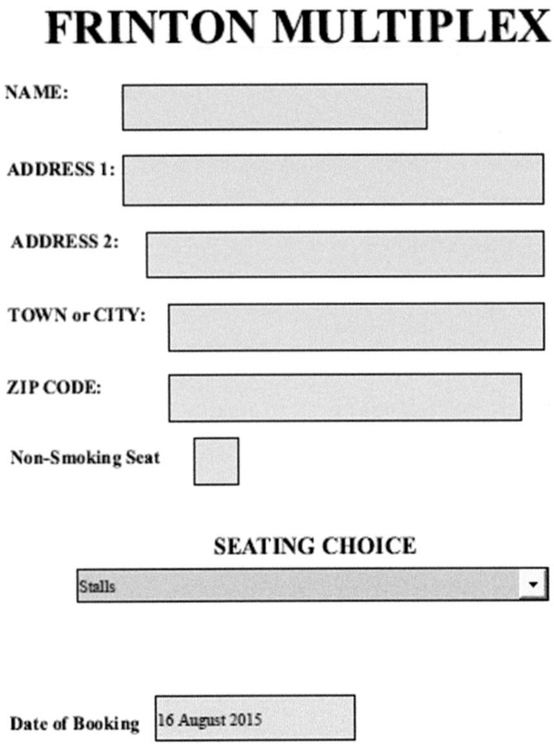

FRINTON MULTIPLEX

NAME:

ADDRESS 1:

ADDRESS 2:

TOWN or CITY:

ZIP CODE:

Non-Smoking Seat

SEATING CHOICE

Stalls ▼

Date of Booking | 16 August 2015

Figure 10-22. *The finished form complete with the current date*

Summary

Thank you for coming along on this exploration of Scribus 1.4.5. I hope you'll agree with me that it is a marvelous page layout system that should suit everyone from publishers, academics, and students to artists and graphic designers.

In this chapter, you learned some of the things that Scribus can do with your PDF files. I have been impressed with the ease with which it is possible to insert hyperlinks, bookmarks, and annotations.

You also learned how to design PDF forms, and how to use interactive elements in the design of these forms. You saw how easy it is to add snippets of JavaScript code to your PDF forms. I hope that you will now want to add more JavaScript code yourself.

More than that, though, I hope that I have encouraged and motivated you to design something in Scribus for yourself. So come on in and meet the Team at

www.scribus.net/meet-the-team/.

Index

■ T, U

Printed in the United States
By Bookmasters